R. Gupta's®

POPULAR MASTER GUIDE

DSSSB–TEACHERS

PGT

HOME SCIENCE

Recruitment Exam

by
RPH Editorial Board

2021
EDITION

RAMESH PUBLISHING HOUSE, NEW DELHI

Published by
O.P. Gupta *for* Ramesh Publishing House

Admin. Office
12-H, New Daryaganj Road, Opp. Officers' Mess,
New Delhi-110002 ℂ 23261567, 23275224, 23275124

E-mail: info@rameshpublishinghouse.com
Website: www.rameshpublishinghouse.com

Showroom
● Balaji Market, Nai Sarak, Delhi-6 ℂ 23253720, 23282525
● 4457, Nai Sarak, Delhi-6, ℂ 23918938

Book Code: R-1319

ISBN: 978-93-5012-018-7

HSN Code: 49011010

Scheme of Examination

DSSSB will conduct **One Tier Exam** for PGT posts having two section:

Section-I

S.No.	Subject	Questions	Marks
1.	Mental Ability and Reasoning Ability	20	20
2.	General Awareness	20	20
3.	English Language & Comprehension	20	20
4.	Hindi Language & Comprehension	20	20
5.	Numerical Aptitude & Data Interpretation	20	20
	Total	**100**	**100**

Section-II

S.No.	Subject	Questions	Marks
1.	MCQs pertaining to Post-Graduation qualification and teaching methodology required for the post.	**200**	**200**

CONTENTS

Previous Paper (Solved)

Delhi Subordinate Services Selection Board (DSSSB)
PGT (Home Science) Teacher Recruitment Exam, 2018

Subject Knowledge – Home Science & Teaching Methodology

1. Which type of diet should be given to high blood pressure patient?
A. High protein and energy diet
B. Low salt diet
C. Low fiber diet
D. Low sugar diet

2. Which method of cooking is best?
A. Frying
B. Boiling
C. Roasting
D. Steaming

3. Symptoms of 'corneal xerosis' is:
A. Wounds in cornea
B. Dryness of cornea
C. High blood pressure
D. All of the above

4. Polyster is a pure:
A. Protein fiber
B. Chemical fiber
C. Regenerated fiber
D. None of these

5. Rayon dyes properly because they are:
A. cellulosic
B. more absorbent
C. tolerate high temperature
D. not affected by acid

6. Best bleach for wool is:
A. Chlorine
B. Calcium chloride
C. Hydrogen peroxide
D. Sodium chloride

7. Which bleaching agent can be used safely both for vegetable and animal fibers?
A. Hydrogen peroxide
B. Oxalic acid
C. Sunlight
D. All of the above

8. Linoleic acid is a:
A. Protein
B. Fat
C. Unsaturated fatty acid
D. Saturated fatty acid

9. Nutritional adequacy of the diet is according to:
A. Age of person
B. Sex
C. Activity pattern
D. All of the above

10. Sucrose is abundant in:
A. Milk
B. Orange juice
C. Sugarcane
D. Grapes

11. The food does *not* come in contact with water while cooking, it is:
A. Frying
B. Grilling
C. Steaming
D. All of the above

12. The important difference between a 'home' and 'house' is:
A. Physical
B. Environmental
C. Emotional
D. Only terminological difference

13. Weight of infant becomes double:
A. from birth to four months
B. in six months
C. in eight months
D. in one year

14. Cephalo-caudal development means:
A. Development from head to legs
B. Development from centre of the body to outwards
C. Both (A) & (B)
D. None of these

15. Learning by curiosity and trial and error method is called:
A. Primary circular
B. Secondary circular
C. Tertiary circular
D. All of the above

16. Boys and girls play ______ in childhood.
A. together
B. separate
C. according to wish
D. do not play

1

17. Why does a child get angry in childhood?
A. by irritating
B. by comparing with other children
C. by favouritism
D. All of the above

18. When menstruation stage starts in girls is called:
A. Menopause   B. Menarche
C. Puberty   D. None of these

19. _______ is helpful in the selection of occupation.
A. motivation   B. skillful
C. tendency   D. All of the above

20. What is the reason of disharmony in relationships?
A. less communication in family
B. not understanding other emotions
C. stress with one another
D. All of the above

21. Housewife should use equipments so that she can save _______.
A. time
B. energy
C. both time & energy
D. None of these

22. Nutrients help in:
A. Body growth   B. Development
C. Maintenance   D. All of these

23. Which nutrient goes out with water if we throw the extra water after boiling?
A. Vitamin B complex
B. Vitamin A
C. Vitamin D
D. Vitamin E

24. Resources can be classified as:
A. Human v/s Non-human
B. Specific v/s general
C. Human, physical and psychic capital resources
D. All of the above

25. _______ are difficult to measure.
A. Values   B. Goals
C. Standards   D. All of the above

26. _______ can be managed more easily.
A. Non-human   B. Human
C. Specific resources   D. General resources

27. Home management is:
A. using resources to attain the set goals
B. getting the work completed
C. supervising individual
D. using efficient methods to complete task

28. Xerophthalmia is the deficiency of:
A. Vitamin A   B. Vitamin D
C. Vitamin E   D. Vitamin K

29. In which year the Government of India passed the 'Consumer Protection Act'?
A. 1987   B. 1988
C. 1985   D. 1986

30. Vitamin B_2 is:
A. Thiamine   B. Riboflavin
C. Niacin   D. Tryptophane

31. Standardized Mark on 'mango powder' is:
A. Agmark   B. ISI
C. FPO   D. None of these

32. 15½ indicated on a care label of a shirt stand for:
A. The collar size   B. Shirt can be ironed
C. Not bleaching   D. Blueing

33. A sedentary man of 60 kg body weight requires energy equal to:
A. 2925 Kcal   B. 1875 Kcal
C. 2225 Kcal   D. 2875 Kcal

34. The minerals _______ and _______ are present in the largest amount in our bodies.
A. Ca and P   B. Ca and K
C. Fe and P   D. K and P

35. _______ present in green leafy vegetables and cereals interfere with absorption of calcium.
A. Oxalates
B. Phytates
C. Oxalates and Phytates both
D. None of these

36. Failure of growth, irritability, skin changes and hair changes are the symptoms of:
A. Kwashiorkor   B. Marasmus
C. PEM deficiency   D. Fluorosis

37. When we add water to make dough, two proteins combine and forms a compound:
A. Gluten   B. Lysine
C. Methoinine   D. Isoleucine

38. When we store fruits for several days in a fridge most of its ______ cannot be retained.
A. Ascorbic acid   B. Thiamine
C. Nicotinic acid   D. All of these

39. RDI for Iron during lactation is:
A. 38 mg   B. 40 mg
C. 30 mg   D. 35 mg

40. The increase in daily recommended allowances by ICMR of Protein in pregnancy is:
A. 14 gm   B. 25 gm
C. 20 gm   D. 15 gm

41. In LTHT method of Pasteurization, milk is heated at:
A. 140°F   B. 145°F
C. 161°F   D. 165°F

42. Artificial silk is:
A. Rayon   B. Polyester
C. Acrylic   D. Acetate

43. The most important test for fibre identification is:
A. Microscopic test   B. Burning test
C. Solubility test   D. Tearing test

44. Tenacity of a fibre is directly related to:
A. length of polymer
B. polymer orientation and strength
C. inter polymer forces of attraction
D. All of the above

45. Fever is a condition when:
A. There is an increase in the body temperature above normal
B. There is an increase in the rate of metabolic activities
C. There is an imbalance between the heat produced and heat eliminated in the body
D. All of the above

46. Dominant paradigm of development is focussed on:
A. Industrial revolution
B. Agricultural development
C. Basic needs of people
D. All options are wrong

47. Which filament fibres are long continuous for thousands of meter?
A. Silk   B. Nylon
C. Polyester   D. All options are right

48. ______ means an increase in size, height, weight and body in general.
A. Development   B. Growth
C. Maturation   D. Progressiveness

49. To moisten meat or other foods to add foods flavour and to prevent drying of the surface of meat is called:
A. Rub in   B. Baste
C. Au-gratin   D. Dredge

50. Design is divided into the following types:
A. Structural and decorative
B. Hard and Soft
C. Vertical & Horizontal
D. All options are wrong

51. A colour scheme is called split complimentary scheme when:
A. Red, orange, orange brown and gold yellow are used together.
B. On a lemon yellow background orange is used.
C. On yellow background blue is used.
D. On yellow background red is used.

52. What does ICSW stands for?
A. International Children's Social Work
B. Integrated Children's Services are Welfare
C. Indian Council of Social Welfare
D. Internationl Cultural and Social Welfare

53. The psychological reason for using clothing is/are:
A. Satisfaction
B. Appear beautiful
C. Attract others towards us
D. All options are right

54. 'Trichinosis' in man is caused by:
A. Pigs   B. Cattles
C. Goat   D. All options are right

55. 'Puppets' are used for/as:
A. Telling stories   B. Teaching aid
C. Illiterate people   D. All options are right

56. Who is the 'Father of Nutrition'?
A. Graham Lusk
B. E.V. Macculum
C. Lavoisier
D. W.O. Atwater

57. Who propsed the theory of Socialization of Human Beings?
A. Carl Jung   B. Karen Horney
C. Erich Fromm   D. Erik. H. Erikson

58. Steroids are produced in greater amount in pregnancy so that:
A. water and sodium are retained in the body.
B. it increases secretion by endometrium.
C. thyroid glands are more active than normal.
D. All options are wrong

59. Coir fibre is made from coconut husk and is a traditional industry in:
A. North India   B. South India
C. East India   D. West India

60. The most suitable method of studying emotions in children is:
A. Survey method
B. Observation method
C. Interview method
D. Experimental method

61. The word 'Calorie' denotes:
A. A nutrient   B. A food
C. A unit   D. All options are right

62. Colour is an important dimension of:
A. Principle of design
B. Element of design
C. Fine art
D. Housing and interior decoration

63. 10 gms of iodized salt provides _______ μg of iodine.
A. 150   B. 100
C. 120   D. 80

64. The Soaps available in the market, use which of the ingredients in their preparation?
A. Oils   B. Colour
C. Perfumes   D. All options are right

65. ABC of Poster is:
A. Attractive, Brief, Clear
B. Attention, Brief, Clarity
C. Attractive, Bold, Clear
D. Attractive, Bold, Colourful

66. Drama and Story telling helps children to develop:
A. Anxiety   B. Frustration
C. Imagination   D. Attachment

67. Broadly soaps can be divided into following categories:
A. Hard soap
B. Soft soap
C. Both Hard soap and Soft soap
D. All options are wrong

68. To present the area of a design most important visually, it is necessary to have:
A. Balance   B. Line
C. Emphasis   D. Harmony

69. It can cause reproductive problems in males:
A. Citrus red 2   B. Metanil yellow
C. Lead chromate   D. Rhodamine B

70. The concept of developmental task was given by:
A. Bandura   B. Havighurst
C. Hawkins   D. Freeman

71. Who started the concept of 'mobile créche?'
A. Dr. Anandalakshmi
B. Dr. Meena Swaminathan
C. Dr. Amita Verma
D. Dr. Meera Mahadevan

72. Load bearning building structure is beneficial as it is:
A. Decorative   B. Beautiful
C. Stronger   D. Easy to construct

73. 'Dumping syndrome' is often experienced by patients who have undergone:
A. Gastrectomy
B. Pancreatactomy
C. Illeostomy
D. Surgery of the oesophagus

74. The component of controlling in which action and outputs are examined in compliance with standard is:
A. Adjusting   B. Changing
C. Checking   D. Assessing

75. The standards for space to be provided all around a building is referred to as:
A. Set back   B. Ventilation
C. Open space   D. Landscape

76. During febrile disorder like typhoid the BMR _______ by _______ percent.
A. increases, 7   B. decreases, 7
C. decreases, 15   D. increases, 5

77. 'Suspense Chart' is also known as:
   A. Organizational Chart
   B. Flow Chart
   C. Strip tease Chart
   D. Tree and Stream Chart

78. Analogous colour scheme make use of the following colours in a colour wheel:
   A. Two or three colours adjacent to each other
   B. Two colours opposite to each other
   C. Three colours forming a triangle
   D. Half of colour wheel

79. A method of developing a pattern from body measurements is called:
   A. Clothing construction
   B. Pattern making
   C. Drafting
   D. All options are wrong

80. Wechsler's Intelligence Scale for Children (WISC) has been designed for children in the age group of:
   A. Birth to 2 years
   B. 2 years to 6 years
   C. 6 years to 16 years
   D. 16 years to 17 years

81. Integrated Child Development Services were started in the year:
   A. 2nd October, 1973
   B. 2nd October, 1975
   C. 2nd October, 1979
   D. 2nd October, 1980

82. ______ is a well considered plan.
   A. Decoration   B. Shape
   C. Lines   D. Design

83. The curriculum of non-formal education should be:
   A. Formally approved
   B. Flexible
   C. Need specific for learner
   D. Culturally based

84. The record of food store inventory is kept in:
   A. Pass Book   B. Stock Register
   C. Cash Book   D. Journal

85. The designers work with the elements of:
   A. Line, Space   B. Texture, Value
   C. Form, Colour   D. All options are right

86. Narrowing of Lumen of artery due to deposition of fat, is called:
   A. Thrombosis
   B. Atherosclerosis
   C. Arteriosclerosis
   D. Myocardial infarction

87. Paper napkins, paper towels, disposable sheets are made of:
   A. Felt wool
   B. Bonded fibre fabrics
   C. Shuttle
   D. Crochet

88. Feedback is a significant component of:
   A. Urbanization   B. Communication
   C. Industrialization D. Globalization

89. ______ present in Green Leafy Vegetables and Cereals interfere with absorption of calcium.
   A. Oxalates
   B. Phytates
   C. Oxalates and Phytates
   D. Inhibitors

90. Maillard reaction takes place in the following cooking procedure:
   A. Prolonged cooking of milk with sugar
   B. Prolonged cooking of milk with salt
   C. Prolonged cooking of milk with vegetables
   D. Prolonged cooking of milk with cereal

91. β-carotene in the body changes into Retinol in:
   A. Liver   B. Pancreas
   C. Gall Bladder   D. Intestine

92. Which of the following is not a theory of clothing?
   A. Modesty   B. Individuality
   C. Protection   D. Adornment

93. Which of the following is not a plain weave fabric?
   A. Percale   B. Calico
   C. Drill   D. Chintz

94. The most durable, long lasting and low maintenance metal used commonly for construction of household equipment is:
   A. Aluminium   B. Iron
   C. Stainless steel D. Copper

95. The fortificant used in iodized salt is:
A. Sodium iodide   B. Potassium iodate
C. Sodium iodate   D. Potassium iodide

96. Serum Vitamin D level _______ are indicative of sub-clinical Vitamin D deficiency.
A. < 20 ng/dl   B. < 10 ng/dl
C. < 30 ng/dl   D. < 5 ng/dl

97. Which of the following is not a hand printing technique?
A. Duplex   B. Screen
C. Block   D. Stencil

98. Which of the following garment finishers is used for finishing number of garments together?
A. Form press   B. Tunnel
C. Buck Press   D. Die Press

99. Electromayography is a method used for measuring:
A. Muscle fatigue
B. Electric phenomenon occurring in the muscle
C. Electric phenomenon occurring in the bones
D. Efficiency of tissues

100. Following fat is the richest source of MUFA:
A. Sunflower Oil   B. Soyabean Oil
C. Coconut Oil   D. Olive Oil

101. Major function of Zinc in the human body is:
A. Haemoglobin synthesis
B. DNA and RNA synthesis
C. Bone health
D. Vision

102. A menu where food items are priced separately is called:
A. Table d' hote   B. Du Jow
C. Set menu   D. A' la carte

103. While washing cotton fabrics colour can be prevented from bleaching by using:
A. Vinegar   B. Common Salt
C. Sodium Carbonate   D. Lissapol

104. Give the correct full form of SASMIRA.
A. Silk And Synthetic Mills and Research Association.
B. Synthetic & Art Silk Mills and Research Association.
C. Silk And Art Silk Mills and Research Association.
D. Standards And Specifications of Mills & Research Association.

105. Sandpaper, cotton and fabric are examples of variation in which element of art?
A. Texture   B. Line
C. Shape   D. Colour

106. Sri Niketan Project of Rural Development was initiated by:
A. Mahatma Gandhi
B. Rabindra Nath Tagore
C. Vinoba Bhave
D. Swami Vivekanand

107. Full form of FSSAI is:
A. Food Security and Standards Association of India
B. Food Security and Safety Authority of India
C. Food Safety and Standards Association of India
D. Food Safety and Standards Authority of India

108. Helicobacter pylorii infection causes the following disease:
A. Peptic Ulcer   B. Typhoid
C. Cholera   D. Constipation

109. Broca's area is an area of the brain that is involved in:
A. Language comprehesion
B. Speech production
C. Motor activity
D. Anger production

110. NCPCR is an autonomous body which stands for:
A. National Commission for the Protection of Child Rights
B. National Council for Prevention and Control of Reproduction
C. National Commission for Poverty Control and Relief
D. National Council for Preschool, Creche and Research

111. Which of the following finishes import lustre to the fabric?
A. Sueding   B. Gigging
C. Ciré   D. Flocking

112. Which of the following thread packages is centreless and is used in quilting and Embroidery machines?
A. Cocoons
B. Spools
C. Cones
D. Vicones

113. These letters R, O, Y help us remember which colour group?
A. Warm
B. Cool
C. Neutral
D. Primary colours

114. Andragogy is the study of teaching:
A. Children
B. Adolescents
C. Young people
D. Adults

115. One of the most effective methods of imparting skill is:
A. Field visit
B. Group discussion
C. Demonstration
D. Project

116. Following is an indicator of deterioration in quality of egg:
A. Egg shell is intact
B. Small air cell
C. Increased alkalinity of egg white
D. Firm chlazae holding the yolk in the centre

117. Which of the following is not a type of buffet service?
A. Finger
B. Trayed
C. Full
D. Fork

118. Which of the following is not a primary property of a fibre?
A. Strength
B. Flexibility
C. Cohesiveness
D. Density

119. Identify the term related to flower arrangement.
A. Feng Shui
B. Ying-Yang
C. Ikebana
D. Alpana

120. _______ applied ethological theory to understand infant-caregiver relationship.
A. Jean Piaget
B. John Locke
C. Albert Bandura
D. John Bowlby

121. In normally distributed population Mean ±1.96 S.D. will cover _____ of population.
A. 90%
B. 95%
C. 98%
D. 99%

122. Haemoglobin level below which a pregnant woman is considered anaemic:
A. 12 g/dl of blood
B. 11 g/dl of blood
C. 11.5 g/dl of blood
D. 10 g/dl of blood

123. The HbAlC level above which a person is diagnosed as Diabetic is:
A. 6.2%
B. 6.5%
C. 6.8%
D. 7.0%

124. Which of the following dyes is cationic in nature?
A. Acid
B. Disperse
C. Basic
D. Direct

125. Wrinkle resistant fabrics are made environment friendly and cost effective by the use of:
A. Formaldehyde
B. Citric acid
C. Xylitol
D. Cross linking citric acid and xylitol

126. 'World Consumer Rights day' is observed on which date?
A. 15th of March
B. 8th of February
C. 10th of December
D. 16th of March

127. _____ consists of procedures that combine conditioning and modelling to eliminate undesirable behaviours.
A. Negative reinforcement
B. Social exclusion
C. Behaviour modification
D. Corporal punishment

128. Innovative entrepreneurs may face a special challenge initially raising:
A. Development capital
B. Structural capital
C. Human capital
D. Seed capital

129. In the preparation of Paneer from Milk, the pH at which casein precipitate is:
A. pH 6.5
B. pH 4.6
C. pH 7.5
D. pH 3.0

130. The functionally active form of Vitamin D is:
A. Cholecalciferol
B. Ergocalciferol
C. Dehydrocholesterol
D. 1, 2 5 Dihydroxycholecalciferol

131. The approach to management which is an effort to control costs of storage space, time and effort:
A. MBO
B. TQM

C. JIT

D. Contingency approach

132. The fastest method of Pattern making is:
A. Flat patterning   B. Drafting
C. Draping   D. Reverse Engineering

133. AATCC stands for:
A. American Association of Textile Chemists and Colourists.
B. All Associations of Textile Chemists and Colourists.
C. Association of American Textiles, Colours and Chemists.
D. Australian Association of Textiles Chemists and Colourists.

134. A step in management process which consists of series of individual purposive decisions which follow a sequence or pattern is:
A. Planning   B. Organising
C. Coordinating   D. Evaluating

135. The programme for promoting functional literacy among adults is:
A. Sarva Shiksha Abhiyan.
B. Sarva Shiksha Adhyayan Programme.
C. National Literacy Mission.
D. National Literacy Motivation Programme.

136. In Mass communication, PSA stands for:
A. Public Service Assessment
B. Public Service Announcement
C. Public Service Access
D. Public Service Account

137. An increase in the alpha, the level of significance, causes:
A. An increase in the probability of Type I error to occur.
B. A decrease in the probability of Type I error to occur.
C. No change in any of the Type I or Type II error.
D. A decrease in the probability of Type I error to occur and an increase in the probability of Type II error to occur.

138. Normal BMI for adult Asians as suggested by WHO is:
A. $18 - 23$ kg/m^2 B. $19 - 24$ kg/m^2
C. $20 - 25$ kg/m^2 D. $21 - 26$ kg/m^2

139. Generally visually impaired persons have visual acuity of:
A. 2/200   B. 20/100
C. 20/70   D. 20/200

140. The female sex hormone is
A. Androgen   B. Prolactin
C. Estrogen   D. Oxytocin

141. Which of the following is sheared from a living sheep?
A. Flannel   B. Fleece
C. Felt   D. Moire

142. Which of the following is a stationary knife?
A. Band   B. Round
C. Straight   D. Die

143. Which of the following is a double pointed dart?
A. Flange   B. French
C. Fish   D. Dressmakers

144. A portion of output re-entered as input to affect succeeding output is:
A. Feedback   B. Deferred resource
C. Throughput   D. Black box

145. The recommended height of the work surface in the kitchen for efficient operation is:
A. 4 inches below the elbow
B. 5 inches below elbow level
C. 3 inches below elbow level
D. 6 inches below the elbow

146. Approaches to understand Women's participation in development have gone through the following phases:
A. Welfare, Women in Development, Gender and Development
B. Welfare, Gender and Development, Women in Development
C. Women in Development, Welfare, Gender and Development
D. Gender and Development, Women in Development, Welfare

147. Putting the last as first, means:
A. Reversals in learning
B. Destination of man
C. Blue print approach
D. Content centric teaching

148. From which plant source gluten is derived?
A. Soya   B. Rice
C. Corn   D. Wheat

149. HDL is synthesized and secreted from:
A. Pancreas   B. Liver
C. Kidneys   D. Muscles

150. Which of the following governs the selection of needle?
A. Type of thread   B. Type of fabric
C. Stitch length   D. Tension of thread

151. Which of the following is not a design repeat?
A. Drop   B. Mirror
C. Rotary   D. Satin

152. The term 'Therbligs' was given by:
A. Prang   B. Gilbreth
C. Denmann W. Ross   D. Mundell

153. Deliberate manipulation of people's beliefs, values and behaviour through words, gestures, images is known as:
A. Publicity   B. Propaganda
C. Persuasion   D. Perception

154. Triggering the mind of participants to finding out solutions for a problem is called as:
A. Colloquism   B. Symposium
C. Debate   D. Brain Storming

155. Which of the following foods are produced by involving lactic acid fermentation?
(*a*) Beer   (*b*) Yogurt
(*c*) Cheese   (*d*) Vinegar
A. (*a*) and (*b*)   B. (*b*) and (*c*)
C. (*c*) and (*d*)   D. (*d*) and (*a*)

156. BARS is a tool used for:
A. Checking quality of food
B. Designing layout plan
C. Performance Appraisal
D. Feedback communication

157. Daily Zinc requirement of an adult man is:
A. 12 mg   B. 8 mg
C. 350 mg   D. 600 mg

158. Infestation of which worm is responsible for the cause of anaemia is rural population?
A. Round worm   B. Hook worm
C. Thread worm   D. Tape worm

159. Following is not a method of nutritional assessment using anthropometry.
A. Skin fold thickness
B. Waist circumference
C. Blood Pressure
D. Mid Upper Arm Circumference

160. The Hippocampus is found in:
A. The circulatory system
B. The human brain
C. Fossils
D. The preschool setting

161. The term not used in traditional Japanese woven textile is:
A. Maya   B. Shashiko
C. Sakiori   D. Zanshi

162. Which of the following amino acids is not present in silk?
A. Glycine   B. Alanine
C. Cystine   D. Serine

163. The managerial and the psycho social subsystems are part of the ______ .
A. Household environment
B. Near environment
C. Large environment
D. Internal environment

164. Which of the following effort is involved in home making activities such as bending, leaning, kneeling and stooping?
A. Muscular effort   B. Physical effort
C. Pedal effort   D. Torsal effort

165. 8th March is celebrated as the:
A. International Environment Day
B. International Sanitation Day
C. International Women's Day
D. International Energy Day

166. Following food is the richest source of ω-3 fatty acids:
A. Coconut   B. Flax seed
C. Olives   D. Groundnut

167. A la carte menu is:
A. Served on a particular day as special
B. Limited choice of fixed price
C. Choices of items listed with its price
D. Series of dishes repeated after a period of time

168. Which of the following is a theory of origin of clothing?
A. Protection   B. Conformity
C. Individuality   D. Track down

169. Organization responsible for preventing unfair or deceptive trade practices in textile and textile products is:
A. AATCC
B. Federal Trade Commission (FTC)
C. Textile Fibre Products Identification Act (TEPIA)
D. ASTM

170. The pictorial view of the proposed house is called:
A. Elevation plan   B. Cross section plan
C. Perspective plan   D. Floor plan

171. Development resulting from on going exchanges between heredity and all levels of the environment is called:
A. Cephalocaudal   B. Proximodistal
C. Genotypical   D. Epigenesis

172. Which one of the following models use only three elements to explain the process of communication?
A. Westley and Machlean's model
B. Berlo's model
C. Leagan's model
D. Aristotle's model

173. Following are disorders of vitamin A deficiency:
(*i*) Xeropthalmia   (*ii*) Night Blindness
(*iii*) Oesteoporosis   (*iv*) Cretinism
(*v*) Kerotomalacia
A. (*ii*), (*iv*) and (*v*)   B. (*i*), (*iii*) and (*iv*)
C. (*i*), (*ii*) and (*v*)   D. (*i*), (*iii*) and (*v*)

174. Following is *not* a method of diet survey:
A. Food frequency questionnaire
B. 24 hrs recall method
C. Food weighment
D. BMI

175. The RDA of Zinc for 16-17 yrs old girls is:
A. 12 mg/day   B. 11 mg/day
C. 8 mg/day   D. 10 mg/day

176. _______ involves universal and irreversible changes due to genetic programming.
A. Pragmatism   B. Secondary aging
C. Imaginary audience   D. Senescence

177. Dry which does not have affinity for cotton fabrics?
A. Basic dye   B. Reactive dye
C. Sulphur dye   D. Vat dye

178. The urge to possess and consume for display of wealth is called:
A. Emulative consumption
B. Conspicuous consumption
C. Customary consumption
D. Competitive consumption

179. The educational and religions activities of families are part of:
A. Household environment
B. Near environment
C. Large environment
D. External environment

180. 'NEEM' stands for:
A. National Extension Education Movement
B. National Elementary Education Mission
C. National Elementary Education Movement
D. National Elementary Extension Mission

181. "Education is something which makes man self-reliant and selfless". This definition of education is given by:
A. Upanishad   B. Rig Veda
C. Bhagavad Gita   D. Gandhiji

182. One of the notable schemes of UGC for nurturing social equity for various beneficiary categories in India is:
A. PWD Act, 1995
B. Post-Doctoral Fellowship
C. SET Examination
D. SSA

183. The Literary rate of Female Dalit of Bihar according to 2011 census is:
A. 38.5%   B. 44.6%
C. 83%   D. 62%

184. Hoy's definition of school culture is the _______ of an organization.
A. Belief   B. Intellectual
C. Emotional   D. Environmental

185. Studies of teacher identity and its impact on instruction consists of 3 broad types of inquiry. Which of the following is not the part of these?
A. Identity formation
B. Physical altitude
C. Characteristics of teacher identity
D. Identity narratives

186. In addition to discourses regarding student demographics and perseverance teachers use the discourse of ______ to define the performance of effective teacher.
A. Perseverance
B. Nurturing
C. Student demographics
D. Perfomance

187. Teacher identity is viewed through the lens of ______ which is closely linked to school culture.
A. Cultural identity
B. Student parameters
C. Classroom environmental
D. Community practice

188. If schools can develop a ______ school culture, they can be more successful.
A. Negative
B. Positive
C. Translative
D. Re-active

189. Effects of technology on different processes does not include:
A. Industrialization
B. Urbanization
C. Modernization
D. Liberalization

190. As of the International Schools Consultancy's List of January 2015, how many International Schools does India have?
A. 1340
B. 410
C. 820
D. 1000

191. Whose directives State, qualifying ages for candidates who wish to take board exams?
A. KSEEB, UGC, CBSE
B. KSERT, NCERT, KSEEB
C. UGC, NCERT and CBSE
D. KGC, UGC, NCTE

192. School culture is touted as a ______ strategy.
A. Perform
C. Reform
B. Civic
D. Critic

193. Which management can be a predictive of school culture?
A. Friendship
B. Entertainment
C. Leadership
D. Risk

194. Actual learning phase step in the process of learning emphasises on:
A. A goal
B. A motive
C. Learning situation
D. A block to achievement of goal

195. Which of the following is not a factor that influences learning?
A. Environmental and other factors
B. Individual difference of learners
C. Learning is a monotonous process
D. Teachers enthusiasm in classroom learning

196. Cognitive characteristics of learners are related to:
A. Learner's personal life
B. Academic performance of the learner
C. Social and emotional perceptive of learners
D. Skills of learner concerned to brain

197. ______ refers to neither influence nor obstruction of previously learned knowledge skill to a new learning situation.
A. Positive transfer
B. Negative transfer
C. Lateral transfer
D. Zero transfer

198. CPD in pedagogy and practice stands for:
A. Continuing Professional Development
B. Classroom Learning Programme Description
C. Competitive Perspective Deterioration
D. Cognitive Pulse Development

199. The follow-up review should be conducted once there has been time and other tasks identified in the action plan:
A. To encourage the review
B. To complete the study unit
C. To evaluate the content
D. To re-consider the objectives

200. How many criterias of successful praise are listed?
A. 10
B. 8
C. 6
D. 18

ANSWERS

1	2	3	4	5	6	7	8	9	10
B	D	B	B	A	C	A	C	D	C

11	12	13	14	15	16	17	18	19	20
D	C	A	A	C	A	D	B	D	D

21	22	23	24	25	26	27	28	29	30
C	D	A	D	A	A	A	A	D	B

31	32	33	34	35	36	37	38	39	40
A	A	A	A	C	A	A	A	C	D

41	42	43	44	45	46	47	48	49	50
B	A	C	D	D	C	D	B	B	A

51	52	53	54	55	56	57	58	59	60
C	C	D	A	D	C	D	A	B	B

61	62	63	64	65	66	67	68	69	70
C	B	A	D	C	C	D	C	B	B

71	72	73	74	75	76	77	78	79	80
D	C	A	C	C	A	C	A	C	C

81	82	83	84	85	86	87	88	89	90
B	D	C	B	D	C	B	B	C	A

91	92	93	94	95	96	97	98	99	100
A	B	C	C	B	A	A	B	B	D

101	102	103	104	105	106	107	108	109	110
B	D	B	B	A	B	D	A	B	A

111	112	113	114	115	116	117	118	119	120
C	A	A	D	C	C	B	D	C	D

121	122	123	124	125	126	127	128	129	130
B	B	B	C	D	A	C	D	B	D

131	132	133	134	135	136	137	138	139	140
C	A	A	A	C	B	A	A	D	C

141	142	143	144	145	146	147	148	149	150
B	A	C	A	C	A	A	D	B	B

151	152	153	154	155	156	157	158	159	160
D	B	B	D	B	C	A	B	C	B

161	162	163	164	165	166	167	168	169	170
A	C	A	D	C	B	C	A	B	C

171	172	173	174	175	176	177	178	179	180
D	D	C	D	A	D	A	B	B	B

181	182	183	184	185	186	187	188	189	190
B	B	B	D	B	B	D	B	D	B

191	192	193	194	195	196	197	198	199	200
C	A	C	C	C	D	D	A	D	C

Delhi Subordinate Services Selection Board
DSSSB–PGT (Home Science) Recruitment Exam, 2015

SECTION-II

Post Specific Subject-Related Questions

1. The word 'textiles' comes from a Latin word textile which means
A. Weave
B. Textile
C. Fabric
D. None

2. Fabrics with low density
A. Have less weight
B. Have less cover
C. Better hand
D. Resiliency

3. Flax and cotton do not show pileing because of
A. Static which is nil
B. Hydrophilic fibre
C. Short length fibre
D. None of the above

4. Artificial silk is
A. Polyester
B. Rayon
C. Acrylic
D. Acetate

5. TPI is a term used in relation to
A. Yarn
B. Fabrics
C. Knits
D. Weaves

6. Staple fibres are short fibres, the length ranges from
A. $\frac{1}{2}$ – 10 cms
B. 1 – 20 cms
C 1 – 30 cms
D. 1 – 40 cms

7. SPI stands for
A. Seam Per Inch
B. Selvedge Per Inch
C. Stitches Per Inch
D. None

8. The factors affecting fashion includes
A. Inflation and Recession
B. Population
C. Income
D. All the above

9. .... is the wedge shape in any pattern that points and ends towards the fullest part.
A. Dart
B. Pocket
C. Seams
D. Placket

10. .... is the line along which the reverse of a collar turns back.
A. Straight line
B. Curved line
C. Half circle
D. Roll line

11. Class 200 series includes all .... stitches.
A. Machine
B. Hand
C. Basic
D. Decorative

12. The term silhouette is
A. Stitching out
B. Stitching in
C. Outer shape of any garment
D. Inner shape of any garment

13. Earlier than this textiles was being looked after by
A. Ministry of Commerce
B. Ministry of Finance
C. Home Ministry
D. None

14. The office of the Development Commissioner for Handicraft is located at
A. Calcutta
B. Madras
C. Mumbai
D. New Delhi

15. The oriental word 'Carbasina' in Sanskrit means
A. Linen   B. Hemp
C. Karpasa   D. None

16. The trade name or 'Acetate' is
A. Tafeta   B. Orgendy
C. Hoisery   D. Viscose

17. In fancy yarns there is combination of
A. Counts   B. Colours
C. Materials   D. All

18. How much yarn is required for weaving a particular length of fabric is termed as
A. Yarn number
B. Yarn weight
C. Yarn count
D. Yarn length

19. Sulphur dyes are basically used for
A. Stone and acid wash
B. Air oxidation
C. Silk
D. None of these

20. Fabric is first treated with dye and then treated with mordant
A. Chrome   B. Meta chrome
C. After chrome D. Scouring

21. One microgram of retinol is equivalent to .... micrograms of carotene.
A 4   B. 6
C. 8   D. 3.8

22. Conjunctival Xerosis means .... of conjunctiva.
A. Hardness   B. Blindness
C. Softness   D. Dryness

23. Failure of growth, irritability skin changes and hair changes are the symptoms of
A. Marasmus
B. Kwashiorkor
C. PEM deficiency
D. Fluorosis

24. 1 Chapati of 20 gms is equivalent to .... rice which yields .... energy and .... protein.

A. $\frac{1}{2}$ cup, 70 K. cals, 2 gms

B. $\frac{1}{3}$ cup, 70 K. cals, 3 gms

C. 1 cup, 100 K. cals, 4 gms

D. $\frac{1}{2}$ cup, 50 K. cals, 2 gms

25. Pulses lacks ....but are rich in ....
A. Lysine, valine
B. Lysine, tryptophan
C. Tryptophan, valine
D. Tryptophan, lysine

26. PFA means
A. Purified Fatty Acids
B. Prevention of Food Adulteration
C. Prevention of Fortified Adulterants
D. Pure Fatty Acids

27. The area of earth where life exists is called
A. Atmosphere   B. Biosphere
C. Lithospher   D. None

28. Ten grams of iodized salt provides .... µg of iodine.
A. 60   B. 100
C. 120   D. 150

29. .... acts as a precursor of niacin.
A. Lysine   B. Histidine
C. Tryptophan   D. Valine

30. Find odd one.
A. NPU   B. BV
C. Douglas bag D. NPR

31. Onions make us cry when shedding. It is because
A. Sulphur compounds
B. Acted upon by enzymes
C. Produce volatile sulphur
D. All of them

32. Egg has all the nutrients for body growth EXCEPT
A. Calcium   B. Niacin
C. Vit. C   D. Vit. E

33. Clinching is
A. Intentional escape of air from loose lid
B. Seality of cans
C. Adding syrup or brine to a can
D. None

34. Phrynoderma (Toad Skin) is caused by
A. Deficiency of essential fatty acids
B. Deficiency of Vitamin A
C. Deficiency of iron
D. Deficiency of Amino acid

35. Genetic code is carried in .... made up of protein
A. DNA   B. RNA
C. Both A and B   D. None

36. Breast feeding is not given when
A. Mother suffers from chronic illness
B. Infant is weak
C. Mother acquires acute infection
D. All the above

37. In case of nausea, vomiting, gas-formation, diarrhoea give
A. Liquid diet
B. Full fluid diet
C. Soft diet
D. Clear liquid diet

38. Glucose is added in the ORS for
A. Absorption of sodium
B. Source of energy
C. Taste
D. None

39. Oral fluids does not include
A. Whey water
B. Barley water
C. Fruit punch
D. Alt the above

40. Crisp food is given by 5th or 6th month to the Infant
A. Diet supplement B. Teething
C. Weaning   D. None

41. A protein present in the blood cells
A. Rh factor   B. pH factor
C. Aa factor   D. None

42. Organ that separates the mover's blood stream from embryo
A. Placenta   B. Uterus
C. Ovum   D. Umbilical cord

43. .... is a process by which minerals and other substances are added to the cartilage and make bone harder.
A. Classification
B. Assimilation
C. Ossification
D. Chromatin

44. .... is a test where high frequency sound waves are beamed at the uterus.
A. Fetoscopy   B. Ultrasound
C. X-ray   D. Eliza test

45. "Child development is a field of study devoted to the understanding of all facts of human growth and development", is a definition given by
A. Berk
B. Harries
C. Hurlock
D. Papivea and Olds

46. 'Vernix Caseosa'
A. Covers entire body of foetus to protect against jerks
B. An agent which causes damage
C. Prevents skin from chapping
D. It is a period of foetus

47. Primary socialization takes place in
A. Infancy
B. Childhood
C. Adolescence
D. All of the above stages

48. Man's special mental abilities can be distinguished at the age of
A. 5   B. 7
C. 11   D. 15

49. The cause of phobia could be
A. Social
B. Emotional
C. Classical conditional
D. None

50. A child with learning disabilities is likely to have difficulties with
A. Maths
B. Reading
C. Illegible hand writing
D. English

51. A process of change which is relatively Independent of experiences
A. Learning   B. Maturity
C. Growth   D. Development

52. .... is a process by which the newborn child is moulded into culture and hence becomes an acceptable person in that society.
A. Interaction   B. Maturity
C. Socialization   D. Development

53. According to Jean Piaget the cognitive development has following stage
A. Sensorimotor period stags
B. Functional stage
C. Post-operational stage
D. All the above

54. Psychoanalytic theory was proposed by
A. Marry landworks
B. Piaget
C. Bowlby
D. Freud

55. .... is the time when sexual maturity is reached.
A. Adolescent
B. Puberty
C. Phallic stage
D. None of the above

56. Cephalocaudal principle tells the development from
A. Inner layer
B. Outer layer
C. Inner to outer
D. Top to bottom

57. The sense of taste is very weak at birth
A. True   B. False
C. Absurd   D. Not related

58. .... is the third part of personality development.

A. Id   B. Ego
C. Super Ego   D. Trust

59. Problems may stem for a child with learning disability because of his inability to
A. Organise time
B. Prioritise activities
C. Grasp verbal and non-verbal concepts
D. Communicate effectively

60. Some behavioural abnormalities that seem to indicate problem children are
A. Stealing   B. Lying
C. Annoying   D. Running

61. .... values are those that stand alone and are important and desirable simply for their own sake.
A. Instrumental value
B. Intrinsic value
C. External value
D. None of these

62. "A value is always important to the person who holds it". Who said this?
A. Clyde Kluck Hohn
B. Piaget
C. Freud
D. Gross and Crandall

63. .... are difficult to measure.
A. Values   B. Goals
C. Standards   D. All of these

64. Police protection, roads and temples etc. are examples of
A. Temporal resources
B. National resources
C. Community resources
D. World society resources

65. Pick the odd one among the characteristics of resources.
A. Useful
B. Accessible
C. Unlimited
D. Inter-changeable

66. The activities which pile up on each other at packed periods are called

A. Work curves   B. Peak loads
C. Time load   D. None of those

67. Due to lack of sufficient Q_2, the person experiences ………….. fatigue.
A. Physiological fatigue
B. Psychological fatigue
C. Boredom fatigue
D. Frustration fatigue

68. Three classes of change was proposed by
A. Mundell
B. Gross
C. Crandall
D. Gross and Crandall

69. ……….. consists of a series of decision making process of using family resources to achieve family goals.
A. Home management
B. Business management
C. Resource management
D. None of the above

70. ………….. is the process of selecting one course of action from a number of possible alternatives to serve the problem.
A. Crux
B. Decision making
C. Feed form and system
D. None of these

71. A step to step description of flow of movements in the task to avoid unnecessary motion
A. Operation chart
B. Pathway chart
C. Process chart
D. Chrono cycle chart

72. Home management is a process of using what you have to
A. Get what you want
B. Get everything
C. Get something
D. None of the above

73. "Getting results through people" is the description of

A. Training   B. Controlling
C. Management   D. None

74. The important difference between a 'Home' and a 'House' is
A. Physical   B. Environmental
C. Emotional   D. Terminology

75. ……….. is one of the sources of value
A. Man   B. Woman
C. Language   D. Culture

76. "……… the family is not only the best conveyor of values, but is the producer of values….." –who stated this?
A. Nickell and Dorsey
B. Gross and Crandall
C. Mundell
D. Leonard Mayo

77. Playing helps to attain good health. It is an example for
A. Intrinsic value   B. Instrumental value
C. Both   D. None

78. Steps in controlling include
A. Incentive   B. Checking
C. Adjustment   D. All

79. Human resources at our disposal include
A. Skills   B. Knowledge
C. Energy   D. Metabolism

80. 'Work is the conscious seeking of the simplest, easiest and quickest method of doing work'. This definition is by
A. Nickell and Dorsey
B. Gross and Crandall
C. Lillian Gilbreth
D. Gilbreth

81. Aprons Bibs and Curtain made of plastic instead of cotton help in reduction of
A. Time   B. Energy
C. Money   D. None

82. Cast iron conducts heat
A. Slowly
B. Bad conductor
C. Surfily and evenly
D. None

83. 'Teflon Coat' the term means to us
A. Trade name
B. Silicon finish
C. Reasonable price
D. Saves time and energy

84. Iron can be prevented from forming rust by
A. A small coat of grease applied on the surface of iron
B. Frequent washing
C. Wiping it clean
D. Not using it on heat

85. Forms are closely related with
A. Circles
B. Square
C. Rectangle
D. Lines

86. A progression of sizes is another technique to achieve rhythm. It is called
A. Balance
B. Emphasis
C. Proportion
D. Gradation

87. When all the element of design are nicely related, the design has
A. Proportion
B. Emphasis
C. Unity
D. Formal balance

88. Amount of lightness or darkness in colour is
A. Hue
B. Value
C. Intensity
D. Complementary

89. "A Text Book of Household Arts" is written by
A. Stella Soundararaj
B. Rutt
C. Friedman
D. Pramila Mehra

90. A combination of vertical or horizontal and diagonal lines produce .... forms.
A. Circle
B. Triangle
C. Square
D. None

91. .... label tells us the composition of a product user to which it can be put, how it is made.
A. Brand
B. Grade
C. Descriptive
D. Informative

92. Environmental noise is a
A. Physical barrier
B. Semantic barrier
C. Technical barrier
D. Social barrier

93. Message has three components
A. Code, content, treatment
B. Knowledge, attitude, interest
C. Initial, derived, terminal
D. None of the above

94. .... function is an important aspect of communication and is undertaken in formal as well as informal organisations.
A. Integrative
B. Instructive
C. Influencive
D. Informative

95. Different roles of extension worker are
A. Guide and expert
B. Enabler
C. Therapist
D. All the above

96. The role of co-ordinator in a satellite programing is
A. Crucial
B. Difficult
C. Time consuming
D. Expensive

97. In planning exhibits the understanding should be
A. Good
B. Simple, attractive, with one idea
C. Expensive
D. Not related

98. A mobile is a
A. Visual medium
B. Pictorial hanging with cords
C. Light weight
D. All the above

99. In oral communication the % of information lost
A. 30%
B. 40%
C. 20%
D. 10%

100. Chart, diagrams, pictures etc. play a significant role in making
A. Eye contact
B. Ideas clear and comprehensive
C. Visual impact
D. None

ANSWERS

1	2	3	4	5	6	7	8	9	10
A	A	C	B	A	D	C	D	A	D

11	12	13	14	15	16	17	18	19	20
B	C	A	D	C	A	D	C	A	C

21	22	23	24	25	26	27	28	29	30
A	D	B	A	D	B	B	D	C	C

31	32	33	34	35	36	37	38	39	40
D	B	A	A	C	D	D	A	C	B

41	42	43	44	45	46	47	48	49	50
A	D	C	B	A	C	D	C	C	A

51	52	53	54	55	56	57	58	59	60
B	C	A	D	B	D	B	C	A	A

61	62	63	64	65	66	67	68	69	70
B	D	A	C	C	B	A	D	A	B

71	72	73	74	75	76	77	78	79	80
C	A	C	C	D	D	C	D	B	A

81	82	83	84	85	86	87	88	89	90
C	C	A	A	D	D	C	B	A	B

91	92	93	94	95	96	97	98	99	100
D	A	A	B	D	C	B	D	A	B

———

Home Science

CONCEPT OF HOME SCIENCE   1

MEANING

Home Science consists of two words, that is, 'Home' and 'Science'. The word 'home' refers to the place of residence where the family lives. The word science refers to knowledge based on facts, principles and laws. By combining these two words the meaning of Home Science can be derived as 'application of scientific knowledge in a systematic manner towards improving the quality of home and family life'.

Since Home Science is concerned with various aspects of daily living that includes food, shelter, clothing, health, resources and services, the subject draws principles from related subjects of arts and sciences. These principles are then applied to promoting healthier and happier living. Home Science thus becomes an art and science of daily living.

MISCONCEPTIONS REGARDING HOME SCIENCE

Although Home Science has evolved into a very vast and detailed area of study, the layperson still has many misconceptions about the subject. It is because of these misconceptions that Home Science is not able to achieve the status and respect that it correctly deserves.

Let us now see what the common man thinks about Home Science.

- **Misconception** – Home Science is limited to cooking, laundry and needlework. The common perception is that these are the only things that are taught in Home Science. Hence parents of young girls readily agree to let them study this subject. They think it helps in preparing them for the responsibilities to come in later life.

Fact – Cooking, laundry, and needlework are only a very small part of what is taught in Home Science. In fact, we learn about every thing that touches our life- the basics of how our body works, what we need to eat to remain healthy, the rules of personal and environmental hygiene that we need to follow, what we should do to avoid illness and how to manage when we or our dear ones become sick. We learn about the different fibres and fabrics available in the market, the factors which influence our selection of fabrics for various uses. Children are an important part of our lives. We are all concerned about raising them safely and sensibly. It is in this course that we learn how they develop before and after birth, what we can do to see that they grow up to be good, responsible adults. We also learn to manage our resources like time, energy, and money so that we get maximum satisfaction out of their use.

- **Misconception** – Home Science is meant only for girls. Many people think that since Home Science teaches only about the home, it should be studied by girls only.

Fact - Today, men and women are sharing the responsibility of a home equally. This is because of a gradual change in the structure of our society. The joint family system is giving way to nuclear families where the man and woman have to manage their lives on their own. With more and more women going out of the home to work, the men have to learn to share the responsibilities. The basic preparation and orientation is given by the subject of Home Science alone. Hence young men are also encouraged to take up study of this subject.

- **Misconception** – People believe that the contents of Home Science are so general that they can be easily learnt from Mother or grandmother at home itself and formal study of any kind is not required.

Fact – Although girls do learn many things by observing their mother and grandmother at work, it is not sufficient. Many things are done traditionally which have a sound scientific basis, for example, pickles are covered with a layer of oil. When asked why, Mother may not be able to explain. But Home Science will explain that the layer of oil prevents contact of pickle with air. This prevents spoilage of the pickle. There are numerous such examples in everyone's lives. It is important to note that it becomes easier to do something when we know why we are doing what we are doing.

- **Misconception–** Studying Home Science does not lead to a career. Since Home Science teaches only about the home and things within the home, it is useless in terms of career development, is what most people think. If a young girl or boy wants to study to become a wage earner, a "serious" subject is to be selected.

Fact - Home Science offers numerous job opportunities to both girls and boys. Jobs in hospitals as dieticians, in boutiques as fashion designer, in hotels as a hostess/ receptionist, in schools as counselors, as teachers in schools and colleges are some of the very common job opportunities open to Home Science learners.

CONSTITUENT AREAS OF HOME SCIENCE

There are five major components which are as follows-

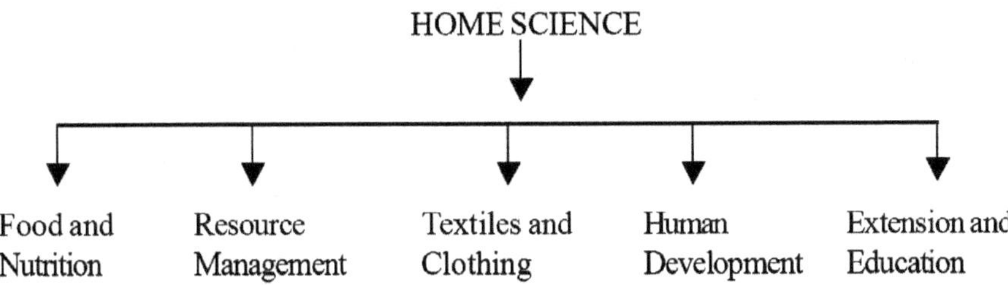

Today this science is so advanced that each compo-nent has its own and independent subdivisions.

These sub-divisions are as follows-

Main Branch	Sub divisions
Food and Nutrition	• Food xcience
	• Nutrition-clinical nutrition and community nutrition
	• Institutional food service
Textiles and Clothing	• Clothing construction
	• Textile science
	• Textile designing
	• Garment designing
	• Care and maintenance of clothes
Resource Management	• Resource management
	• Housing and Equipment
	• Interior decoration
	• Consumer education
Human Development	• Child welfare
	• Adolescence, marriage and family guidance
	• Care of the elderly
Education and Extension	• Preparing home science educators
	• Community services and welfare
	• Non-formal Education

FOOD & NUTRITION 2

Life cannot be sustained without adequate nourishment. Man needs adequate food for growth and development and to lead an active and healthy life. **Nutrition** is the science of foods, the nutrients and other substances therein, their action, interaction and balance in relationship to health and disease. **Health** is defined by The World Health Organisation as the state of complete physical, mental and social well being and not merely the absence of diseases. Therefore Food plays an important role in maintaining a person's nutritional and health status.

CLASSIFICATION OF FOODS

Foods are classified according to their functions in the body.

Energy Yielding Foods

This group includes foods rich in carbohydrate, fat and protein. They may be broadly divided into two groups.

1. Cereals, pulses, roots and tubers: Cereals provide in addition to energy large amounts of proteins, minerals and vitamins in the diet. Pulses also give protein and B vitamins besides giving energy to the body.
2. Fats, Oils and pure carbohydrates like sugars: Sugars provide only energy and fats provide concentrated source of energy.

Body Building Foods

Foods rich in protein are called body building foods. They are classified into two groups.

1. Milk, egg, meat & fish. They are rich in proteins of high biological value. These proteins have all the essential amino acids in correct proportion for the synthesis of body tissues.
2. Pulses, nuts and oilseeds: They are rich in protein but may not contain all the essential amino acids required by the human body.

Protective Foods

Foods rich in protein, vitamins and minerals have regulatory functions in the body like maintaining the heartbeat, water balance, temperature, etc.

Protective foods are broadly classified into two groups.

(i) Foods rich in vitamins and minerals and proteins of high biological value: milk, egg, and fish.
(ii) Foods rich in certain vitamins and minerals only: green leafy vegetables and fruits.

COOKING

The process of subjecting foods to the action of heat is termed as cooking.

Objectives of Cooking

- Improves the taste and food quality.
- Cooking food to the required temperature for a required length of time can destroy all harmful microorganisms in food.
- Cooking improves digestibility.
- Cooking increases variety.

Mehods of Cooking

1. Moist heat methods

- **Boiling:** Boiling is cooking foods by just immersing them in water at 100°C and maintaining the water at that temperature till the food is tender. It does not require special skill and equipment. It is time consuming.

- **Simmering:** When foods are cooked in a pan with a well fitted lid at a temperature just below the boiling point 82°-99°C , it is known as simmering. It is a useful method when foods have to be cooked for a long time to make it tender.

- **Poaching:** This involves cooking in the minimum amount of liquid at a temperature of 80°-85°C. Foods generally poached are eggs and fish.

- **Stewing:** This is a gentle method of cooking in a pan with a tight fitting lid, using small quantities of liquid to cover only half the food. The liquid is brought to a boiling point and then the heat applied is reduced to maintain the cooking at simmering temperature ie., 98°C. Apples can be cooked by this method.

- **Steaming:** This method requires the food to be cooked in steam. This is generated from vigorously boiling water or liquid in a pan so that the food is completely surrounded by steam and not in contact with the water or liquid. Here the food gets cooked at 100°C.

- **Pressure cooking:** In pressure cooking escaping steam is trapped and kept under pressure so that the temperature of the boiling water and steam can be raised above 100°C thus reducing cooking time. Foods cooked in pressure cooker are rice, dhal, vegetables and meat.

2. Air as medium of cooking

- **Grilling:** Grilling consists of placing the food below or above or in between a red-hot surface. This results in the browning of the food.

- **Pan broiling or roasting:** When food is cooked uncovered on heated metal or a frying pan, the method is known as pan-broiling. Example: Chapathis.

- **Baking:** Here food gets cooked by hot air inside the oven. Foods baked are generally brown and crisp on the top and soft and porous in the centre. Examples: Cakes and breads. The temperature that is normally maintained in the oven is between 120°C-260°C.

3. Fat as medium of cooking

- **Sauteing:** This method involves cooking in just enough of oil to cover the base of the pan. Foods cooked by sauteing are generally vegetables used as side dishes in a menu.

- **Shallow fat frying:** Here food is cooked on a tava with little oil. Examples: Chapathi, cutlets, etc.

- **Deep fat frying:** Food is totally immersed in hot oil and cooked. The temperature maintained is 180° - 220°C. Example: Samosa, Bajji, etc. The taste of the food is improved along with texture.

4. Other cooking methods

- **Braising:** Braising is a combined method of roasting and stewing in a pan with a tight fitting lid. Meat is cooked by this method.

- **Microwave cooking:** 1. Door release button. 2. See-through oven window. 3. Door safety lock system. 4. External air vents. 5. Control panel. 6. Identification plate. 7. Glass tray. 8. Roller ring.

Electromagnetic waves from a power source called magnetron are absorbed by the food and food becomes hot at once. Microwave cooking enhances the flavour of food because it cooks quickly with little or no water and thus preserves the natural colour of vegetables and fruits.

Solar Cooking

Food is a mixture of many different chemical components. The study of food science involves an understanding of the changes that occur on these components during food preparation. Study of food science also includes understanding the nutritive value of different foods and methods of preserving them during cooking.

Solar cooker works on solar energy. Solar cooker consists of well insulated box, the inside of which is painted dull black and is covered by one or more transparent covers, the purpose of which is to trap the heat inside the solar cooker. The temperature maintained is around 140°C. Cost of the cooker and the maintenance cost is low. It takes longer time and special vessels need to be used.

FOOD SCIENCE

Food is a mixture of many different chemical components. The study of food science involves an understanding of the changes that occur on these components during food preparation. Study of food science also includes understanding the nutritive value of different foods and methods of preserving them during cooking.

Cereals

The principle cereal crops are rice, wheat, maize, jowar, ragi and bajra. Cereals are the main source of energy. Rice provides 345 calories and 6.8 grams of protein per 100 grams and wheat provides 341 calories and 12.1 grams of protein per 100 gms. Ragi is a rich source of calcium and iron. Wheat and ragi are rich in fibre. Whole grain cereals are an important source of B vitamins in our diet.

Principles of cooking

- **Gelatinisation:** When starch granules are mixed with water and cooked the grains absorb water and swell. This process is known as gelatinisation.
- **Dextrinisation:** If starch is subjected to dry heat, it is converted to dextrin, giving a brown colour. This is called dextrinisation.

Gluten Formation

Glutenin or glutelin and gliadin are proteins present in wheat. During the mixing of a dough the long strands of glutenin evidently becomes aligned in the direction of mixing and forms a film that envelopes the starch granules in the dough. In the presence of water and with mechanical agitation, the protein fraction forms a tough elastic complex called gluten, which is capable of retaining gases and by doing so, a leavened product is obtained.

Due to its elastic property, the dough can be rolled to prepare chapathis or puris.

Pulses

Pulses are edible fruits or seeds of pod bearing plants. The major pulses which are used are red gram dhal, bengal gram dhal, black gram dhal and green gram dhal.

Composition and nutritive value

Pulses contain 55 to 60% starch. Every 100 grams of pulses provide about 350 calories and 22 grams of protein. Pulses are excellent source of B complex vitamins particularly thiamine, folic acid and pantothenic acid. Soyabean provides 43 grams of protein per 100 grams. Whole grams are good sources of protein, B-vitamins and fibre.

Principles of cooking

Many pulses particularly whole grams, which have hard outer covering need soaking prior to cooking. Addition of sodium bicarbonate hastens the cooking process, but is not advisable because it destroys the B vitamins.

Vegetables

The term vegetable is used to refer to those plants or parts of plants that are served raw or cooked as a part of the main course of a meal.

Composition and nutritive value

Nutritionally they are classified into 3 groups,

(i) **Green Leafy Vegetables:** They are good sources of β-carotene, calcium, riboflavin, folic acid, ascorbic acid, iron and vitamin K.

(ii) **Roots and Tubers:** They are good sources of calories and fairly good sources of Vitamin C. eg. Potato,. Carrots etc.

(iii) **Other Vegetables:** They contribute to the fibre content of the diet. Ladies finger and cluster beans are a good source of folic acid.(eg.) Brinjal, Ladies finger, etc.

Fruits

Fruits are the ripened ovary or ovaries of a plant together with adjacent tissues. Fruits are fleshy or pulpy in character, often juicy and usually sweet with fragrant, aromatic flavours.

Composition and nutritive value

Fruits are very poor source of protein and fat. They are good source of fibre, β-carotenes and vitamin C.

Milk and Milk Products

Milk is one food for which there seems to be no adequate substitute. The milk products include curd, butter, skimmed milk, condensed milk, khoa, paneer and cheese.

Composition

Milk is a complex mixture of lipids, carbohydrates, proteins and many other organic compounds and inorganic salts dissolved or dispersed in water. The chief carbohydrate present in milk is lactose, a disaccharide although trace amounts of glucose, galactose and other sugars are also present. The protein present in milk is caesin.

Nutritive value

Milk provides 67 calories and 3.2 grams of protein per 100ml. Milk has good quality protein. Dairy foods are a major source of calcium and riboflavin.

The ratio of calcium phosphorus in milk is regarded as most favourable for bone development. In addition, dairy products contain other nutrients such as vitamin D and lactose which favour calcium absorption.

Milk is not a good source of niacin, but it is an excellent source of tryptophan. Milk is a very poor source of vitamin C and iron.

Pasteurization

The microorganisms present in milk are killed using a method called pasteurization, where milk is heated to 65°C for 30 minutes or 72°C for 15 seconds and cooled rapidly.

Eggs

Although eggs of all birds may be eaten, the egg of chicken is used more often than any other birds.

Composition

The chief protein of egg white are ovalbumin, conalbumin, ovamucin and avidin. The major proteins in egg yolk are lipoprotein which includes lipoviteliins and lipovitellinin. The fat in the egg yolk contains triglycerides and phospholipids (ie) lecithin.

Nutritive value of egg / 100 g

NUTRIENT	AMOUNT
Energy (Kcal)	173
Protein (g)	13.3
Fat (g)	13.3
Calcium (mg)	60.0
Phosphorus (mg)	220.0
Iron (mg)	2.1
Retinol (mcg)	420
Thiamine (mg)	0.1
Riboflavin (mg)	0.4
Niacin (mg)	0.1
Folic acid (mcg)	78.3
Vitamin BI2 (mcg)	0.2

One egg weighs between 40-50g. Egg contains good quality protein. Egg yolk is a good source of iron, vitamin A, riboflavin, folic acid and vitamin B_{12}.

Flesh foods

The term flesh foods include meat, poultry and fish.

Meat

The term meat refers to the muscles of warm-blooded, four legged animals, the chief ones being cattle, sheep and pigs. Meat provides 86 calories and 19.4 grams of protein per 100gm. Meat is an excellent source of some of the B complex vitamins. Liver is an excellent source of iron and vitamin A. Tender cuts of beef, lamb and pork may be cooked by roasting, broiling, pan-broiling, frying, braising, stewing and pressure-cooking.

Poultry

The term poultry is applied to all birds used as food and includes chicken, duck, geese, turkey and pigeons. Of these chicken and turkey are most commonly used for their meat.

Poultry meat has high protein content and contains all the essential amino acids required for building body tissues. Poultry flesh is a good source of B vitamins and minerals.

Moist heat methods are applied to older and tougher birds and dry heat methods are applied to young tender birds.

Fish

Edible fish are categorised as either fin fish or shell fish. Fish is an excellent source of protein. They contain around 20 % protein. Fresh water fish contains n-3 fatty acids, the consumption of which reduces the incidence of heart diseases. Fish is rich in calcium. Fish liver oils are excellent source of vitamins A and D. Fish are good source of niacin and vitamin D.

Fish is usually cooked by dry heat methods of cooking like broiling, baking and frying. Moist heat method is also effectively used to protect the delicate flavour of the fish.

Spices

Aromatic food substances, which enhance flavour, are classified into spices, herbs and seasonings. Spices are usually dried roots, barks or seeds used whole, crushed or powdered. Example: cloves. Herbs are usually the fresh leaves. Example: coriander leaves. Seasonings are the bulbs used fresh like onion and garlic.

Role of spices in cookery

- Spices are used as flavouring agents. Example: garam masala added to pulav.
- Spices are used as colouring agents. Example: turmeric added to lime rice.
- Spices give pungency. Example: ginger.
- They act as preservatives. Example: fenugreek powder added to pickles.
- They act as souring agents. Example: dry mango powder.
- Spices act as thickening agents. Example: poppy seeds added to kurma.
- They have antibacterial and anticarcinogenic properties. Example: turmeric, garlic.
- Spices reduce blood sugar and blood cholesterol levels. Example: fenugreek seeds.

Beverages

Beverages may be classified according to their functions in the body.

- Refreshing. Example: fruit juices.
- Nourishing. Example: milk shakes.
- Stimulating. Example: coffee and tea.
- Soothing. Example: warm milk and hot tea.
- Appetising. Example: soups.

Points to remember while making beverages

- Beverages should be served as soon as possible after preparation in order to retain fresh natural flavour.
- Hot beverages should be served hot and cold beverages ice cold.
- Beverages should be served in attractive glass tumblers.
- Beverages must not be diluted too much with either water or ice.

Alcoholic beverages

Beer

The principle raw materials of beer manufacture are malted barley, rice and corn, which supply carbohydrates for fermentation by yeast into ethyl alcohol and carbon dioxide.

Wine

As grapes mature, the wine yeast saccharomyces ellipsoideus naturally accumulates on the skin. When the crushed grape is placed at a temperature of about 27°C the juice proceeds to ferment yielding ethyl alcohol, carbon dioxide and traces of flavour compounds.

IMPORTANT NUTRIENTS

Nutrients are the constituents in food that must be supplied to the body in suitable amounts. These include carbohydrates, fats, proteins, minerals and vitamins.

CARBOHYDRATES

Carbohydrates are sugars or polymers of sugars such as starch, that can be hydrolyzed to simple sugars by the action of digestive enzymes or by heating with dilute acids.

Carbohydrates are classified as monosaccharides or simple sugars (glucose, fructose), disaccharides or double sugars (sucrose, lactose) and polysaccharides which include many molecules of simple sugars (starches, dextrins).

Functions

1. The body uses carbohydrate as a source of energy. One gm of carbohydrate provides 4 kilocalories.
2. They are the major source of energy for muscular work.
3. The main source of energy for the central nervous system is glucose.
4. The body mainly uses carbohydrate as the source of energy, thus sparing the tissue protein breakdown for energy purpose. This is called "protein sparing action of carbohydrates".
5. In the liver, carbohydrates have special functions to perform. They include detoxifying action and a regulating influence on protein and fat metabolism.
6. The heart muscle mainly uses glucose as a source of energy.
7. Excess of calories is stored in the form of fat in the adipose tissue.
8. Consumption of indigestible polysaccharides or fibre prevents constipation and reduces the incidence of heart diseases, diabetes mellitus and colon cancer.

Sources of carbohydrates

Foods	Carbohydrate %
RICH SOURCES	
Sugar, jaggery,	85 - 99
Cereals and millets	63 - 79
Dried fruits	67 - 77
GOOD SOURCES	
Pulses	56 - 60
Milk powder, full fat	38 - 39
Milk powder, skimmed	54 - 55
Roots and tubers	22 - 39
FAIR SOURCES	
Fresh fruits	10 - 25
Milk	4
Nuts and oil seeds	10 - 25

FATS

The term lipid or fat is applied to a group of naturally occurring substances characterised by their insolubility in water. The lipids present in the diet of animal and human body includes triglycerides, phospholipids and cholesterol.

Functions

1. Fats are a concentrated source of energy. One gram of fat provides 9 calories.
2. Fat is essential for the absorption of fat soluble vitamins like vitamin A, D, E and K.
3. Fats improve the palatability and gives a satiety value (ie) feeling of fullness in the stomach.
4. Fats are deposited in adipose tissue and thus serve as a reserve source of energy during starvation and illness.
5. They protect vital organs in the body by forming a lining on top.
6. They act as insulators against heat and cold.
7. They are the essential constituent of the membrane of every cell.
8. Phospholipids are present in the plasma in combination with proteins as lipoproteins

which are involved in the transport of fat and cholesterol.

9. Phospholipids are present in large amounts in the nervous system and essential for its function.

10. Cholesterol serves as a precursor for the formation of bile acids.

Sources of fats

Food	Fat %
RICH SOURCES	
Pure oils and fats	100
Ghee and vanaspathi	100
Butter	80-81
GOOD SOURCES	
Nuts and oil seeds	40-60
Milk powder, fullfat	26
Eggs	14
Meat and fish	10-15
FAIR SOURCES	
Milk, cow's	4
Milk, buffalo	7
Pulses (whole)	3-5
Cereals and millets	2-3

PROTEINS

Dietary protein performs all three functions of nutrients. It is needed for growth, maintenance, and repair of body tissues. It regulates key processes within the body and only excess protein can be used as a source of energy.

Functions

1. Proteins are required for the growth and maintenance of tissues.

2. It is needed for the formation of essential body compounds.

3. It regulates water balance in the body.

4. It helps in the transport of nutrients.

5. It is required for the maintenance of appropriate pH.

6. It is also a source of energy. One gram of protein provides 4 calories.

7. It fights the body against diseases.

8. It helps in detoxifying action.

Sources of proteins

Food	Protein %
RICH SOURCES	
Meat, fish and liver	18-20
Eggs	14
Milk powder, full fat	26
Cheese	18-20
Pulses, dry	18-24
Nuts and oilseeds	18-26
Soyabean	35-40
GOOD SOURCES	
Cereals and millets	6-12

MINERALS

1. Calcium

Calcium makes up between 1.5-2% of body weight. Almost 99% of this calcium is found in the hard tissues of the body, namely the bones and teeth.

Sources of calcium

Food stuffs	Calcium (mg/100g)
Rich sources	
Milk powder, sesame seeds with husk and small dried fish	1.20-1.45
Good sources	
Ragi, milk and green leafy vegetables and small fish eaten with bone	0.10-0.33

Functions

1. It is essential for the formation of bones and teeth.

2. It is essential for clotting of blood.

3. It regulates the permeability of capillary walls.

4. It is essential for the contraction of heart and muscle.

5. It regulates the excitability of nerve fibres and nerve centres.

6. It acts as an activator for the enzymes present in the gastric juice.

2. Phosphorus

Phosphorus constitutes approximately 1% of the weight of the human body, Upto 90% of this is found within calcium phosphate crystals in the bones and teeth.

Functions

1. It is necessary for the formation of bones and teeth.

2. It is essential for carbohydrate metabolism.

3. It is a constituent of certain co-enzymes.

4. It is an essential constituent of nucleic acids and nucleoproteins which are integral parts of the cell nuclei.

Sources of Phosphorus

Food stuffs	Phosphorus (g/100g)
Cereals, Millets, Pulses, nuts and Oilseeds	0.20 - 0.65
Dried fish	1.2 - 1.3
Milk powder	0.76 - 0.82
Meat, fish and eggs	0.31 - 0.41
Milk	0.09 - 0.11

3. Iron

Most of the iron in the body is found in the blood, but some is present in every cell bound to iron containing enzymes.

Functions

1. It is required for the transport and storage of oxygen in cells & tissues.

2. It acts as co-factors of enzymes and other proteins.

3. It is required for the formation of red blood cells.

Sources of iron

Food stuffs	Iron (mg/100g)
Rich sources	
Sesame seeds, jaggery and green leafy vegetables	10-20
Good sources	
Cereals and millets	3-8
Liver	7-9
Meat and egg	2-3

4. Iodine

Functions

Iodine is a constituent of thyroxine, the active principle of the thyroid gland. The thyroid gland plays an important role in energy metabolism and in the growth of the body.

Sources

Iodine is present only in small amounts in common foods, the quantity of iodine present depending on the iodine content of the soil. Iodised salt and seafish are good sources of iodine.

VITAMINS

Vitamins may be defined as organic compounds occurring in small quantities in the different natural foods and necessary for the growth and maintenance of good health in human beings.

A. Fat soluble vitamins

1. Vitamin A

Functions

1. Vitamin A plays a critical role in vision in dim light.

2. Vitamin A is essential for the integrity of the mucous secreting cells of epithelial tissues.

3. It is essential for normal bone formation.

4. Vitamin A deficiency causes degeneration of the myelin sheath.

5. Vitamin A is essential for the synthesis of mucoproteins and glycoproteins.

6. It is essential for normal reproduction.

Sources

Vitamin A is present only in foods of animal origin, such as liver, eggs, milk and fatty fish. All plant foods contain only carotenoids which is converted to vitamin A in the body .Papaya, mango, carrots, green leafy vegetables and other yellow, orange coloured fruits and vegetables are good sources of b-carotene.

2. Vitamin D

Functions

1. Vitamin D promotes the absorption of calcium and phosphate from the small intestines.
2. This also acts on the bones directly promoting calcification.
3. It regulates the concentration of calcium in blood plasma.

Sources

The good sources of vitamin D includes sunlight, fish liver oils, butter, cheese, ghee and milk.

3. Vitamin E

Functions

1. It is essential for normal reproduction in man.
2. It is required for the normal functioning of the immune system.
3. It is an antioxidant, which reduces the incidence of heart diseases.

Sources

Vegetable oils and fats, nuts and oilseeds and whole grams are the richest natural sources of vitamin E.

4. Vitamin K

Functions

Vitamin K is essential for blood coagulation. It is required for the synthesis of various substances needed for blood clotting.

Sources

The concentration of vitamin K is highest in dark green leafy vegetables, but it is also found in liver, pulses, cereals and some tubers.

B. Water soluble vitamins

1. Vitamin C or Ascorbic acid

Functions

Vitamin C is essential for

1. Formation of collagens and intercellular cement substances.
2. Absorption of iron and incorporation of plasma iron in ferritin.
3. Bone formation.
4. Adrenal cortex function.
5. Neuro transmitter synthesis.
6. Aids in calcium absorption.
7. Drug detoxification.
8. Activation of hormones.

Sources

The rich sources of vitamin C includes amla, guava and other citrus fruits. Good sources include green leafy vegetables and fruits like papaya and tomato.

2. B Complex Vitamins
Thiamine or Vitamin B_1

Functions

1. Thiamine is essential for growth.
2. It is essential for maintaining the nerves in normal condition.
3. It plays an important role in carbohydrate metabolism.

Sources

Diets based on whole wheat, millets, raw hand pounded rice or parboiled rice usually supplies thiamine in the diet. Organ meats, pork, liver, eggs and whole grams are fair sources of thiamine.

3. Riboflavin or Vitamin B_2

Functions

1. Riboflavin is involved in the regulatory functions of some hormones involved in carbohydrate metabolism.
2. The retina contains free riboflavin, which is converted by light to a compound involved in stimulation of the optic nerve.

3. Riboflavin plays, an important role in many enzyme systems involved in the metabolism of carbohydrates, fats and proteins.

4. It is involved in the formation of red blood cells in the bone marrow.

Sources

Rich sources of riboflavin include milk and milk products, eggs, liver, and dried yeast. Good sources are green leafy vegetables, whole cereals and millets, meat and fish. Fair sources include milled cereals, cereal products and roots and tubers.

4. Niacin or Nicotinic Acid

1. Nicotinic acid is essential for the normal functioning of the skin, intestinal tract and the nervous system.

2. Nicotinic acid is a component of two coenzymes NAD and NADP, which take part in several enzymatic reactions.

Sources

The rich sources of niacin are groundnuts, dried yeast and liver. Good sources are whole cereals, legumes, meat and fish. The fair sources include milled cereals, maize, milk and eggs.

5. Pyridoxine or Vitamin B$_6$

Functions

1. Pyridoxine like other vitamins functions as a co-enzyme.

2. It is essential for growth of infants and prevention of macrocytic anemia.

Sources

Meat, pulses, wheat and dried yeast are good sources while green leafy vegetables and other cereals are fair sources of this vitamin.

6. Folic acid

Functions

1. It is essential for the maturation of red blood cells.

2. It is required for the normal growth and division of all cells.

3. It plays a role in the metabolism of some amino acids.

4. It prevents megaloblastic anaemia.

Sources

Fresh green leafy vegetables, yeast, liver and eggs are rich sources of this vitamin. Cereals, pulses, nuts, oilseeds and other vegetables like ladies finger and cluster beans are good sources of this vitamin.

7. Vitamin B$_{12}$

Functions

1. It promotes the maturation of erythroid cells.

2. It is involved in biochemical-processes essential for DNA synthesis and division of cells.

3. It is required for the synthesis of myelin, the white sheath that covers the nerve fibers.

4. It stimulates appetite and improves the general health of the patient.

5. It cures the neurological symptoms of pernicious anemia.

Sources

Vitamin B$_{12}$ is normally present only in animal foods like liver, egg, mutton and milk.

8. Pantothenic Acid

Functions

It is involved in the synthesis of amino acids, B$_{12}$ and hemoglobin.

Sources

The best sources of pantothenic acid are liver, kidney, egg yolk, yeast and fresh vegetables. Milk and meat are fairly good sources.

9. Biotin

Functions

Biotin takes part as a coenzyme in several metabolic functions of carbohydrate and lipid metabolism.

Sources

Liver, kidney and yeast extracts are good sources. Pulses, nuts and chocolate are fair sources of this vitamin.

MENU PLANNING

Menu planning is the process of planning and scheduling intake of meals for a general or specific individual requirements.

PRINCIPLES OF PLANNING MENUS

1. A good menu plan should meet the nutritional requirements of each member of the family.
2. Meal pattern must fulfill family needs.
3. Meal planning should save time and energy.
4. Meal planning should satisfy the budget of the family.
5. Meal plan should give maximum nutrients.
6. The meal planned should consider individual likes and dislikes.
7. Planned meals should provide variety.
8. Meals should give satiety.
9. Menus should include available foods.

Balance Diet

Balanced diet is one which contains different types of foods in such quantities and proportions so that the need for calories, proteins, minerals, vitamins and other nutrients is adequately met and a small provision is made for extra nutrients to withstand short duration of leanness.

A balanced diet should provide around 60-70% of total calories from carbohydrate, 10-12% from protein and 20-25% of total calories from fat.

PRINCIPLES OF PLANNING MENUS FOR DIFFERENT AGE GROUPS

INFANCY (0-12 MONTHS)

Breast milk is not only the best but it is a must for the infant, only breast milk should be given to the infant upto the age of 6 months.

The advantages of breast-feeding are as follows.

1. Breast milk protects the baby against several diseases like diphtheria, poliomyelitis, influenza and other bacterial diseases.
2. The composition of human milk is best suited to the infants, aiding in easy digestibility.
3. Breast feeding is associated with reduced need for hospitalization and improved child survival.
4. An infant derives a sense of security and belonging in being held.
5. It is economical to breast feed an infant.
6. Breast feeding is an important birth control method.
7. Breast feeding enables the mother to shed extra weight accumulated during pregnancy and the uterus comes back to normal size faster when the mother breastfeeds the infant.
8. Human milk is always fresh and at the right temperature.
9. Low danger of incorrect formula and overfeeding.
10. There is evidence to suggest that breast fed babies have better IQ scores later in life and their mental ability is improved.

Weaning

Weaning begins from the moment supplementary food is started and continues till the child is taken off the breast completely. The types of supplementary foods include liquid supplements (fresh fruit juices, soup from green leafy vegetables), solid supplements mashed well (cereal and starchy gruels) and solid supplements unmashed (cooked cereals, pulses and vegetables).

Preschool Children (1-6 Years)

1. The diet should include a variety of foods.
2. The food should be interesting and attractive (eg) chapathis and puris can be made into different shapes.
3. Child should never be forced to eat more than he can take.
4. Food preferences of the child should be taken into consideration.
5. Flavour or color of the milk can be changed to encourage the child to drink more milk.
6. Milk can be given in other forms like milk shakes, ice creams etc.

7. Regularity of meal times is essential.

8. The person feeding the child should not show any dislike of that food in front of the child.

9. The child should never be hurried while taking the food.

10. Different cooking methods and new attractive combinations encourage the child to eat more.

Some suggested recipes include noodles, tricolor sandwiches, milk shakes and ice creams.

School Children (6-12 Years)

1. Menus need to provide variety in colour, texture, taste and flavour.

2. Children do not like to spend too much time at the table for eating. So menus have to provide dishes that are quick to eat and yet satisfying nutritionally.

3. Nutritional requirement should meet their increasing activity and growth.

4. Children have varying appetites and often prefer snacky meals at frequent intervals to a few large ones.

5. New foods are likely to be accepted if it is given in a form, which can be easily handled, and they should be offered at regular intervals until the child learns to accept it.

6. The young child should be encouraged to eat with the rest of the family to help him to learn good eating habits.

Adolescence (13-18 Years)

1. Adequate well balanced nutritious foods should be taken to prevent obesity or under nutrition.

2. An adolescent girl should take enough calcium rich foods in her diet to increase bone density, which delays the onset of osteoporosis.

3. No meal of the day should be missed.

4. Avoid empty calorie foods such as carbonated beverages and junk foods.

5. Iron rich foods may be included in the diet to prevent anemia.

6. Calorie and protein rich foods should be taken to support the growth spurt.

7. Include fruits and vegetables in the diet to meet the vitamins, minerals and fibre requirement.

8. Eating habits should be independent of emotions.

Adults

1. Foods from all five food groups should be included in every menu.

2. It is better to include two cereals in one meal.

3. To improve the cereal and pulse protein quality, minimum ratio of cereal protein to pulse protein should be 4:1.

4. Foods rich in fiber should be included in the diet.

5. Every diet should contain atleast one medium size fruit.

6. Inclusion of salads or raitha not only helps in meeting the vitamin requirements, but the meals would be attractive and have high satiety value due to the fiber content.

7. One-third of calories and protein requirement should be met by lunch or dinner.

8. Processed foods contain a variety of food additives. They may not be nutritionally balanced unless fortified.

9. Fried foods cannot be planned, if oil allowance is less or low in calorie diets.

10. At least five servings of fruits and vegetables should be included in a day's diet.

Old Age

After the age of 35, the basal metabolic rate decreases due to reduced muscle mass and other metabolically active tissue mass. Also there is reduction in physical activity which affects the energy needs.

Dietary modification

The dietary modification to be made in old people's diet and the reason for modification is given in the following table.

Modification of diet during old age

Dietary modification	Reason
Foods must be soft, easily chewable.	Problems of dentition, fallen teeth or dentures.
Foods should be easily digestible.	Decreased production of digestive enzymes.
Restricted fat in the diet, inclusion of PUFA.	Susceptible to heart disease.
Foods rich in fibre should be given.	To prevent constipation and reduce cholesterol level. Also to prevent colon cancer.
Coffee, tea and cola beverages should be restricted.	May result in insomnia due to over stimulation.
Foods rich in calcium like milk should be given.	To compensate the bone loss and reduce the incidence of osteoporosis.
Green leafy vegetables can be given liberally.	Source of nutrients like carotene, calcium, iron, riboflavin, folic acid and vitamin C, besides supplying fibre, Rich in antioxidants.
Foods of the elderly should consist of familiar foods. New foods are difficult to accept.	Unfamiliar or changes in the food pattern may lead to psychological problem like depression.
Clear soup at the beginning of meal.	Aids digestion.
Small and frequent meals instead of three heavy ones.	Favour more complete digestion and free from distress.
A glass of hot milk just before going to bed.	May induce sleep.
Heavy meal at noon and light evening meal.	Sleep is less likely to be disturbed.
Too many sweets with lot of fats and sugar should be avoided.	Too much of sugar may cause fermentation, discomfort due to indigestion and cause tooth ache and may increase cholesterol level. May lead to obesity.
Plenty of fluid	To prevent constipation and dehydration.

Pregnant women

A women who has been well nourished before her pregnancy with reserves of several nutrients so that the needs of the growing foetus can be met without affecting her health. Infants who are well nourished in the womb, have an enhanced chance of entering life in good physical and mental health. Mother's diet should produce adequate nutrients, so that maternal stores do not get depleted and produce sufficient milk to nourish her child after birth.

Dietary modification

1. Nutrient dense foods are those that give the most nutrients per calorie consumed. This type of foods should be included in a pregnant women's diet.

2. Each meal should contain foods from all five food groups.

3. Small and frequent meals at regular intervals should be planned.

4. Usually a daily diet containing 3 cups of milk or its equivalent, two servings of meat, fish, poultry, eggs or a source of complete protein, a dark green or yellow vegetables and a generous serving of citrus fruits will provide a foundation for a nutritionally adequate diet.

5. Plenty of water at least four to six glasses in addition to what is contained in the form of milk and other beverages should be taken daily throughout pregnancy. This will help keep the bowels regular.

Lactating mothers

The nutritional link between the mother and the child continues even after birth. The newborn baby depends for some period solely on breast milk for his existence.

Lactating mother's nutritional requirements should meet her own daily needs, provide enough nutrients for the growing infant and furnish the energy for the mechanics of milk production. Diet of lactating mother and her nutritional status during pregnancy affect to a certain extent the quality and quantity of breast milk.

Dietary guidelines

1. Nutritional requirements are maximum during lactation compared to any other age group in a woman's life. Hence the diet should be balanced and meet the nutritional requirement.

2. Number of meals can be increased.

3. The diet can include lactogogues like garlic, nuts, etc which stimulate the production of milk.

4. It is better to control constipation by including raw and cooked fruits and vegetables, whole grains and adequate amount of water.

5. No food need to be withheld from the mother unless it causes distress to the infant.

6. If the mother loses rapid weight while breast feeding, her calorie intake is to be increased. Some suggested recipes include badam kheer, garlic chutney, fried snacks and custards.

FOOD ADULTERATION AND FOOD LAWS

Adulteration is defined as the process by which the quality or the nature of the given substance is altered. Adulteration of food may endanger health if the physiological functions of the consumer are affected due to either addition of a deleterious substance or the removal of a vital component. Adulteration means not only intentional addition of substances which adversely affect the nature of substances and quality of foods, but also their incidental contamination during growth, harvesting, storage, processing, transportation and distribution.

TYPES OF ADULTERANTS

Adulterants may be intentional or unintentional or incidental. The former is a willful act on the part of the adulterator intended to increase the margin of profit. Incidental contamination is usually due to ignorance, negligence or lack of proper facilities.

Intentional Adulterants

Intentional adulterants are sand, marble chips, stones, mud, chalk powder, water, mineral oil and coaltar dyes. These adulterants cause harmful effects in the body.

Incidental Adulterants

Incidental adulterants are pesticide residues, tin from can, droppings of indents and larvae in food & metallic contamination with arsenic, lead, mercury, etc. can also occur incidentally. The following table shows the toxic effects of some metals and chemicals.

Arsenic	Fruits sprayed by lead arsenate, drinking water	Dizziness, chills, cramps paralysis leading to death.
Barium	Foods contaminated by rat poison (barium carbonate)	Violent peristalsis, muscular twitching and convulsions.
Cadmium	Fruit juices and soft drinks, that come in contact with cadmium and plated vessels, crabs, oysters and kidneys.	Excessive salivation, liver, kidney damage, prostrate cancer, multiple fractures (painful 'itai -itai' disease reported from japan due to cadmium poisoning.)
Cobalt	Water, beer	Cardiac failure.

Copper	Acid foods in contact with tarnished copper ware.	Vomiting, diarrhoea, abdominal pain.
Lead	Some processed foods, water	Paralysis, brain damage, blindness.
Mercury	Mercury fungicide treated seed grains of mercury contaminated fish particularly pike, tuna and shell fish.	Paralysis, brain damage and blindness
Tin	Canned foods	Colic, vomiting, photophobia.
Zinc	Foods stored in galvanized ironware	izziness, vomiting.
Pesticides	All types of foods.	Acute or chronic poisoning causing damage to liver, kidney, brain and nerves leading to death.
Diethyl stilbestrol	Present in meat of stilbestrol fed animals and birds.	Teratogenesis, carcinogenesis.
Antibiotics	Meat from animals fed with antibiotics.	Drug resistance, hardening of arteries, heart diseases.

The incidental poisoning can be prevented by:

- Regular market surveys to warn people of dangerous build up of toxins in foods.
- Using safer pesticides like synthetic pyrethroids or malathion.
- By washing vegetables thoroughly before cooking
- By teaching farmers to use pesticides judiciously

FOOD LAWS AND STANDARDS

Effective means of food quality can be achieved by legislative measures, certification schemes and public participation and involvement in the programme. The following acts has been passed by the government of India to prevent food adulteration and to maintain food quality.

1. Prevention of Food Adulteration Act

This act was passed in the year 1954. The act prohibits the manufacture, sale and distribution of not only adulterated foods but also foods contaminated with microorganisms and toxicants and misbranded foods. PFA specifies microbial standards for pasteurized milk, milk powder, skimmed milk powder, infant milk food and malted milk food. According to PFA, an article of food shall be deemed to be adulterated,

i. If the article is not upto the standard prescribed.

ii. If the article contains any other substances which affects the nature or quality of the substance.

iii. If any inferior or cheaper substance has been substituted wholly or partly.

iv. If any constituent of the article has been wholly or partly abstracted.

v. If the article has been prepared, packed or kept under unsanitary conditions whereby it has become contaminated or injurious to health.

vi. If the article consists of decomposed or diseased animal or vegetable substance or insect - infested or otherwise unfit for human consumption.

vii. If the article contains any poisonous or other ingredient which renders its contents injurious to health.

viii. If any colouring matter other than that prescribed and in amounts not within the prescribed limits of variability is present in the article.

ix. If the article contains any prohibited preservative or permitted preservative in excess of the prescribed limits.

x. If the quality or purity of the article falls below the prescribed standard or its constituents are present in quantities which are in excess of prescribed limits of variability.

2. Essential Commodities Act, 1954

The main objectives of this act is to maintain supply of essential commodities to the public by proper regulation, prevention of black market and making it available to the public at reasonable price. A number of control orders have been formulated under this act

(a) Fruit Products Order, 1955

This lays down statutory minimum standards in respect of the quality of various fruits and vegetable products and processing facilities. Packaging fruits and vegetables of a standard below the minimum prescribed standards is an offense punishable by law. This order is operated by the food and nutrition board of the Ministry of food processing industries.

(b) Milk and Milk Products Order, 1992

The milk and milk products order is to set sanitation and hygiene standards for dairy plants and establish an advisory board to advise the government on production, sale, purchase and distribution of milk and milk products.

(c) Meat Products Order, 1973

This makes it illegal to transport meat unless it has been prepared and processed according to the provisions of the inspection. The order also lays down rules and conditions for procedure to be adopted for the selection of disease free animals, slaughter house practices for further treatment of the meat so as to maintain the meat in a wholesome manner devoid of pathogens.

The following agencies have also laid down quality standards for foods.

(i) **Bureau of Indian Standards (BIS):** Standards are laid for vegetables and fruit products, spices and condiments and animal products and processed foods. Once these standards are accepted, manufacturers whose products conform to these standards are allowed to use BIS label on each unit of their product.

(ii) **The Agmark Standard:** The word AGMARK is derived from Agricultural Marketing. The AGMARK standard was set up by the Directorate of Marketing and Inspection of the Government of India by introducing an Agricultural product Act in 1937.

A sample AGMARK seal is given below.

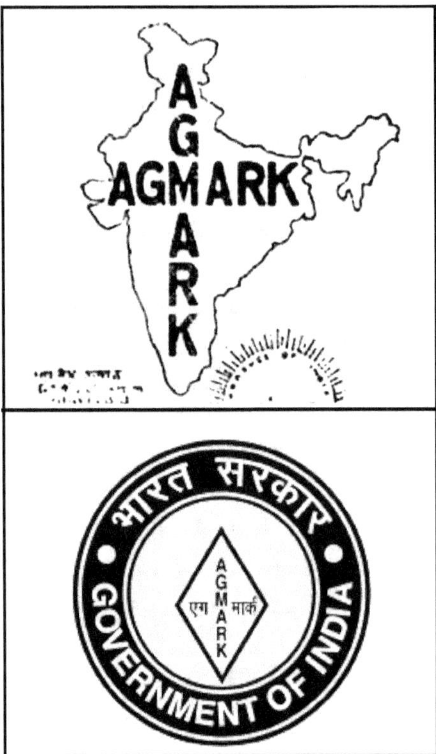

Fig.: Agmark Standards

The quality of a product is determined with reference to the size, variety, weight, colour, moisture, fat content and other factors are taken into account. The act defines quality of cereals, spices, oil seeds, oil, butter, ghee, legumes and eggs and provides for the categorization of commodities into various grades depending on the degree of purity in each case. Grading of commodities like tobacco, spices, basmati rice, essential oils, etc. which are meant for export is compulsory under AGMARK. AGMARK ensures the quality of the product to the importers. In India consumer awareness about the various aspects of PFAis lacking. If consumer cooperation is not forth-coming, controlling adulteration is not an easy task.

FOOD PRESERVATION

When food is available more than the present use, it is preserved for future consumption. Foods such as fruits and vegetables have a short growing season and preservation makes them available for use throughout the year and avoids wastage of surplus crops.

Principles of Food Preservation

1. Prevention or delay of microbial decomposition.

    (a) By keeping out microorganisms – asepsis

    (b) By removal of microorganisms - filtration

    (c) By hindering the growth and activity of microorganisms - low temperature, drying.

    d) By killing the microorganisms - heat or radiation.

2. Prevention or delay of self decomposition of food -By destruction or inactivation of food enzymes, (eg) blanching.

3. Prevention of damage caused by insects, animals and mechanical causes.

Methods of Food Preservation

All methods used for preserving foods are based upon the general principle of preventing or retarding the causes of spoilage-microbial decomposition, enzymatic reactions and damage from mechanical causes insects and rodents.

PRESERVATION BY LOW TEMPERATURE

(i) Freezing

Freezing may preserve foods for long periods of time provided the quality of food is good to begin with and the temperature is maintained in freezers. In slow freezing process or sharp freezing the foods are placed in refrigerated rooms at temperatures ranging from - 4°C to 29°C. In quick freezing process the lower temperatures used - 32° C to -40° C freeze foods so rapidly that fine crystals are formed and the time of freezing is greatly reduced over that required in sharp freezing.

(ii) Dehydrofreezing

Of fruits and vegetables consists of drying the food to about 50 percent of its original weight and volume and then freezing the food to preserve it.

PRESERVATION BY HIGH TEMPERATURE

Pasteurisation

Pasteurisation is a heat treatment that kills part but not all the microorganisms present and usually involves the application of temperatures below 100°C. The heating may be by means of steam, hot water or dry heat and the products are cooled promptly after the heat treatment. Usually milk is pasteurized. Three general methods are used now-a-days.

(a) **Holding or Batch system (Holder method):** This consists in bringing the milk or cream to a temperature usually 65° C and holding at that point for at least 30 minutes followed by rapid cooling.

(b) **High Temperature Short Time Method (HTST) (Flash method):** This consists of raising the temperature of the milk to at least 72° C for 15 seconds followed by quick cooling.

(c) **Ultra High Temperature System (UHTS):** In this system, milk is held for 3 seconds at 93.4° C. After pasteurisation the milk is cooled rapidly to 7° C or lower.

HEALTH | 3

CONCEPT OF HEALTH

Health is the state of being free from disease. But this is not a complete definition of health. According to the World Health Organisation, "Health is a state of complete physical, mental and social well-being and not merely an absence of disease." It means that health includes being physically fot, mentally relaxed, happy and free from worries and socially one is able to get along with people, have confidence in dealings with other people in society, help others and is sensitive to their needs.

Indicators of Good Health

Physical	Mental	Social
- energetic	- happy	- get along well with others
- good posture	- contented	- pleasant mannerism
- normal weight and height	- confident	- help others
- body organs functioning normally	- sensitive to other people's needs.	- fulfil responsibility towards others
- clear, clean skin	- free from tensions and anxieties	
- bright eyes	- relaxed	
- shining hair		
- clean breath		
- good appetite		
- good sleep		

FACTORS CONTRIBUTING TO HEALTH OF THE FAMILY

A family includes the young and old, men and women, each with different needs and health requirements. Let us discuss requirements for good health of a family here.

1. Nutritious Food

Why do we need food? We need to eat so that we get energy, build muscles and bones and protect our body from disease. We must eat a balanced diet, which means our food must have carbohydrates, proteins, fats, vitamins and minerals in the right quantity. The 'right quantity' depends on the age, sex, work of a person, status of health etc. A growing child needs more protein, an adult needs more carbohydrate, sick people need different types of food depending on the disease. A person with diabetes should not be given sweets. Food eaten at the proper time is a healthy habit. We should avoid eating in between meals. Children should be encouraged to eat fruits and vegetables and less of fried and 'fast' food like hamburgers and pizzas. Consumption of sweets, chocolates and 'cola' drinks should be minimal.

2. Personal Hygiene

There are four major aspects of personal hygiene:

(i) Cleanliness

(ii) Physical exercise

(iii) Rest and sleep

(iv) Healthy habits

Let us study more about these aspects.

Cleanliness

Hands: These must be cleaned regularly. We are continually handling a variety of things like furniture, books, coins, currency notes, animals etc. All these carry germs which may be picked up by your hand and fingers and transferred over other parts of the body or into your mouth through food. To avoid getting any infection through these modes remember the following:

- Never put your fingers into your mouth.

- Never turn the page of your book or newspaper by applying saliva to your finger and likewise never count the currency notes in a similar manner.

- Any time holding the currency notes or other objects in between the lips is even more risky as you may catch germs.

- After using toilets (latrines) always wash your hands very well with soap or with clean charcoal ash but never with any soil (mitti).

- Indian culture of washing hands before and after meals is certainly a hygienic practice, which must never be forgotten.

- Shaking hands, though very common, is a potential source of transmission of germs.

Skin: In order to keep the skin healthy take a bath daily because regular bathing does the following:

- Keeps the skin clean and free of germs

- Removes the body odours given out in perspiration

- Keeps the sweat pores open

Also, change undergarments daily and wash them daily. Use handkerchief/disposable napkins for nose.

Hair: The hair should be kept clean by frequent washing and regular combing. This keeps them healthy and free of parasites (like the head lice) and dandruff. Applying oil to the hair in moderate quantities at frequent intervals is required.

Teeth: The teeth should be cleaned at least twice a day, i.e., before going to bed, at night and after getting up in the morning. The mouth should be washed after every meal. This removes most of the extra food particles stuck in between the teeth. Too many sweets and chocolates is harmful to both your teeth and gums. When teeth and gums are not clean and healthy one is likely to get bad breath.

Breathing by nose: Always breathe by nose and never by mouth. Nose filters out the dirt and germs from the in-going air, thus protecting from many diseases.

Eyes: The eyes must be cleaned and washed with clear water two or three times every day. Otherwise sticky white/yellow dirt sticks on inner sides of the eyes. Never share towels with others, even in the same family. Applying kajal may some times lead to eye infections specially if the same applying stick is shared by others.

Ears: The ears should be kept clean. If you do not wash ears every day you can see dirt depositing on the insides of the ears. The wax inside may be cleaned by a soft moistened swab (phurari). Never put pointed object into the ears.

Nails: Nature has provided nails for efficient working of fingers in holding and manipulating objects. These are also an item of personal beauty. But long or untrimmed nails gather dirt and germs underneath. So, always keep nails trimmed and clean.

3. Physical Exercise

Some kind of physical exercise is necessary for all age groups. Children, adolescents and the young specially need it. Physical exercise improves blood circulation. As a result, all the organs of the body receive the required oxygen and nourishment for normal healthy growth.

There are a variety of physical exercises:

- Brisk walking, running or jogging, aerobics, yoga, etc.
- Playing fast games like kabaddi, kho-kho, football, hockey and other such sports
- Wrestling, dund-baithak, judo, karate, etc.

For older people long gentle walks and yogasanas are excellent for keeping fit.

4. Posture

Correct posture is also important for health as well as for impressive personality. Posture means the manner in which one sits, walks, stands and works.

5. Rest and Sleep

During the day we work a lot and our body muscles get tired. Similarly, our brain too gets tired because we read and memorize and do so many other things mentally. Resting for a short while after intense work and sleep at night refreshes our body for more work the next day. Sleep provides a good rest not only to the tired brain but also to the fatigued body muscles.

How much to sleep?

- Very young infants sleep for most of the day.
- For the adults 6-7 hours of continuous sleep is sufficient.

The room or the place where you sleep should be well ventilated to allow fresh air to come in, also it should be free of noise and disturbance.

6. Healthy Habits

Some important healthy habits ones are as follows:

- Take your food at regular hours
- Go to bed at regular timings
- Clear your bowels (passing stools) every day, preferably in the mornings.
- Say 'no' to any temptation of even just trying once to taste drugs (stimulants and sedatives). Similarly, don't smoke or chew tobacco or even eat pan masala and keep away from alcoholic drinks.
- Never spit, urinate or defecate on the roadside or in public. Use only public latrines and that too carefully, without making them dirty.

DEFICIENCY DISEASES

PROTEIN ENERGY MALNUTRITION (PEM)

The term protein energy malnutrition covers a wide spectrum of clinical stages ranging from the severe forms like kwashiorkar and marasmus to the milder forces in which the main detectable manifestation is growth retardation. It is widely prevalent among weaned infants and pre-school children in India and other developing countries.

Causes

1. **Social and Economic Factors:** Poverty that results in low food availability, overcrowded and unsanitary living conditions and improper child care are frequent causes of PEM. A decline in the practice and duration of breast feeding combined with inadequate weaning practices are the important causes of PEM.

2. **Biological factors:** Maternal malnutrition prior to and or during pregnancy is more likely to produce an underweight new born baby. Infectious diseases are major contributing and precipitating factors of PEM. Diarrhoea, measles and respiratory and other infections result in negative protein and energy balance.

3. **Environmental factors:** Overcrowded and or unsanitary conditions lead to frequent infections like diarrhoea. Agricultural patterns, droughts, floods, earthquakes, wars and forced

migrations lead to cyclic, sudden or prolonged food scarcities. Post harvest losses of food can occur due to bad storage conditions and inadequate food distribution.

4. **Age:** It mostly affects infants and young children whose rapid growth increases nutritional requirement. The long term intake of insufficient food can result in marasmus before one year. Kwashiorkar is common after 18 months.

The five forms of PEM are as follows :

i. Kwashiorkor

The important Clinical signs and symptoms of kwashiorkor are:

- Growth failure due to general lack of proteins and calories.
- Mental changes such as apathy and irritability.
- Muscle wasting.
- Oedema occurs at first in the feet and lower leg and then may involve the hands, thigh and face.
- Moon face.
- Fatty and enlarged liver
- Loss of appetite, vomiting and diarrhoea
- Characteristic skin changes which include dark pigmented brownish black areas of skin on buttocks and back of thighs called as crazy pavement dermatosis.
- Hair changes
- Anaemia
- Vitamin A deficiency.

ii. Marasmus

The signs and symptoms of marasmus are:

- severe growth retardation
- loss of subcutaneous fat
- severe muscle wasting
- he child looks appallingly thin with shrivelled body, wrinkled skin and bony prominence.

iii. Marasmic Kwashiorkar

The child shows a mixture of some of the features of marasmus and kwashiorkar.

iv. Nutritional Dwarfing or Stunting

Some children adapt to prolonged insufficiency of food-energy and protein by a marked retardation of growth. Weight and height are both reduced and in the same proportion, so they appear superficially normal.

v. Under Weight Child

Children with sub-clinical PEM can be detected by their weight for age or weight for height, which are significantly below normal. They may have reduced plasma albumin. They are at risk for respiratory and gastric infections.

Treatment

Treatment strategy can be divided into three stages.

- Resolving life threatening conditions
- Restoring nutritional status
- Ensuring nutritional rehabilitation.

There are three stages of treatment.

1. **Hospital Treatment:** The following conditions should be corrected. Hypothermia, hypoglycemia, infection, dehydration, electrolyte imbalance, anaemia and other vitamin and mineral deficiencies.

2. **Dietary Management:** The diet should be from locally available staple foods - inexpensive, easily digestible, evenly distributed throughout the day and increased number of feedings to increase the quantity of food.

3. **Rehabilitation:** The concept of nutritional rehabilitation is based on practical nutritional training for mothers in which they learn by feeding their children back to health under supervision and using local foods.

Prevention

- Promotion of breast feeding
- Development of low cost weaning

- Nutrition education and promotion of correct feeding practices
- Family planning and spacing of births
- Immunisation
- Food fortification
- Early diagnosis and treatment

DEFICIENCY OF VITAMINS

1. Vitamin A: (Retinol)

The important deficiency states due to lack of vitamin A in the diet are:

(i) Night Blindness: In the early stages of vitamin A deficiency, the individual cannot see well in dim light. In advanced deficiency, the subject cannot see objects in dim light.

(ii) Xerosis Conjunctiva: The conjunctiva is dry, thickened, wrinkled and pigmented. The pigmentation gives conjunctiva a smoky appearance.

(iii) Xerosis Cornea: When dryness spreads to cornea, it takes on a hazy, lusterless appearance.

(iv) Bitot's Spots: Greyish glistening white plaques, formed of desquamated thickened conjuctival epithelium, usually triangular in shape and firmly adhering to the conjuctiva.

(v) Keratomalacia: When xerosis of the conjuctiva and cornea is not treated, it may develop into a condition known as keratomalacia.

(vi) Follicullar Hyperkeratosis: The skin becomes rough and dry.

2. Vitamin B$_1$ (Thiamine)

Thiamine deficiency causes the disease, beriberi, in human beings. Two forms of beriberi namely wet beriberi and dry beriberi occurs in adults. The first symptoms are anorexia (loss of appetite) with heaviness and weakness of the legs. There is pain and numbness in the legs. The subjects feel weak and get easily exhausted. Oedema is the important feature of wet beriberi. The calf muscles are swollen. The pulse is fast and bouncing. The heart becomes weak and death occurs due to heart failure. In infantile beriberi, the first symptoms are restlessness, sleeplessness and cardiac failure.

3. Vitamin B$_2$ or Riboflavin

Riboflavin deficiency is characterized by

(a) **Angular stomatitis:** The lesions at the angles of the mouth are termed as angular stomatitis.

(b) **Glossitis:** The tongue in general is acutely inflamed called as glossitis.

(c) Skin lesions occur on the nasolabial folds and on the ears.

(d) **Cheilosis** which is the dry chapped appearance of the lips.

(e) Behavioural abnormalities occur in riboflavin deficient children.

4. Vitamin B$_3$ (Niacin)

Niacin deficiency causes the disease *pellagra* in humans. Pellagra is also called *Disease of 3D's*. Because the disease has the symptoms of diarrhoea, dermatitis and depression. The disease is characterized by the following.

(a) **Glossitis and diarrhoea:** These are the two outstanding symptoms. Nausea and vomiting are seen in most cases.

(b) The *dermatitis* is the most characteristic symptom of the disease. The commonest sites are the back of the fingers and hands, the forearms, and the neck.

(c) Milder mental disturbances consisting of irritability, depression, inability to concentrate and poor memory are common in niacin deficiency.

5. Vitamin B$_6$ or Pyridoxine

Pyridoxine deficiency results in the following

(a) Hypochromic microcytic anaemia.

(b) Sleep disturbances, irritability and depression

(c) Angular stomatitis, glossitis and cheilosis in pregnant and lactating mothers.

6. Pantothenic Acid

The visible signs of deficiency include nausea, vomiting, tremor of the outstretched hands, irritability and burning feet syndrome.

7. Folic Acid

Folic acid deficiency causes megaloblastic anaemia mainly in pregnant women of low income groups.

8. VITAMIN B$_{12}$

Vitamin B$_{12}$ deficiency causes perinicious anemia in humans. Soreness and inflammation of the tongue are commonly observed. Parasthesia (numbness and tingling) occurs in fingers and toes. Persons living exclusively on vegetarian diets develop vitamin B$_{12}$ deficiency.

9. Vitamin C (Ascorbic Acid)

Severe Vitamin C deficiency results in the development of the disease scurvy. The disease is characterized by

(a) General weakness followed by shortness of breath, pain in bones, joints and muscles of the extremities.

(b) Swollen and tender joints, haemorrhages in various tissues and pain in joints.

(c) Bleeding gums and loose teeth.

In infantile scurvy, the infant screams if picked up or moved or handled. There is pain and tenderness of the limbs.

10. Vitamin D (7 - dehydro cholestrol)

Disease caused by vitamin D deficiency are:

(i) Rickets: The chief signs in fully developed active rickets are found in the chest wall (beading), waists and ankles (thickening) and various deformities (knock - knees and bow legs). The child is restless, fretful and pale with flabby and toneless muscles, which allow the limbs to assume unnatural postures. Development is delayed so that the teeth often erupt late and there is failure to sit up, stand, crawl and walk at the normal ages. There is usually a protuberant abdomen so called potbelly.

(ii) Osteomalacia: It may be called as adult rickets. It occurs generally in pregnant women. The changes in bone are similar to rickets. Skeletal pain is usually present and persistent and ranges from a dull ache to severe pain. Muscular weakness is often present and the patient may find difficulty in climbing stairs or getting out of a chair.

11. Vitamin E (Tocopherol)

Vitamin E deficiency in animals causes several disorders such as reproduction failure, liver necrosis, etc.

12. Vitamin K

Vitamin K deficiency leads to haemorrhagic conditions.

DEFICIENCY OF MINERALS

1. **Calcium:** Calcium deficiency may lead to osteoporosis, which is a condition associated with a loss in bone density and bone mass and is primarily found in middle age and elderly women. Its major symptoms are increased vulnerability to bone fractures. Episodes of severe bone pain are usually due to fractures of the brittle bones and may occur after minimal trauma.

2. **Magnesium:** The principal clinical features are depression, muscular weakness, vertigo and liability to convulsions.

3. **Iron:** Iron deficiency anemia is widely prevalent among children, adolescent girls, and expectant and nursing mothers in all developing countries. The clinical features are the results of diminished oxygen carrying power of the blood due to low haemoglobin content. The symptoms are as follows - the skin may appear pale, fingernails can become thin and flat and spoon shaped nails called *koilonychia* may develop.

Other symptoms include fatigue, breathlessness on exertion, dizziness, headache, dimness of vision, sleeplessness, parasthesia, (tingling sensation in arms and legs) and chest pain. In severe cases there may be some oedema of the ankles. There is tendency for children below 3 years with iron deficiency anemia to eat mud (Pica).

4. **Iodine:** If sufficient iodine is not taken in the diet, enlargement of the thyroid takes place, resulting in the disease called *goitre*.

In children severe iodine deficiency may result in serious retardation of growth called cretinism. Iodine deficiency can be treated with administration of iodised salt in the diet. In India, the endemic belt of goiter and cretinism mainly lies along the slopes, foothills, and plains adjacent to Himalayas. Several pockets of endemic goitre are being identified in the Aravalli hills in Rajasthan, Subvindhya hills of Madhya Pradesh, Narmada valley in Gujarat, hilly areas of Orissa, Andhra Pradesh and tea estates of Karnataka and Kerala.

5. **Zinc:** One form of severe zinc deficiency is Acrodermatitis Enteropathica in which severe dermatitis usually appear in the first few months of an infants life.

Hypoguesia (impaired taste) and Hyposmia (impaired smell) appear in moderate zinc deficiency, which can be cured with zinc supplementation.

THERAPEUTIC DIETS

Therapeutic nutrition is concerned with the nutritional requirements of patients suffering from different diseases and prescribing the right type of diets for them. The objectives of diet therapy are as follows:

(i) The correction of the existing dietary deficiencies and to maintain the patient in good nutritional state.

(ii) Formulation of the diet to meet the needs of the patient taking into consideration his food habits.

(iii) Education of the patient regarding the need for adherence to the prescribed diet.

Diet therapy in most instances is not a remedy in itself but is a measure which supplements or makes the medical or surgical treatment more effective.

Factors to be Considered in Planning Therapeutic Diets

(i) The underlying disease conditions which require a change in the diet.

(ii) The possible duration of the disease.

(iii) The factors in the diet which must be altered to overcome these conditions.

(iv) The patient's tolerance for food by mouth.

The normal diet may be modified to

(i) Provide change in consistency as in fluid and soft diets.

(ii) Increase or decrease the energy value.

(iii) Include greater or lesser amounts of one or more nutrients, for example, high protein, low sodium, etc.

(iv) Provide foods bland in flavour.

MODIFICATION OF DIETS IN DIFFERENT NUTRIENTS

Modifications in diets in diseases may involve changes in different constituents such as

(i) Bland diets, omitting spices and condiments.

(ii) Low fibre or high fibre diets.

(iii) High protein or low protein diets.

(iv) High fat or low fat diets.

(v) High carbohydrate or low carbohydrate diets.

(vi) High calorie or low calorie diets.

(vii) Low sodium diets.

The types of changes required in the diets in different diseases are:

1. **Modification in Carbohydrate Content:** High Carbohydrate diet may be indicated in liver diseases and in pre-operative conditions. Restricted Carbohydrate diet is essential in the treatment of diabetes mellitus.

2. **Modification in Calorie Content:** Diets with increased calorie content are required in fever, infections and hyperthyroidism. Low calorie

diets are used for the treatment of obesity and heart diseases.

3. **Modification in Protein Content:** High protein diets are prescribed in protein - calorie malnutrition, and cirrhosis of the liver. Low protein diet may be necessary in nephritis and hepatic coma.

4. **Modification in Fat Content:** Moderately high fat diet is used in the treatment of severe under-nutrition. Low fat diet is essential in heart diseases, obesity and diseases of the liver.

5. **Modification in Mineral Content:** High calcium diet is essential in the treatment of rickets and osteomalacia, while a diet restricted in calcium is desirable in kidney stones. Sodium restricted diets are essential in the treatment of hypertension, cardiac failure and kidney diseases.

6. **Modification in Fibre Content:** Diets rich in fibre are prescribed for the treatment of constipation, while low fibre diets are essential in the treatment of diarrhoea, peptic ulcer and dysentery.

ROUTINE HOSPITAL DIETS

1. Clear Fluid Diet

This diet is made up of clear fluids that leave no residue, and it is non gas forming, non irritating and non stimulating to peristaltic action. This diet can meet the requirement of fluids and some minerals and can be given in 1 to 2 hour intervals. The foods which can be included are barley water, dhal water, tea and coffee without milk, etc.

2. Full Fluid Diet

This diet bridges the gap between the clear fluid and soft diet In this diet, foods which are liquid or which readily become liquid on reaching the stomach are given. It is used following operations, in acute gastritis, acute infections and in diarrhoea. This diet is given at 2 - 4 hours interval. The foods included are kanji, milk shakes, lassi, custards, etc.

3. Soft Diet

It may be used in acute infections, following surgery, and for patients who are unable to chew. The soft diet is made up of simple, easily digested food and contains no harsh fibre and no rich highly seasoned food. In this diet, three meals with intermediate feedings should be given,

SPECIAL FEEDING METHODS

1. Tube Feeding

This is done by passing a tube into the stomach or duodenum through the nose which is called nasogastric feeding or directly by surgical operation known as gastrostomy and jejunostomy feeding. The type of foods supplied through the tube may be

- natural liquid foods
- solid foods blenderised to make liquid food
- commercially supplied polymeric mixtures or elemental diet like Complan, Horlicks, etc.,

The advantages of tube feeding are

- Adequate nutrition could easily be given by this method.
- Foods and drugs which may not be liked by the patients can be administered.

2. Parenteral Feeding

Here the nutrient preparations are given directly into a vein. This method may be used to supplement normal feeding by mouth but can provide all the nutrients necessary to meet a patient's requirements. Then it is known as total parenteral nutrition or TPN. The nutrients given in TPN are glucose, emulsified fat, crystalline aminoacids, Vitamins including B12, folic acid and vitamin K, electrolytes like sodium, potassium, calcium and magnesium, trace elements like Zinc, Copper, Iodine and Water.

DIET IN DIFFERENT DISEASES

1. Fevers

Fever is an elevation in body temperature above the normal. Fever are of three types:

(i) Short duration fever: typhoid, influenza,

(ii) Chronic fever: tuberculosis

(iii) Intermittent fever: malaria.

General Dietary Considerations

Energy: A high calorie diet is prescribed because there is increase in the metabolic rate. Around 2500 - 3000 calories is prescribed.

Protein: About 80 – 100g of protein is prescribed. High protein beverages may be used as supplements to the regular meals.

Fats: Fried foods and highly concentrated foods are avoided because it cannot be digested easily.

Vitamins: Fevers apparently increase the requirement for Vitamin A, B Complex vitamins and Vitamin C.

Fluid: The fluid intake must be liberal to compensate for the losses from the sweat. 2500 - 5000ml is necessary, including soups, fruit juices and water.

Bland, readily digested food and soft foods should be given to facilitate digestion and rapid absorption. Small quantities of food at regular intervals of 2 - 3 hours will permit adequate nutrition without overtaxing the digestive system at any time.

Foods to be Included: Fruit juices with glucose, coconut water, barley water, custards and cereal gruels.

Foods to be Avoided: Oily foods, ghee, spices, fried foods and rich pastries.

2. Peptic Ulcer

The term peptic ulcer is used to describe any localized erosion of the mucosal lining of those portions of the alimentary tract that come in contact with gastric juice. The symptoms of peptic ulcer are epigastric pain, discomfort and gas formation in the upper part of abdomen, weight loss and iron deficiency anaemia.

Dietary Guidelines

1.Bland diet, which consists of mechanically, chemically and thermally non-irritating foods should be given.

2. Moderate use of seasonings is permitted.

3. Regularity of meal times is essential. Small frequent meals are given.

4. In between meals, protein rich snacks should be taken.

5. Meals should be eaten in a relaxed atmosphere and the person should forget personal or family problems while eating.

6. Foods should be eaten slowly and chewed well.

7. Milk and cream can be included because it helps in healing of the ulcer.

8. High protein foods should be included because it helps in healing of the ulcer.

Foods to be Included: Milk, cream, butter, custards and well cooked cereals.

Foods to be Avoided: Strong tea, coffee, alcohols, pickles, spices and condiments and fried foods.

3. Diarrhoea

Diarrhoea is the passage of stools with increased frequency, fluidity or volume compared to the usual for a given individual. Nutritional care includes the replacement of lost fluids and electrolytes by increasing the oral intake of fluids, particularly those high in sodium and potassium such as soups and juices.

Oral Rehydration Solution (ORS) is given which is made by mixing one glass of boiled cooled water with one pinch of salt and one teaspoon of sugar. When the diarrhoea stops, starchy foods like rice, potato and plain cereals can be given followed by protein foods. Fat need not be limited if the individual is otherwise healthy.

4. Liver Diseases

Liver is a vital organ, which secretes bile and takes part in the metabolism of carbohydrates, fats and proteins and in many other vital metabolic processes. The diseases of the liver include:

(i) **Infective Hepatitis:** This is otherwise called as viral hepatitis. The symptoms include anorexia, fever, headache, rapid weight loss, abdominal discomfort and jaundice, (ie) yellow discolouration of the skin and body tissues.

(ii) **Cirrhosis of Liver:** Cirrhosis is a condition in which there is destruction of the liver cell due to viral infection, alcohol and toxins. The symptoms include anorexia, nausea, vomiting, pain, muscle cramps, weight loss, fever, jaundice and ascites. i.e. accumulation of fluid in the abdomen.

(iii) **Hepatic Coma:** This results from entrance of certain nitrogen containing substances such as ammonia into the cerebral circulation without being metabolized by the liver. The precipitating factors are gastro intestinal bleeding, severe infections, surgical procedures and excessive dietary protein. The symptoms include confusion, restlessness, irritability, inappropriate behaviour and drowsiness. Treatment consists of dietary protein restriction and increased calorie intake.

Dietary management of hepatitis and cirrhosis

Energy: A high calorie diet is prescribed. The calorie requirement is between 2000 - 2500 calories.

Proteins: Protein requirement varies according to the severity of the disesase. In severe jaundice 40g is given while in mild jaundice 60 - 80g of protein is permitted.

Fats: About 20g of fat is given. Coconut oil, which contains medium chain fatty acids are given because it does not require bile acids for digestion.

Carbohydrates: High Carbohydrate content in the diet is essential to supply enough calories so that tissue proteins are not broken down for energy purposes.

Vitamins: They are essential to regenerate liver cells. Vitamin supplementation is essential for patients with liver diseases.

Foods Included: Cereal porridge, bread, rice, skimmed milk, fruit juices, biscuits and non stimulant beverages.

Foods Avided: Pulses, bakery products, concentrated sweets, fried foods, whole milk and cream.

5. Heart Diseases

Heart disease affects people of all ages, but is most often caused by atherosclerosis. The term atherosclerosis is used to describe a condition in which lipids are deposited in the intima of blood vessels. The important contributory causes for the development of atherosclerosis are

- High calorie intake
- High saturated fat and cholesterol intake.
- Increased level of cholesterol in blood.
- Sedentary life.
- Stress and strain.

Dietary Management

The objective are maximum rest for the heart and maintenance of good nutrition.

Principles of Diet

Energy: The calorie intake should be just adequate to meet the requirements. For obese patients, it may be necessary to reduce calorie intake.

Fats: Fats should be restricted to not more than 20% of the total calories consumed. The diet should consists of polyunsaturated fatty acids, (eg) sunflower oil.

The diet should contain adequate amount of proteins and vitamins. Fishes are a good source of n-3 fatty acids. Consumption of 100 - 200g of fish 2-3 times a week helps to prevent heart disease. Three or four smaller meals are suggested instead of two big meals. Regular exercise and relaxed mental attitude help to reduce blood pressure. Smoking and drinking of alcohol should be stopped.

6. Hypertension

World Health organisation (WHO) defines hypertension as a condition in which systolic pressure exceeds 160 mm Hg and diastolic pressure exceeds 95 mm Hg. Cardio vascular diseases, renal diseases, tumours of the brain or adrenal glands, hyperthyroidism or diseases of the ovaries or pituitary may cause hypertension.

Predisposing factors of hypertension are heredity, stress, obesity and smoking.

Headache, dizziness, impaired vision, failing memory, shortness of breath, pain over the heart, gastrointestinal disturbance and unexplained tiredness are some of the symptoms.

Dietary Management

Energy : About 20 kcal/kg of ideal body weight are prescribed.

Protein : A diet of 60 g protein is necessary to maintain proper nutrition.

Fats : As they are prone to atherosclerosis it is advisable to avoid a high intake of animal or hydrogenated fat. About 20 g of fat is permitted.

Sodium : A low sodium diet should be given in severe hypertension, salt in cooking and salt on the table should be avoided. The other foods rich in sodium to be avoided are pickles, papad, chips, cheese, salted butter, canned foods, sauce, ketchup, baked foods where baking powder is used and foods where sodium salts are used as a preservative.

Fibre: A high fibre diet should be given.

Foods Included: Salads, Steamed foods, low sodium foods.

7. Kidney Diseases

(i) Nephritis

This condition affects mostly children and young adults. Streptococcal infections causes inflammation of the glomeruli. The symptoms are haematuria (blood in the urine), proteinuria (protein in the urine), oedema, shortness of breath, anorexia, tachycardia (increased heart beat), decreased urine output and elevated blood pressure. The dietary management include:

- High calories - 2000K calories
- Low protein because the kidney cannot excrete the waste products of protein metabolism like urea and uric acid

- Restricted fluid
- Restricted sodium
- Restricted potassium

Foods Included: Rice, sago, ash-gourd and sugar.

Foods Avoided: Salt, pickles, nuts, jaggery, pulses and meat.

(ii) Nephrosis

This can be caused due to progressive nephritis, diabetes mellitus and toxins. The symptoms include proteinuria (protein in the urine), hypoalbuminaemia (low serum albumin levels), oedema and increased serumcholesterol. High carbohydrate, restricted protein, moderate fat, restricted fluid and restricted sodium diet is recommended for a nephrotic patient. Vitamin supplements especially vitamin C should be given.

(iii) Kidney Stones (Urolithiasis)

Urinary calculi or kidney stones are usually found to be lodged in the urinary tract, namely kidney, ureters, bladder or urethra. The causative factors are warm climate, occupation, urinary tract infection, heredity and hyperthyroidism. The majority of stones are made up of calcium phosphate, calcium oxalate, uric acid or magnesium ammonium phosphate. The diet should provide adequate fluids and restrict foods rich in calcium, oxalate and uric acid.

8. Diabetes Mellitus

Diabetes mellitus is a chronic metabolic disorder that prevents the body to utilize glucose completely or partially due to the deficiency in the secretion of insulin. The predisposing factor of diabetes mellitus are mainly heredity and stress. The symptoms of diabetes mellitus are

- Increased thirst (polydypsia)
- Increased urination (polyuria)
- Increased hunger (polyphagia)
- Weight loss
- Glycosuria (sugar in the urine)

- Hyper glycemia (increased blood sugar level)
- Skin irritation or infection
- Weakness, loss of strength.
- Delayed wound healing.
- Fluid and electrolyte imbalance.

A blood sugar level between 80-120 mg per 100 ml is considered to be normal.

Dietary Management

- Simple Carbohydrates like sugar and honey are avoided.
- The diet should provide high fibre. Salads should be included in every meal.
- Whole grams and sprouted grams should be included in the diet
- Wheat is preferred to rice because it is high in fibre and reduces the rate at which glucose is absorbed in the blood.
- Poly unsaturated fatty acids are included in the diet.
- High protein intake helps to increase insulin production and promote satiety.
- Three main meals and three in between meal snacks are taken.
- Patient should avoid fasting and feasting.
- Vitamins and minerals are supplemented to meet daily requirements.
- Low fat diet is preferred to prevent atherosclerosis.

Foods to be Avoided: Simple sugars, honey, sweets, dried fruits, cake, fried foods, alcohol, nuts and sweetened juices.

Foods to be Restricted: Fats, cereals, meat and egg.

Foods to be Included: Green leafy vegetables, fruits except banana, coffee or tea, skimmed milk, butter milk, salads and lemon.

9. Food Allergy

Food allergy may be defined as normal tissue reactions that may occur in some individuals after consuming a particular food or groups of food. Food allergens consist mostly of proteins like milk and eggs and also include tomato, brinjal, orange, potato and chocolate. The signs and symptoms of food allergy include:

1. Skin lesions such as rashes and eczema.
2. Nausea, vomiting and diarrohea
3. Headache, cold and asthma.
4. Redness, swelling, burning and itching of the eyes.
5. Irritation of the nasal mucous membrane.

The procedures adopted for the diagnosis are history of the consumption of foods and skin tests. Elimination diets (i.e) exclusion of certain foods or food groups in the diet for some time are used in the treatment of food allergy. Drugs like antihistamines and corticosteroids are also given to treat allergy.

FOOD BORNE INFECTIONS AND FOOD POISONING

Raw foods such as meat, fish, milk and vegetables grown on sewage purchased from the market are likely to be contaminated with harmful microorganisms. These are generally destroyed during cooking or processing of the food. Some of the microorganisms may survive due to inadequate heat processing. Further, some of the foods if consumed in the raw state can cause food poisoning Recent studies have shown that food grains when stored in humid atmosphere are infected by pathogenic fungus which can cause serious illness.

BACTERIAL INFECTIONS

Some of the important diseases caused by pathogenic bacteria contaminating foods are discussed below:

1. **Typhoid and Paratyphoid:** Shell fish and vegetables grown on sewage are common carriers of typhoid and paratyphoid. Foods kept exposed for sale are liable to be infected by typhoid and paratyphoid bacteria as flies can transmit these bacteria from infected material to exposed foods. The symptoms include vomiting, diarrhoea and fever.

2. **Botulism:** Botulism is usually caused by consuming canned foods contaminated by botulinum spores. The causative organism is clostridium botulinum and it produces an endotoxin, which is highly toxic. The exotoxin can be inactivated by heat The incubation period is 8-36 hours. The onset of the disease is sudden. The signs and symptoms include disturbed vision, dizziness, and sometimes headache, abdominal pain and physical exhaustion. The toxin affects the central nervous system causing paralysis affecting speech and swallowing. Death from respiratory or cardiac failure occurs after a few days.

3. **Clostridium Perfringens Food Poisoning:** This is mostly associated with consumption of defectively processed pre cooked meat product. The causative organism is clostridium perfringens and the symptoms are abdominal pain and diarrhoea. The incubation period is 8 – 12 hours.

4. **Salmonella Food Poisoning:** The causative organism is Salmonella typhosa. Defectively processed meat, fish and egg and raw vegetables grown on sewage are mainly involved in transmitting the infection. The symptoms are vomiting, diarrhoea and fever. The incubation period is 12 – 48 hours and the duration is for 1 – 7 days.

5. **Staphylococcal Food Poisoning:** The causative organism is staphylococcus aureus. This organism produces an exotoxin and the poisoning is due to the presence of exotoxin in the contaminated food. The toxin is heat stable. Pre cooked animal foods are most commonly involved in this type of poisoning. The symptoms are vomiting, diarrhoea and abdominal pain. The incubation period is 2 – 6 hours.

6. **Streptococci:** Streptococci are the causative agents for sore throat and scarlet fever.

7. **Shigella:** This group causes bacillary dysentry. The symptoms are loose motions with mucous and blood and abdominal pain. It is caused mainly from consuming raw milk to which unclean water has been added and cooked food kept exposed. Flies are the common carriers of this disease, transferring the bacteria from infected material to food.

VIRAL INFECTIONS

This is caused through water polluted with sewage. The viruses however only multiply in living cells and not in food. The various diseases spread include hepatitis, cholera and poliomyelitis.

FUNGAL CONTAMINATION OF FOODS

1. **Fusarium and Cladosporium:** This is caused due to the consumption of cereals and millets infected with fusarium and cladosporium.

2. **Aspergillus Flavus:** This fungus can grow in moist groundnuts, soyabean, cottonseed, legumes and cereals. It produces toxins called as aflatoxins. These can cause liver damage and cancer.

TOXICANTS NATURALLY OCCURING IN SOME FOODS

Some foods contains toxic substances which may cause serious illness when consumed in large amounts. An important example is the legume - Lathyrus sativus, which contains a toxin. When consumed in large amounts, the subjects develop a crippling disease known as lathyrism. Some varieties of mushrooms contain toxic substances which when consumed produce serious ill effects.

INSECT AND RODENT CONTAMINA-TION OF STORED FOODS

1. Insect Infestation

Insect infestation of food grains causes heavy losses and damage to the quality of grains in storage. Taste, flavour, hygienic quality and acceptability of the food grains are affected due to the presence of insect excreta, insect fragments and dead insects. The content of B-Vitamins and the nutritive value of the proteins are also lowered.

2. Rodents

Damages caused by rodents to stored foods are as follows:

(i) They consume large quantities of food grains.

(ii) The hygienic quality of the grain is affected by the excreta of the rodents and also by some disease producing microorganisms present in the food grains. They cause diseases like leptospirosis and plague.

TEXTILES AND CLOTHING

4

Clothing is one of the basic needs for mankind. It protects the body from heat and cold, but also brings out one's personality, enhances beauty, gives comfort and expresses the status of living.

FIBERS

Fibers are very small visible units from which fabrics are made by one process or another. Take a yarn or thread and untwist until it comes apart, or pull a single strand from an opened cotton ball or from a bunch of wool. The small fine, individual hair-like strands are fibers. Thus, a fiber may be partly described as being a slender filament or fine strand of sufficient length, pliability and strength, to be spun into yarns and formed into cloth.

PROPERTIES OF FIBER

The fibers possess certain essential properties. These are the primary and secondary properties.

The primary properties include :

(a) High length to breadth (width) ratio

(b) Tenacity or Fiber strength

(c) Flexibility or Pliability.

(d) Cohesiveness or spinning quality of fibers, and

Secondary properties of fibers are not essential but desirable for consumer satisfaction. These include :

(a) Physical shape

(b) Specific gravity

(c) Luster

(d) Moisture regain

(e) Elastic recovery

(f) Elongation

(g) Resilience

(h) Thermal behavior

(i) Resistance to biological organisms

(j) Resistance to chemical and other environmental conditions.

CLASSIFICATION OF FIBRES

Fibres come as short fibres and long fibres and their length is an important property of fibres. To see a short fibre, take a ball of cotton and pull out fibres from it. Notice that these fibres are quite small. Now try and pull out fibres from a nylon fabric. These, you will see, are longer fibres. The short fibres are called staple and the long ones are called filament.

Fibres also can be classified according to their origin. Some fibres are obtained from natural sources i.e. from plants, animals or minerals. These are called natural fibres. The other fibres are manmade.

(a) Natural Fibres

There can be vegetables fibres, animal fibres and mineral fibers. Let us study these in detail.

(i) **Vegetable Fibres:** Fibres that come from plants are called vegetable fibres and can be obtained from different parts of a plant. Cotton is an example of seed hair. Similarly, fibres can be obtained from the stem of a plant e.g. jute and flax, and from the leaves like pineapple fibres. Fibres are also obtained from the outer covering of a fruit, like coir from coconut husk. All the plant fibres are made up of cellulose.

(ii) **Animal Fibres:** Sheep is the most common animal whose hair is used as wool. Some other animals are camel, goat, and rabbit. Silk is also an animal fibre. It is the secretion of an insect called the silkworm. The animal fibres are made up of proteins.

(iii) **Mineral Fibres:** Natural fibres obtained from the minerals are called mineral fibres, eg. asbestos.

Natural fibres are usually staple fibres with the exception of silk which is a filament fibre.

(b) Manmade Fibres

There is another class of fibres called the manmade fibres. As the name suggests these fibres are not obtained directly from nature but made by using chemicals. Manmade fibres are of two types:

1. Regenerated fibres

2. Synthetic fibres

Let us find out more about man-made fibres.

(i) **Regenerated fibres:** These are made from natural raw material eg., cellulose, (waste cotton fibres or wood pulp) or protein depending upon the fibre to be made. This natural raw material is regenerated with the help of chemicals. Rayon is a regenerated cellulose fibre.

(ii) **Synthetic fibres:** On the other hand Synthetic fibres are obtained from chemical substances and are totally synthetic in nature, e.g., Nylon, Polyester, Acrylic (Cashmilon). Manmade fibres are generally filament fibres. Of course, they can always be cut in to small pieces to form staple fibre, if required.

Let us put the two classification together:

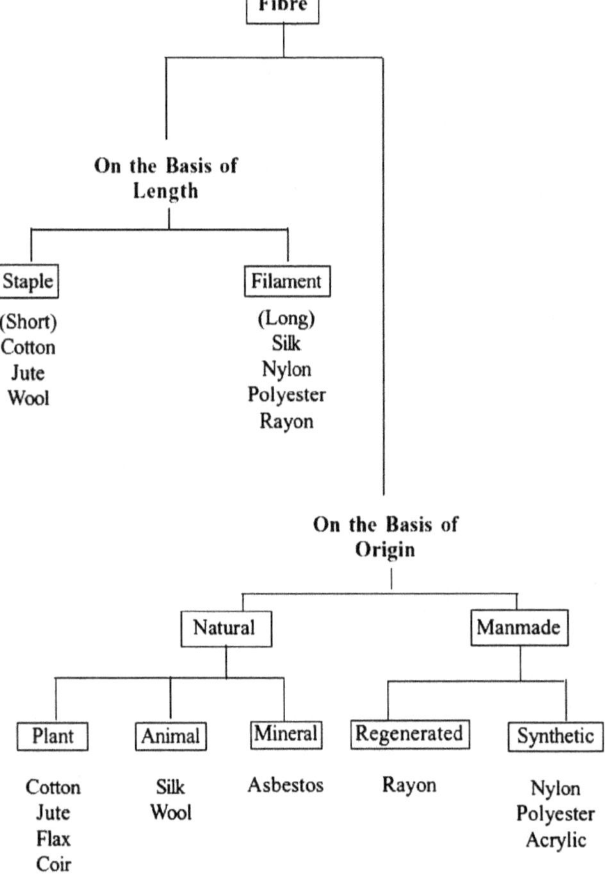

NATURAL FIBERS

Natural Fibres include cotton, silk and wool.

COTTON

Cotton referred to as the "King of fibers" is most important textile fibre in the world. Cotton fabrics were made by the ancient Egyptian, Chinese and of course Indian civilizations.

The cotton fiber is a long cell made up of countless cellulose molecules. Cotton is removed mechanically from the seed balls by the cotton gin. The ginned cotton is then pressed into bales and sent to the factories to be spun into yarns.

Properties of cotton

Cotton fiber is a single cell and varies in length from ½ to 2½ inches. The width varies between 12 to 20 microns.

Physical properties

1. The cotton fibers vary in colour (i.e) white to cream.
2. Cotton has low luster, elasticity & resilience.
3. It is 25% stronger when wet than dry and absorbs moisture.
4. Cotton fabrics shrink and hence they are made shrink resistant.

Thermal properties

1. Cotton burns quickly and readily with a smell of burning paper.
2. It is a good conductor of heat.
3. It will scorch when ironed with too-high temperatures.

Chemical Properties

1. Cotton is resistant to alkali.
2. Strong acids disintegrates cotton.
3. It is resistant to organic solvents.
4. Mercerized cotton can be dyed easily.

Biological Properties

1. Cotton is damaged by fungi such as mildew and bacteria.
2. Silverfish lives on cellulose, so it damages cotton fibers.
3. Moths and beetles do not attack or damage cotton.

Uses of cotton

Cotton is the most widely used fiber because it is inexpensive, easy-care, high absorbency, excellent launder ability and good colourfastness. It is not only used for apparel but also for household and industrial applications.

SILK

Silk has been considered as one of the most elegant and luxurious of fibers. It is popularly known as the Queen of fabrics. The method of raising silk worms and removing the silk filaments from the cocoons, and of using the silk in weaving for garments was discovered by Hsi-Ling-Chi, a little Empress of China.

Commercial silk is produced by the cultivated silkworm, Bombyx mori, a caterpillar, that feeds on mulberry leaves. The eggs laid by the moth are stored in winter and spread out on trays to hatch in a warm shed. Mulberry leaves are placed as soon as the worms appear, for them to eat.

When the worm is fully grown, it starts spinning its cocoon on straw placed on the trays. The silk fluid from special glands issues from two holes, one on either side of the head, called spinnerets.

The fluid hardens as it comes in contact with the air and two long fibers which are stuck together with silk gum are formed. The cocoons are heated to kill the pupa inside, otherwise the moths would destroy some of the silk. Some are allowed to become moths to provide eggs.

Properties

Physical

1. Silk filaments are very fine and long.
2. It is one of the strongest fibers.
3. It has good elasticity and moderate elongation and resilience.

4. Silk fabrics have good resistance to stretch & shrinkage when dry-cleaned.

Thermal

1. Silk burns directly in the path of flame.
2. It extinguishes itself when removed from flame and gives an odour of burning hair.
3. Silk scorches if ironed at too high temperatures.

Chemical

1. Silk is damaged by strong acids and alkalis.
2. Silk is not affected by cleaning solvents.

Biological

1. Silk is resistant to attack by mild dew, bacteria and fungi.
2. Carpet beetles will eat it.

Use

Silk fabrics are noted for their soft, luxurious handle, rich luster, warmth, resilience, and crease resistance, strength and excellent draping quality. A wide range of fabrics are made ranging from sheer chiffon to firmer dress and suiting material, to heavy brocades to the rich pile velvet. Silk serves best for ceremonial occasions, evening or day wear and lingerie.

WOOL

Wool is a natural protein fiber and considered as Man's best friend. Sheepskin, including the hair, was probably used long before it was discovered that fibers could be spun into yarns or even felted into fabric. The earliest fragments of wool fabric have been found in Egypt but Mesopotamia is the birth place of wool.

Wool can be sheared from the living animal or pulled from the hide after the animal has been slaughtered for its meat. Sheared wool is called fleece or clipwool and wool taken from the hides of slaughtered animal is called pulled wool which is inferior in quality to fleece or clip wool.

The quality of wool is expressed by numbers. The higher the numbers, the finer the wool and better the quality. The finest wool is from young sheep. Very fine wool of excellent quality is shorn from lambs when eight months old.

Properties

Physical

1. Wool fibers varies in length from 1½ -15 inches
2. Wool after scouring is yellowish - white or ivory in colour. Other wool may be grey, black, tan or brown.
3. Fine & medium wool have more luster than coarse wool.
4. Wool has a natural crimp. The crimp increases the elasticity and elongation properties of the fiber.
5. Wool is weak but has exceptionally good resilience and moisture absorption.

Thermal

1. Wool bums slowly with a slight sputtering and is self extinguishing.
2. A crisp, black, bead-shaped residue is formed and gives a burning hair smell when removed from flame.
3. Wool scorches easily.

Chemical

1. Wool is susceptible to damage by alkaline solution. Even 5% of NaOH will dissolve wool.
2. It is resistant to mild acid but strong concentrated sulphuric acid decomposes wool fibers.
3. Solvents have no damaging effect on wool fibers.

Biological

1. Wool is resistant to bacteria and mildew but if moisture is present both may destroy wool fiber.
2. Wool being protein fiber is a good food source for carpet beetle and the larvae of clothes moth.

Uses

Woolen and worsted fabrics are used throughout the world. They are crease resistant, flexible, elastic, absorbent, warm and comfortable. A major problem with wool fabric is the tendency to shrink. Crimp decreases when wet and increases when dry. Wool can be dry-cleaned but laundering is difficult. Wool can be dyed and has good colourfastness property.

MAN-MADE FIBERS

These include viscose rayon, polyester and nylon.

RAYON

Rayon is regenerated cellulose fiber.

Manufacture

There are three main steps in making rayons. They are,

1. To obtain pure cellulose from the raw material.

2. To form a thick, thread - like liquid from the cellulose.

3. To spin the liquid into hardened filaments of regenerated cellulose.

For viscose, spruce wood or cotton linters, which yield the cellulose, are used as raw materials. They are treated with caustic soda and carbon bi sulphide to form a thick liquid.

Spinning: The liquid is forced through a spinneret into an acid bath to harden the long filaments, which are stretched and twisted to form the yarn. This is called wet stretch spinning. The stretching makes the fibers stronger and the acid and other chemicals in the bath cause the cellulose to re-form or to be regenerated.

Delustering: The filaments have metallic luster, if not treated. They are delustered by putting a white pigment in powder form into the spinning solution.

Dyeing may be carried out after the yarn is spun or pigments may be added to the spinning solution.

Properties

Physical

1. Viscose rayon though resembles silk in appearance, its physical and chemical properties are quite different. However, some properties are like those of cotton.

2. Viscose is absorbent, a burn rapidly, is not elastic, it has low dry strength, much reduced strength when wet and greater stretch.

Thermal

1. Rayon fibers burn rapidly with a yellow flame and give a light grey residue.

2. Afterglow results after extinguishing the flame.

3. Very high temperatures disintegrate the fibers.

Chemical

1. Rayon fibers disintegrate in acids.

2. Strong alkali solution causes rayon to swell and produce a loss of strength.

Biological

1. Mildew and bacteria damage the fibers.

2. Silverfish also destroys rayon fibers.

Uses

Rayon fibers are used extensively in apparel and home furnishing fabrics. It is also used in automobile tyres and various industrial applications. Simple, complex and textured yarns can be made from rayon fibers.

POLYESTER

During the early stages of fundamental research for Du Pont was done by the Carothers team on polyester fibers. In 1941, J.R. Whinfield and J.T. Dickson of Calico Printers Association introduced a successful polyester fiber. Dacron polyester has become one of the most used of all synthesized fibers.

Manufacture

Polyester are the product of the reaction between a dihydric alcohol and dicarboxylic acid. Ethylene glycol and terephthalic acid polymerize by condensation reaction to form the polyester polymer. Dimethyl terephthalate is more frequently used than terephthalic acid because it is easily obtained in pure form. The resultant molten polymer is forced through spinneret and then cooled where it solidifies. It is later cut into small chips, dried and stored until needed for filament formation. The fibers can be used for weaving or knitting.

Properties

Physical

1. Polyester is transparent and white or off - white in colour. The fiber strength varies due to differences in the formulation of the polymer.

2. There is no loss of strength when the fiber is wet.

3. Polyester has good elasticity, resilience and wrinkle resistance.

4. The fibers are heat-set to prevent shrink and stretch during use.

5. Polyester like cotton and linen has high degree of wickability. This wicking property carries exterior moisture through to the inside, or body perspiration through to the outside.

Thermal

1. Polyester will burn and produce a dark smoke and an aromatic odour.

2. It forms a grey colored bead.

3. Heat setting is essential if polyester fabrics are to possess the easycare, wrinkle free properties.

Chemical

1. Polyester has good resistance to weak than strong alkalis.

2. It is not affected by acids, but prolonged exposure to strong acids at high temperature may destroy the fiber.

3. It is resistant to organic solvents.

4. Polyester exhibits good resistance to sunlight when behind glass, but prolonged exposure to sunlight weakens the fiber.

Biological

1. Beetles and other insects cut their way through the fabric.

2. Microorganisms will attack fabrics that have been applied with finishes.

Uses

Polyester fibers have immediate consumer acceptance because of their easy-care and wrinkle-free properties. They require no-ironing, easy to launder and quick to dry. Polyesters are not only used as apparel but also in industrial use items such as laundry bags, calendar sheeting, press covers, conveyor belts, fire hoses, fish netting, ropes and protective clothing. An important use of polyester is for surgical implants.

NYLON

Nylon is a man-made fiber developed by Du-Pont company in 1927-29. It was discovered that when a glass rod came in contact with some viscous material in a beaker was pulled away slowly, the substance adhered to the rod and a fine filament was formed which hardened when exposed to cool air. It had excellent stretchability producing a flexible and strong fiber.

Manufacture

Nylon 6,6 means it has six carbon atoms per individual molecule. Nylon is made by linear condensation polymerization process of the two chemicals, hexamethylene diamine and adipic acid. After polymerization it is extruded in a ribbon form and chipped into small flakes or pellets. The polymer is melted and extruded through a spinnerette into cool air. Thus the nylon filaments are formed which are stretched to give strength and fineness.

Properties

Physical

1. Nylon is transparent and can be made bright or dull.

2. It is the strongest of man-made fibers.

3. It has good elasticity, good recovery from creasing and wrinkling.

4. It has low moisture absorbency and resistance to perspiration.

Thermal

1. Nylon melts away from flame and forms a gummy grey residue that hardens as it cools.

2. Nylon is heat set but very high temperatures discolour the fabric.

Chemical

1. Nylon is unaffected by alkalis.

2. Acids disintegrate nylon fibers.

3. Except phenol all other solvents are harmless.

4. Prolonged exposure to sunlight has a destructive effect on nylon and weakens the fabric.

Biological

1. Ants, crickets, and cockroaches will eat nylon fabrics if trapped in creases or folds.

2. Mildew has no effect on the fiber.

Uses

Nylon is widely used for apparel, home furnishing and industry. It is a leading fiber in the manufacture of hosiery and lingerie for it wears well, has good elastic recovery, dimensional stability, shape retention and abrasion resistance. It is also used as carpeting materials and upholstery fabrics.

YARNS

The quality of cloth, its suitability for different purposes, and its performance in wear and cleaning cannot be assumed entirely from a knowledge of its fibers. The method by which the fibers have been combined to form yarns, and the ways in which the yarns have been interlaced to form the material are very important.

Yarns are composed of textile fibers. Yarns play an important role in determining the characteristics of the great variety of fabrics. Much of the beauty, variety and texture of fabrics is due to yarn differences.

Yarn as defined by ASTM (American Society of Testing Materials) is "A generic term for continuous strand of textile fibers or filaments in a form suitable for knitting, weaving or otherwise interwining to form a textile fabric".

CLASSIFICATION OF YARNS

Yarns are classified as simple, complex and textured yarns.

1. A simple yarn is composed of two or more simple single yarns plied or twisted together. A ply yarn consists of two or more singles twisted together and a cord yarn consists of two or more ply yarns twisted together

2. Complex or Novelty yarns are different from simple yarns in structure, size, twist and effect. Complex yarn may be composed of single or ply. Complex ply yarns are composed of a base or core, an effect and tie or binder yarn. The base yarn controls the length and stability of the end product. The effect yarn forms the design and the tie or binder yarn holds the effect yarn so that it will remain in position.

3. Textured yarns have greater apparent volume than other yarns of similar fiber count and linear density. The yarns have a relatively low elastic stretch and the greater volume is achieved by physical, chemical or heat treatment.

PROCESSING OF YARNS

Yarns are made from fibers by two processes - General which is common to many yarns and texturizing to obtain special textured effects such as extra bulk, stretch or a combination of these properties in the fabrics made from them.

The General processes include opening, picking, cleaning, blending, degumming, scouring, carbonizing, carding, combing, drawing, spinning, throwing, slashing, rewinding as discussed in the earlier chapters in the manufacture of natural fibers. No fiber goes through all these processess. Texturing process are primarily applicable to manmade fibers and particularly to thermoplastic fibers.

Texturizing imparts a permanent curl, loop or crimp to the individual filaments, so that when they are recombind, the yarns are more or less fuzzy - appearing and have stretch, bulk or both. Textured yarns do not have free fiber ends to pull out, roll up, or pill. They are more opaque, have a different appearance, feel, warmth and more absorbent.

Yarns thus formed are now used in the manufacture of fabrics. Woven fabrics consists of sets of yarns interlaced at right angles in established sequences. One of the process of fabric manufacture is weaving.

WEAVING OF FABRICS

Weaving is the process most used for the manufacture of textile fabrics. In weaving two or more set of yarns are interlaced at right angles to each other. The warp yarns run in the lengthwise direction in a woven fabric also called as ends. The filling yarns run in the crosswise direction also called as picks. Extra warps yarns at each side form a selvedge which is parallel to the warp yarns.

The machine for weaving is a loom. Loom are of different types varying in their complexity from the most primitive to the most modern, operate on the same principles.

The essential parts of the loom are - the warp beam which holds the lengthwise yarns is located at the back of the loom and release yarns as needed. The harness is the frame which holds the heddles in position. The heddles are the wire or metal strips with an eye at the centre through which individual yarns are threaded. The harness can be raised or lowered to produce the shed. The reed is a comb-like device which determines the cloth width and acts as a beater bar. The filling yarns are carried by shuttles or bobbins across from side to side. The cloth beam is present at the front of the loom which rolls the fabric as it is woven.

The basic weaving operation includes :

Shedding : The harness can be raised or lowered which has the warp yarns by means of heddles to form the shed. The filling yarns pass from one side of the loom to the other through the openings of the warp yarns.

Picking : The filling yarns are carried by the shuttle across the shed, laying the filling in position.

Battening or Beating consists of evenly packing the filling yams into position in the fabric with the reed.

Taking up involves the taking up of the newly made fabric on the cloth beam and Letting off involves releasing thread from the warp beam for the weaving operation.

Types of Weaves

1. Plain Weave

It is the simplest weave and therefore inexpensive to produce. Many fabrics that you commonly wear like mulmul dupattas, organdy and chiffon sarees are all plain weave. Each and every weft yarn goes alternately under and over the warp yarns across the width of the fabric. If the yarns are close together, the plain weave has a high thread count and the fabric will be firm and will wear well.

Plain weave is of two types-

1. **Rib Weave:** Rib or line effect is created by using thin yarns with thick yarns or single yarns with doubled yarns in any one direction of the fabric.

2. **Basket Weave:** Two or more weft yarns are interlaced as a unit with corresponding number of warp yarns to give a basket like effect. Mattee fabric commonly used for cross stitch embroidery is an example of such a weave.

2. Twill Weave

This basic weave has a clear diagonal line on the face of the fabric. The denim or jean fabric you wear is twill weave. It is a very strong and durable weave. It is therefore commonly used in men's suit and coat fabrics. Twill weave fabrics show soil less quickly than plain weave.

3. Satin Weave

This basic weave has a beautiful shiny surface because of long floats on the surface of the fabric.

In the satin weave warp yarns float over several weft yarns before interlacing with a weft yarn and so on. However, the long floats snag easily therefore satin weave is not as strong as plain or twill weave.

KNITTING

Knitting is making of cloth with the help of needles to create a series of interlocking loops with a single yarn.

This fabric making method gives us a very comfortable and stretchable fabric which does not wrinkle. Due to its elasticity, it can fit various sizes. Knitted fabrics are used not only for sweaters but also for hosiery articles like vests, socks, underwears, etc. It is specially suited for winter wear. Knitted wool keeps as warm since it has many air spaces which trap the body heat and provide warmth.

In a knitted garment you will see the following:

Courses: These are the series of successive loops lying in crosswise direction.

Wales: These are the lengthwise or vertical columns of loops.

Weaving Vs Knitting

	Property	Weaving	Knitting
1.	Number of yarns	Two sets of yarns interlaced at right angles.	One set of yarn interlooped with itself.
2.	Equipment required	A loom-could be a handloom or automatic loom.	Needles - could be hand knitting or machine knitting.
3.	Fabrics are	Firm, smooth, stable and maintain their stiffness.	Wrinkle resistant, stretchable, limp and fit the body.
4.	Care and maintenance	Need proper washing and ironing before re-use.	No ironing required but while drying have to be dried flat on ground.
5.	Designs	Can be created by using different yarns (types and colours) and also weaves.	Are created by using various knitting yarns and by changing stitches or colour
6.	Used for	Apparels, upholstery, curtains, draperies, table linen, bed linen, etc.	For undergarments, hosiery, sweaters, T-shirts socks, stockings, etc.

FINISH AND COLOUR APPLICATION

Fabrics which reach the consumer are finished by one treatment or other. Except for the white fabrics, colour is applied to all the fabrics. "A Finish is any treatment given to a fabric to change its appearance'. The fabric can be finished so as to be smooth, shrink resistant, easy care, flame resistant, etc.

CLASSIFICATION OF FINISHES

Finishes can be classified as:

(a) Renewable and Durable

(b) Routine (Basic) and Special

Routine finishes are applied to almost all fabrics with an aim to improve their appearance. Special finishes are applied with a specific purpose or end use in mind.

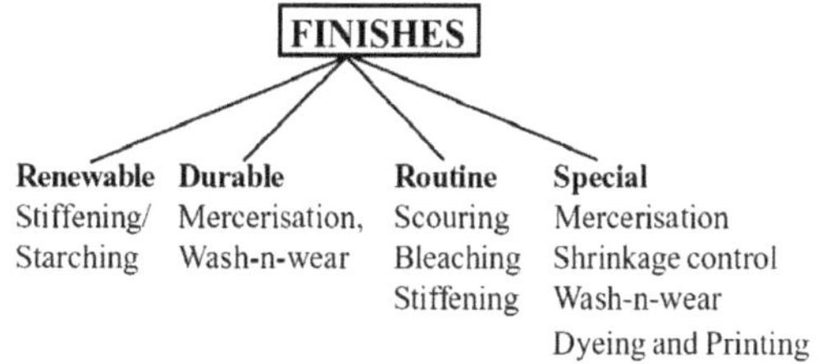

We come across the problem of fabric losing its stiffness after washing or the fabric crushing badly after wearing. What do you do in such a case? You starch the fabric and iron it after every wash. This is called a renewable finish. That means, these finishes last only till washing or drycleaning but some finishes stay on the fabric for its entire life, eg., resistance to crease or the wash 'n' wear finish. These are not affected by washing, drycleaning or ironing. These finsihes are called durable finishes and they cannot be applied at home. Some of the finishes which are durable could also be special or routine.

SOME COMMON FINISHES

Scouring: Fabrics can be scoured by immersing them in 2- 4 percent of caustic soda (NaoH) with addition of wetting agents and emulsifiers under heat to remove waxes, foreign matter and discolouration.

Bleaching : Bleaching is done to fibers, yarns and fabrics to make them white or prepare them for dyeing and printing. It is a chemical finish where sodium chloride or hydrogen per oxide bleach is used to bleach the fabrics. The chemical for bleaching depends on the textile fiber. Cellulose fabrics such as cotton can be bleached with sodium hypochlorite whereas silk and wool respond well to hydrogen peroxide.

Calendering (Pressing) : Calendaring is also called pressing done on cotton, wool, silk as well as rayons. It is a mechanical process where the fabric is fed between flat, heated plates and pressed under heat and pressure. As for wool the fabric is fed between needle boards, which help retain the pile finish. Calendering must be renewed after each laundering or cleaning.

Heat Setting : Mostly thermoplastic fibers are given heat-setting finish to produce fabrics which are wrinkle resistant, good elastic recovery, and give relative permanent design details such as pleats, planned creases and surface embossing. The fibers are exposed to a certain temperature called the glass transition temperature (Tg temperature) where they are shaped. If at any later period the fabric is exposed to temperature higher than Tg temperature the fabric may take a new shape. So fabrics should be laundered or dried under the Tg temperature.

Mercerization: Mercerization is a chemical finish mostly done on cotton fabrics. The fabric is immersed in 16-27 percent of sodium hydroxide and fed between rollers for a specific period of time. Then it is passed on a tentering frame to have specified dimensions. At last it is washed and dried. This process causes the fabric to have increased luster, improves dying characteristic and strength.

Sizing: Sizing is a process of stiffening materials to yarns or fabrics. Sizes is composed of starch or resin. Starch is applied mostly to cellulose fabrics to improve its luster and to add strength. Resin when applied reacts with the fiber molecules and chemical change occurs in the fiber. Starch is applied to the fabric which then passes between rollers that pad the starch into the fabric and remove excess solution. Thus a fabric with additional stiffness and improved luster is obtained.

Tentering: Tentering is a mechanical finish where the fabric is held horizontally by each selvedge between pins. There is a tenter frame which moves with a speed slightly higher than the speed with which the chains holding the fabric are moving. This process straightens the fabric which involves many finishing processes like mercerizing, resin finishing and drying.

Weighting: Weighting is a process applied to silk fabrics. After removal of gum (i.e) degumming, the silk fabric, becomes very soft. To make the silk fabric heavy and stiff, the Federal Trade Commission ruled out that silk fabric can be given stiffness by addition of 10% stannous chloride a metallic salt. If this 10% exceeds very high the silk fabric tends to crack and split. Weighted silk has body and density but they are not durable and can be damaged by sunlight, air and perspiration.

Water proofing: Water proof finishes are those that prevent water entering the fabrics. These fabrics do not allow air also to enter and thus not suitable for wearing apparel. Earlier, rubber, oxidized oil or varnish were used to waterproof fabrics. Modern fabrics are coated with synthetic polymers.

DYEING AND PRINTING

Dyeing and printing are the methods of applying colour to white fabrics. Dye is a substance which is fixed more or less permanently on the fabric which evokes colour.

The processes of producing colours and designs are called dyeing and printing. Dyeing gives a solid colour to the fabric whereas printing is an application of dye at specified areas to create a design. It is very important for the dyed and printed fabric to be 'colourfast', otherwise, if the colour runs on washing, rubbing or ironing the design is destroyed.

A simple test to check colourfastness is to rub a wet white hanky against the coloured fabric. If colour comes on it, the colour is not fast and the fabric should not be bought. If you have bought a cotton fabric whose colour runs, wash it only in cold water with salt added to it. This will help in fixing the colour to some extent.

TYPES OF DYES

Dyes are classified according to hue produced, chemical class, method of application and the types of fibers to which they are applied. Some of the different dyes include :

1. **Direct Dyes :** Direct dyes are water soluble and are applied mostly to cellulosic fibers. These dyes are dissolved in water and salt is added to control the absorption rate of the dye by the fiber. Then the cloth which is to be dyed is immersed. Direct dyestuffs have relatively excellent light fastness and good colourfastness to sunlight.

2. **Acid Dyes :** Acid dyes are used on protein, acrylic and nylon fibers. They have no affinity for cellulosic fibers and are not suitable for fibers which are sensitive to weak acid solutions. They have excellent lightfastness and some have good colourfastness to dry cleaning and perspiration.

3. **Basic Dyes :** Basic or cationic dyes are excellent for colouring acrylic fibers. They are mostly used as "topping" colours to give brilliant colour effects on fabrics. Because of the variety of colour effects produced, it is successfully used on modified nylon and modified polyester.

4. **Vat Dyes:** Vat dyes have excellent colourfastness property and is suitable on all cellulosic fibers and man-made fibers. It is not suitable on protein fibers because of the alkaline bath which will damage the fibers. There is a wide choice of colours in vat dyes and they withstand hard wear and are fast colours.

5. **Reactive Dyes:** Reactive dyes are suitable for mostly all fiberscellulosic, wool, nylon, silk, acrylics, as well as blends. Bright colours with excellent wash fasteness & colourfasteness are obtained. Colour fasteness to crocking, perspiration and fume fading are excellent.

STAGES OF DYE APPLICATION

When we go to the market we find it is not only fabrics which are dyed but sewing threads and knitting yarns are also available as dyed materials.

Dyeing may be done during

(i) **Fibre Stage:** Both natural and manmade fibers can be dyed at this stage. It gives very uniform dyeing and fast colours. But there is a lot of wastage during further processing of fibres.

(ii) **Yarn stage:** Sometimes yarns are also dyed, especially when they have to be sold as such. Hence in embroidery thread, sewing threads and knitting yarn, dyeing is done at the yarn stage.

(iii) **Fabric stage:** This is the most popular stage of dyeing. Most of the fabrics which are dyed in a single solid colour are dyed at this stage. This method is a fast method and it is easy to match colours. Blended fabrics can also be dyed.

(iv) Garment dyeing: Sometimes, after stiching the garment, there is a need to dye it, for example, dupattas for suits are dyed after making.

PRINTING

Designs are applied on fabrics by means of printing. Printed fabrics are defined as those that have been decorated by a motif, pattern or design applied to the fabric after it has already been constructed. Printing can be done by two basic methods -Resist printing and Direct printing.

RESIST PRINTING

Resist printing is done by preventing the dye to enter some specific portions of the fabric by some methods.

1. **Tie and Dye :** Fabrics are made into tiny puffs with some object inside and tied with a waxed thread wherever the dye has to be prevented. The fabric is immersed in the dye solution. If two or more colours are desired the thread is removed and the fabric retied. After drying the object is removed. Other methods of tie and dye include folding the fabric and stitching it and pulling the threads to draw the fabric to resist the dye from penetrating into the fabric, called as tritik.. Tie & dye fabrics are quite popular in apparel and home furnishings.

2. **Batik :** A resist method developed by the Javanese involves wax as the resist substance. A copper cup called tjanting is attached to a reed handle. The wax is taken in this tjanting and applied in the design areas, wherever necessary to resist the dye. The fabric is immersed in dye solution. The wax resists the dye from entering the fabric. In some places it forms cracks and forms fine lines in the design. The fabric is later washed in boiling water to remove the wax.

3. **Screen Printing:** A screen resist is made by covering a frame with bolting cloth of silk, metal or nylon filament yarns. The fabric is covered with a film and the design areas are cut out of the film. Some areas of the mesh are left open to allow the dyestuff to pass through and print the fabric. The frame is laid on the fabric, and the dye is placed at one end of the frame. A rubber knife moves the dye across the screen and forces the dye through the open mesh of the fabric, One screen is prepared for each colour. Screen printing is considered by many textile authorities to be newest method of decorating fabrics.

4. **Discharge printing :** Discharge printing is used to print designs on fabrics which has been previously dyed. A reducing bleach is used which removes the base dye and leaves a white pattern on a coloured ground. Dark fabrics with white designs such as polka dots are examples of discharge printing.

DIRECT PRINTING

Direct printing is the method of applying colour directly on to the fabrics by one of the following methods.

1. **Roller Printing:** Designs are engraved in metal rolls and arranged around a main cylinder and locked into place. Many rolls can be used. A trough containing the dye solution along with a doctor blade which scrapes of the excess dye is placed for each roll. The large cylinder is covered by a padded blanket and a grey cloth is used on top of the printing blanket.

   The cloth to be printed is on the outer surface. The layers move together, the rolls take up the dye from the trough print on the cloth as it comes and goes to the drying oven which sets the colour on the fabric. Roller printing is steadily increased during the past decades for its quality prints and unusual patterns produced.

2. **Block printing :** Block made of wood or metal are engraved with designs. Each block prints only one colour. The blocks are dipped in dye solution. Only the raised portion in the blocks picks up the dye and is then pressed on the fabric, forcing the dye to be printed on the surface.

3. **Duplex prints:** Duplex prints are produced by modified direct roller print equipment. The design is made by a machine, which is set up

to print on both the face and back of the fabric.

4. **Photographic prints:** Photographic prints are made similar to that used in making photograph. A negative is placed on the fabric and light is transmitted to it and the design is developed. The fabric is washed and the design is as permanent as a photo.

5. **Transfer printing:** Transfer printing involves heat and pressure. The dye in the desired design, is first printed onto a special paper. The paper is laid on the fabric and the design is transferred by-sublimation. The dye is changed from solid state on, the paper to vapour and again changes to solid and fixes on the fabric. The heat sets the colour on the fabric. Transfer printing is suitable for nylon and some acrylic fabrics.

IDENTIFICATION OF FIBRES

The vast variety of fabrics available today, makes their identification important. You know that variety is created by using different fibres in combination. Knowledge of the fibre content of a fabric is therefore necessary to know its suitability, use and care. Sometimes you may have been cheated by an imitation fibre, like a fabric looking like silk but turning out to be artificial silk or imitation silk. Labels and salespersons are not always able to guide you.

Burning test is a simple and reliable test and can be done alongwith the visual inspection of the fabric. It can help you to choose the fabric according to your requirements. The burning test does not identify the fibre in particular but indicates its group. Cotton, flax and rayon will have similar results when burnt as they are all basically cellulosic in nature.

(a) Visual Inspection

You can identify a fabric by its appearance but accuracy in identifying comes through experience. The appearance properties of different fibres given earlier in this lesson can help you in identifying a fabric e.g., Silk is smooth, shiny and fine. Cotton

is also smooth but looks dull, wool is most definitely rough.

(b) The Burning Test

The burning test is a good preliminary test. Although it does not identify fibres specifically, it provides valuable data regarding appropriate care. The procedure is as follows:

1. Select one or two yarns from the warp of the fabric.

2. Untwist so that the fibres are in a loose mass.

3. Hold yarns in forceps; move them towards the flame from the side.

4. Observe the reaction as they approach the flame.

5. Move them into the flame, and then pull them out of the flame and observe the reaction.

6. Notice any odour given off by the fibre.

7. Observe ash or residue formed.

8. Repeat for the filling yarns of the woven fabrics.

Home tests for colourfastness of fabrics

- **Dry cleaning:** Take a sample fabric, approximately 2 by 4 inches, and immerse in cleaning solution for 10 to 20 minutes. Observe to determine whether any colour has bled into the cleaning solution, then dry and compare the sample with an original piece to determine colour change.

- **Laundering:** A small fabric sample can be taken from seam allowance or hem of a fabric. Take one cup of water and one teaspoon of soap or synthetic detergent in a jar. Add the fabric sample. Shake the jar frequently and allow the fabric to remain in solution for 10 minutes. Observe the colour of the wash water. Rinse the sample in warm water atleast twice and observe any loss of colour into the rinse water. Dry the sample and compare it with the original fabric to determine whether any colour change has occurred.

- **Sunlight:** Textile fabric that is exposed to sunlight for many hours each day such as curtains and draperies should be colourfast to sunlight or sunfast. Expose the fabric to sunlight between 10.00 am and 4.00 pm, standard time, the period between may and September, Keep a record of the number of hours of exposure. Compare the sample with an original at frequent intervals.

- **Ironing:** Colour may be altered by ironing or pressing with either dry or wet heat. When dry heat is used, the fabric will usually return to its normal colour after cooling. Press the: sample fabric with iron set at the temperature recommended for the fibre. Observe any colour change. If colour does change, observe the fabric as it cools to determine whether it returns to its original shade.

- **Rubbing and Crocking:** Place small square of white cotton fabric preferably muslin or percale over the forefinger. With even pressure rub the white fabric atleast ten times over a coloured one. Observe to see whether the colour rubs off onto the white square of fabric. Repeat with the white square of fabric that has been moistened thoroughly. Either by test, using home methods or laboratory equipment, or label information a consumer has the ability to determine, to some degree atleast, the care a product will require.

Table: Burning Test of Fibres

Name	Approaching Flame	In Flame	Removed From Flame	Odour	Residue
(a) Natural Cellulose fibre– Cotton, Linen	Does not shrink away and catches fire on contact.	Burns quickly.	Continues burning, shows an afterglow.	Like burning paper.	Light, feathery, gray in colour.
Manmade cellulose fibre– Rayon	-do-	-do-	-do-	-do-	Light, fluffy very small amount.
Protein Fibre– Wool	Curls away from the flame.	Burns slowly.	Stops burning after removing from flame.	Like burning hair.	Small black bead, brittle, crushable.
Silk	-do-	Burns slowly and sputters in flame.	-do-	-do-	Bead-like, black, crushable.
(b) Manmade Synthetic– Polyester	Melts and shrinks away from the flame.	Burns slowly and melts.	-do-	Smell of chemicals.	Bead formed, hard, tough, black-brown in colour.
Nylon	-do-	-do-	-do-	Synthetic or chemical odour.	-do-
Acrylic	-do-	Burns quickly and sputters.	Continues to burn, melts and molten fibre drops.	Acidic (vinegar) odour	Irregular black beads, hard but crushable.

CLOTHING CONSTRUCTION - BASIC PRINCIPLES OF DRAFTING, FLAT PATTERN AND DRAPING METHODS

DRAFTING

It is the method of developing a pattern from body measurements. It is really one reliable way, even for a beginner, to make a master pattern that proves to fit exactly each part and all positions.

It is an engineering type method based on a set of body measurements. Success in drafting depends on the accuracy of the set of measurements.

FLAT PATTERN

Flat pattern work starts with a commercial basic pattern. The pattern work consists of changing the basic pattern to create new designs. Work is done on paper on a flat surface. It is often necessary to make the pattern up in fabric to get the full effect of the design that has been created. For dress designing there are five basic pieces:

(i) front blouse

(ii) back blouse

(iii) front skirt

(iv) back skirt

(v) sleeve

Following procedure needs to be followed in securing a master pattern.

1. Select a simple dress pattern nearest your size. Have it of five basic pieces. The front blouse dart may be from shoulder or under arm but the vertical dart at waistline makes sewing and fitting easier.

2. Copy on plain paper. Alter this pattern to fit by slashing and spreading or over lapping. If need be it can be redrawn.

3. Cut out the garment, with 1/2"seam in armholes and neckline, 1" elsewhere. No hem is needed at bottom of skirt, but an 1" seam or hem at centre front in both blouse and skirt makes it easier to dress and fit. Stay stitch on all seam lines and dart lines. Then, base stitch all darts and silhouette seams to create three units i.e. blouse, sleeve and skirt.

4. Fit by changing size of darts and seam allowances. Tucks may be pinned in some areas as a guide to altering the basic pattern both for length and width.

5. Correct the pattern on the basis of changes made. Re-pin circumferences and have more fittings until satisfactory. At the second fitting, concentrate on sleeve and arms hole. Make neckline, waistline and wrist line comfortably and curve to fit naturally.

6. At last fitting extend the basic "dressmaker" darts, which give a semi-casual effect. This fitting will tighten the garment slightly in width.

7. Check the pattern. Use a ruler on all darts, shoulders and underarm seams, and skirt seams below the hipline. Notches should be retained only in the sleeve and armholes, and darts cut out. Then this foundation pattern can be quickly traced around to begin pattern work.

8. Save the muslin garment to use later in establishing other dart or seam locations.

9. After each use of your foundation pattern, refine lines in the light of later fittings.

10. Save copies of your most used 'patterns as basic blocks for quick changing of details.

Successful dress designing for an individual begins with a pattern of the right size based on actual body measurements and not age.

DRAPING

It is an artistic approach in which the person makes her pattern by fitting cloth to the curves of a dress form. In this method, she has the pleasure of seeing how the garment will look as the pattern develops. Draping is advantageous because without cutting it teaches one how to work for the entire effect rather than for minute detail. It forces the draper to carry the fabric from neck to hem and from front to back, and also to the idea simple and natural so as to give a mere impression of the design. The result is bound to be smooth, easy flowing line rather than overworked detail. The fabric needs to be handled carefully and therefore, pin it only where necessary.

Just as the flat lay figure gives a basis for sketching space divisions in relation to the two-dimensional silhouette, the dress form provides a three dimensional shape, the actual size of the figure on which to experiment with fabric.

Inconsistency in scale of major space divisions or inappropriateness of detail to the entire figure, becomes apparent at once. The challenge is to retain the figure's most pleasing attributes and to emphasize them through the lines of the dress and by subtle illusion to modify the less desirable proportions.

Since the dress is for the wearer rather than wearer for the dress, the form as a source of design inspiration is the nearest approach to figure itself.

Valuable suggestions do come from draping the uncut fabric on yourself. You see your, features, the tilt of your head, your characteristic posture in relation to the fabric and the, times into which you drape it; and immediately you can sense the harmony or disharmony between the draped fabric and yourself. Draping also teaches one not only to recognize an fitting garment but to correct fitting errors. It is one of the oldest method of pattern designing.

To conclude one can say that flat pattern designs developed from draped patterns will be utterly cold, set and lifeless unless one has had experience in working with fabric on the form. Such designs may be accurate, but they will lack the finer line placement gained through the draping experience. Therefore, draping has its own advantages.

TEXTILE DESIGNING - PRINCIPLES AND CONCEPTS

Good taste in a dress involves not only consideration of beauty but critical judgement of suitability and appropriateness which suits to your eyes or complexion within fashion trends and with your budget limit. So it implies visual perception of and intellectual concepts as well.

ART PRINCIPLES OR PRINCIPLES OF DESIGN

Few are born with good taste in dress and others are not. We can acquire the good taste on dress by applying the principles of design and you may become a creative designer who plans and makes beautiful clothes and accessories. All designers work with the elements of line, texture, form, colour, space, values, etc. There designs are not used alone but are combined in useful appropriate ways to produce charming, interesting, graceful and dignified effects.

In judging a dress design consider the structural overall design, silhouette (outline shape) of a garment, shapes and lines within and the decorative features and details which must be related to the structure. In using the principles, you will find them interrelated and are involved in each and every design.

Design

Design is a deliberate or well considered plan. It is the composition and atrangement of paths, form, colour and fabric, line for introduction of a style, During the fabric/clothing construction one should use the various principles of design in the correct manner. Design is divided into two types. Those are the structural and the decorative designs.

1. Structural design

This type of design is composed and is the arrangement of lines, colours, forms and shapes. It is the type of design which forms the outline of any shape like it gives the silhouette to any structure. Lets take the curves and shape of the dress—the curves which go along with the curves of the body is a the structural design e.g. a plain dress with no outer decoration on it. Requirements of structural design are:

— It should be suited to the purpose.

— It should be simple and well proportionate.

— It should be suited to the material by which it is made, and to the process that will be followed in making it.

2. Decorative design

It is the surface enrichment of structural design. Any type of colours or materials that have been applied to structural design for the purpose of adding a richer quality to it, constitute its decorative design. Structural design is more important than decorative design e.g. a decorative design in a dress will have outer showy. Requirements of a good decorative design:

— Decoration should be used in moderation.

— The decoration should be placed at structural points and it should strengthen the shape of the object.

— There should be enough background and

space to give simplicity to the design. Surface pattern should cover the surface.

— Decoration should be suitable for material and purpose served.

Structural and decorative designs are the main points through which we can make a dress. While making a dress first we will think and take in consideration all the structural design points.

Firstly we will take the shape or the form of the dress. The shape or silhoutte of the dress should go along with the shape of the body. We should give curves to the dress everywhere they are needed like at the waist area we should give the darts to make the dress similar to size to the waist. Then we should see the necklines and the sleeves of the dress they should go along with the body a person has. For example a round faced person should not wear round necks but she should wear oval necks.

Then a person having fat arms should not emphasize on the arms but on the other parts of the dress so that the interest will not go to the arms. We should also see the height and size of a person for whom the dress is stitched. Like a person who is short and fat should wear a dress with vertical lines and a person who is tall and slim should wear a dress with horizontal stripes.

Also the different parts of a dress like the sleeves, collars, belts, gathers, etc. should appear to fit with the whole dress. If the structure of the dress. is well suited then the dress, looks beautiful. Secondly, the decoration on the dress should be planned so as to enrich the structural design. Beautiful decorative effects on dress may be obtained through the use of well planned tuckings, cordings or bands of the same material of the dress. Then the threads used for embroidery on the material should be suitable. Heavy material requires a bold, free design and delicate design need fine texture.

There, are five elements of design-line, colour, form, texture, and size. Lines are of various types and each one of them have different effect in clothing construction. Usually following lines are used.

Vertical lines: These types of lines carry eye from top to bottom and bottom to top. These lines give a feeling of length in a dress: These lines are important for a person having short height and fat. They give an impression of dignity, and strong direct discipline.

Horizontal lines: These lines carry eye from right to left and left to right. They break the effect of vertical line and create a feeling of width. These lines are used in piping, collar, buttons, yoke, and lace. They give a feeling of repose, solidity, down to earth feeling and tranquility.

Diagonal lines: These are also known as slanting or oblique lines. These lines decrease the effect of width and increase the effect of height. They suggest sophistication, refinement and arouse interest.

Curved lines: These lines create a circular feeling in collar, cuff, yoke and neckline. They are also used in button, tape, piping and provide softness, gracefulness, feminity to the dress. These lengthwise curves help in giving a feeling of increased height and horizontal-wise curves decrease the height and increase width. Analysis of these lines help in correct selection of the garment.

V-shaped lines: The longer the length of the 'V' the greater the effect of height it gives. If the top portion of the V is increased in width it gives an illusion of increased breadth. These lines are used in necklines, waistlines, piping. By the use of these lines a short stature person appears tall.

Broken lines: These lines keep changing their direction after some distance or they do not remain same throughout the length and width. These lines are mixture of different types of lines and bring about variations in dress designing. By their correct size, they can break the effect of width.

There are five principles of design—proportion (systematic distribution of space), balance (weight), rhythm (flow or continuity), emphasis (importance of design) and harmony (suitability of design).

1. Proportion

Proportion deals with areas or systematic distribution of spaces with each other and within hold, so that all the parts of a design are in harmony. It also means relations between sizes or areas to one another. In this the general proportion of the costume must be in harmony with the proportion of the human body. For example we use rectangle, oval, triangle in the neckline than square, circle because the first one gives a pleasing proportion to the face.

Also the dimension more than 1/2 and less than 2/3rd of a frock is more pleasing than the exact mathematical division and darts should be put at the waist so as to give a narrow shape. Also heavy busted people should not wear light filling clothes. Dress should be planned as such to increase or decrease her apparel size. For a design to be pleasing the part should be close enough together but varied enough to apply interest- e.g. the human figure is considered to be of beautiful proportion if it was divided into eight equal parts from which three parts falls above waist line and five parts below waist line.

A space divided into the proportion of 2:3 or 3:5 is more pleasing than one divided as 2:2, 2:6, e.g. A garment is more pleasing if its yoke does not divide the blouse into half strips in a fabric and if not a same width through out the garment. Unequal division of space i.e. 3:5, 2:3 or another interesting division like 2:2 and 4:4. For example, if a girl wearing a blouse and skirt and the end of blouse is broad below the waist line and the skirt ends above the knee length then this distribution becomes half/half (equal proportion) and it appears to be monotonous but if the blouse is shorter and the skirt is little longer then the design becomes more interesting.

Proportion also applies to the relation between size of the design on a fabric and size of a wearer. A large whole design is proportional to a tall person because the area on which design spreads is greater at the same time a large design will overpower a short person because the area is small.

2. Balance

Balance provides good weight distribution. This principle of design produces a feeling of rest and repose and it is obtained by grouping shapes and colours to maintain a feeling of equal attraction from side to side, front to back or top to bottom.

The arrangement of colour depends upon the principle of see-saw. For example, a dress with red and blue colour in which since red is prominent so it should be more towards the centre so as to balance.

For a design to have balance it is necessary to have equal gravitational pull i.e. the pull of attention or interest must be equal. Balance are of two types: formal balance/symmetrical balance and informal balance.

Formal Balance: It is also called symmetrical or even balance. It is an arrangement of objects exactly alike or same on both sides of a design. To obtain formal balance garments both sides has to be identical. For example, formal balance of garment having same pockets, pleats, tucks or dats on both the sides.

Informal Balance: It is also called as asymmetrical or uneven balance. It is unequal distribution of details of a design in a garment. Though both sides are not same in informal balance so care must be taken in order to that one side of the garment does not seem heavy or crowded for the second side.

3. Rhythm

It is a pleasing sensory motion which gives continuity design. It is an art principle which suggests a pleasing movement throughout the design. The process of leading the eye from one part of design to the other is termed as rhythm. Rhythm is that movement of eye which is smooth, even lively but gliding and orderly. Rhythm may be provided by repetition, transition, gradation and opposition.

In **repetition** details of a design are repeated at regular-intervals. Repetition may be achieved by repeating long row of buttons, pockets, pleats, seams, long drafts, frills etc. in a dress or by repeating line, texture and colour in a fabric.

Transition is a gradual margin of two lines from different directions. In this the angle of two opposing lines is softened by a curved shape e.g. trimmings, ruffles.

Gradation is the rhythm that suggests a gradual increase or decrease in shapes and sizes such as tucks of increased length or increase in the size of a print on a fabric, less frills to more frills, colours may progress from bright to dull shades, textured from dull to shiny or rough to smooth.

Opposition is more or less contradiction of lines in a garment. This can be achieved through constructional lines or decorative braid or trimmings. It can also be achieved by use of plaid material e.g. Checks.

Radiation is a starting of lines from a centre point and flowing out and this effect is produced by bows.

4. Emphasis

It creates interest and centre of attraction of design. It is that principle of design that gives character, or dominant interest to a dress. One can apply this principle to clothes by accentuating one's good points and concealing one's defects—e.g. if you have a nice complexion and beautiful eyes then focus attention to your face by choosing pleasing colours, pretty necklines and collars etc. Defects can be minimized by making them as inconspicuous as possible—e.g. if you have large hips, avoid horizontal lines in. a design too full or too light skirts and a combination of a light skirt and a dark blouse.

Repetition and extreme contrast both emphasized—e.g. a round face appears rounder with a round collar. Pretty ankles are emphasized either by pretty shoes or contrast shoes or details around the neckline of the skirt.

Emphasis can be applied to a dress design by proper grouping and placing of parts of the design i.e. pockets, tucks, frills etc. by using contrast of light and textured materials or by introducing unusUiallines or colours. Simplicity of a design is the key note to all good design, when doubtful it is better to under-emphasize rather than overemphasize in a design.

5. Harmony

It conveys unity throughout the design by their choice and use of lines, shapes, colours and ideas. When all the principles of art will be followed, complete harmony will be the result.

1. Space must be interestingly distributed.

2. Shapes must be similar and properly balanced.

3. Structural and decorative lines must be consistent.

4. Textures must be pleasingly combined.

5. Ideas must be related.

It also means selection and arrangement of objects and ideas and it also shows the unity of ideas and objects. In order to secure harmony in a dress certain points are to be kept in mind. To achieve harmony for the neckline there can be any three types of lines used:

1. Lines which follow or repeat one another.

2. Lines which contrast with one another.

3. Transitional line.

For the neck opening if the shape of the neck repeats the shape of the face, it emphasizes it. e.g. if the person is having square face, wear square necks. If the neckline contrast the shape of the face thus it also emphasizes. So we should take transitional line which neither repeats but modifies and softens the features and include gracefulness and also horizontal line worn near the neck shortens and hardens the shoulders. e.g. boat neck. Long pointed neckline will give unusual and slenderness to the face. e.g. deep 'V' neck and also collar 'V' neck. Secondly we should see the harmony of texture in this and also notice the texture of the clothes should be nice and also if we want to combine two types of clothes then we should see that they come in the same class. e.g. silk with satin, and not with cotton. Thirdly, the harmony of ideas. In this we should have an idea of what size of embroidery, etc. should be done. e.g. a short person should not wear dress with big flowers and also a huge person should not wear a dress with tiny flowers. The colours for kids should be light.

CARE AND MAINTAINANCE OF TEXTILE MATERIALS AND GARMENTS; LAUNDARY AGENTS: METHODS AND EQUIPMENTS

1. Brush garments thoroughly and often keep them free from dust. Empty out pockets. Shake

well before brushing. Sun and air to kill the grubs and keep the moths away.

2. Garments which have been worn should not be put away until they have been thoroughly aired. Cupboards, boxes and clothes-closets should be aired frequently.

3. Washable garments should be laundered frequently. Woolen coats, suits and shawls should be sponged and pressed. Garments which cannot be laundered should be dry-cleaned occasionally. Do not let a suit to become too dirty before sending it to the dry-cleaner.

4. Suits and overcoats should be hung away on clothes hangers. The sleeves of coats will keep the shape much better if they are stuffed with tissue paper. Make sure that the shoulders sit properly on the hanger.

5. Light often fades the colour of fabrics, hence protect them wi'th covers made for that purpose. Keep such garments in dark closets which can be frequently aired.

6. Do not put away garments in a damp condition. Moist atmosphere causes mildew, which penetrates into the fibre, changes its colour and may even cause it to fall to pieces. This can be easily prevented by brushing the garment each time after wearing, and hanging and storing it away in a dry place in a perfectly dry condition. Protect textiles from destructive insects. The moth grubs feed upon woolen fabrics, carpets, furs, and feathers. The moth is grey in colour. These pests can be prevented as follows:

(a) **Spraying:** Wool and its storage place may be sprayed with a fluid or dust insecticide in which D.D. T. is incorporated to give it a measure of permanent protection obtained.

(b) **Repellants:** Such as tobacco, dried neem leaves, cedar chips, camphor and moth-balls which are sometimes recommended are of doubtful value and cannot be relied on. These repellants, however, will not have any effect upon the eggs or larvae in the garments. Moth balls are effective only as long as a sufficient concentration of vapour is maintained. Naphthalene flakes are more efficient than the traditional moth balls. Para-dichloro-benzene is the best repellant, but it is not so cheap.

(c) **Packing:** Pack away all woolens and furs wrapped in newspapers, as the moth dislike printer's ink. The box may be lined and covered with tarred paper. Cedar chips, sandal wood dust, dry eucalyptus and neem leaves are good as long as their odour lasts.

(d) **Fumigation:** with a poisonous gas, e.g. hydrocynic acid. It destroys grubs and moths, but it is dangerous to use and calls for specialists' handling.

(e) **Addition of an insecticide to the wool:** This er.tails adding- a substance to the wool which either poisons the larvae or renders the wool indigestible.

STAIN REMOVAL

Linen or any other material should be washed the moment it is stained. The stains are easy to remove when they are fresh; otherwise it becomes permanent and difficult to remove. It is easy to remove a stain when one can identify it. Stains are divided into various types based on their nature.

Animal stains: These include blood, egg, milk, meat, juices, ice cream etc. These stains contain proteins, hence heat should be avoided while removing them. Reagents used are cold water, salt, soap, borax solution, and a few drops of ammonia.

Vegetable stains: These are acidic, therefore, alkaline reagents should be used to remove them. For example, tea, cocoa, coffee, fruit juices, wine and glass. Warm water, borax, glycerin, hydrogen peroxide, benzene, and starch paste can be used to remove stains.

Dye stains: These may be acidic or alkaline, hence the reagent used for removal of stain, should depend on the nature of the stain. Water, soap, dilute alkali, dilute acid, alcohol, cold bleaching powder solution are some of the reagents used to remove the stains.

Mineral stains: These are iron, mould, and ink stains. Mineral stains are compounds of a metal and dye. Therefore acidic reagents should be used first to act on the metal, followed by dilute alkaline solutions to neutralize the acid reagent and to remove the dye. Various reagents used to remove these stains are water, soap, cut tomato, lime, sour milk, starch paste, oxalic acid, borax solution, and methyl alcohol.

Grease stains: These are caused by the grease and specific colouring matter in it;hence grease solvents and grease absorbents should be used. Oil, paint, varnish, butter, and tar stains are the examples of this kind which can be removed by water, solvent soap, french chalk, fuller's earth, kerosene, turpentine, and alcohol.

LAUNDERING

Laundering of clothes consists of two processes—the process of removing dirt from the clothes and the process of finishing them to regain the appearance of neatness as a new fabric. The methods used for removing dirt and cleaning the clothes depend on the nature of the fabric and the kind of dirt. The loose dust particles may be removed by shakilig, brushing or by the action of pedesis in steeping. For removing the dirt, it is necessary to remove the grease first from the fabrics by means of emulsification or absorption; and thus liberate the dust particles. The essential factor in the process of cleansing, therefore, is the use of a grease solvent or absorbent to remove the grease and an application of hard or delicate pressure to remove the dust. The application of pressure is done in four ways:

1. Application of friction.
2. Application of light pressure.
3. Application of the principle of suction.
4. Washing machines.

Application of Friction

This method should be applied to the washing of strong and durable fabrics, e.g. household linen and cotton clothes. Friction may be applied by means of hand-rubbing or by means of some appliance, such as a brush or a scrubbing board.

But this method is not advisable as it cause uneven friction on clothes, stretches the clothes in parts and thus, the clothes wear out much quicker.

1. **Hand Friction or Rubbing:** This is suitable for washing small articles which are lightly soiled, e.g. blouses, handkerchiefs, etc. Wring out the article from the steeping water and place it in hot water. Squeeze it and then wring it out of the hot water. Apply soap all over the article holding the material between the hands, rub one part of the material on another. This causes a permanent lather to be formed in the rubbed portion, which cleanses the material. Rinse the article in hot water.

2. **Special Scrubbing by Brush:** This method is suitable for strong fabrics and for articles which are very dirty such as jharans and apron, overalls, cuffs and neckbands of coats. Place the article in hot water, and squeeze it to saturate it in hot water and wring it out. Spread on a flat surface and apply soap. Scrub the material in one direction, away from the worker, causing a permanent lather in the fabric. Sprinkle some water on the surface while scrubbing. Rinse the article in hot water, to remove the dirty soap.

3. **Rubbing and Scrubbing:** This consists of both rubbing and scrubbing. This method is suitable for any articles of strong fabric that are soiled. Place the scrubbing board in a tub or sink, half filled with hot water. Wring the article out of the steeping water. Place it in hot water. Squeeze out a portion of the article and place it flat on the board; apply soap on it, rub the part of the board to cause a permanent lather in the fabric. Continue this till the whole article is soaped and rubbed well. Rinse out the article in hot water to remove the dirt.

Application of Light Pressure

This method should be applied to the washing of fine texture.

Kneading and Squeezing: This method is suitable for coloured articles and delicate fabrics, e.g. coloured cotton, silk, woolen and lace. The process consists of kneading and squeezing of the articles by hand in the soap solution; since the application of pressure is very light, it does not damage the texture, colour or weave of the fabric.

Make a soap solution with hot water, add sufficient cold water to the solution to get the correct temperature suitable for the fabric. Shake the solution thoroughly to get a lather. Place the article in the solution, squeeze it well to saturate it with the soap; knead and squeeze part of the article at a time. Continue this process till the whole article is cleansed. At the end of the process, there should be some lather left over. Disappearance of lather indicates that the article is still dirty and needs more soap, and use of several soap water is, therefore, required to cleanse the article. The very dirty portions of the articles, such as the neck-bands and the sleeve-bands should be lightly rubbed with the hand or a soft brush using extra lather.

Application of Suction or Suction Washing

This method is suitable for cleansing small and large articles of any fabric or colour. It is generally used to cleanse heavy articles, such as trousers, coats, blankets, which are not possible to clean by kneading and squeezing, and which will not stand friction.

Prepare soap solution using a suitable soap. Adjust the temperature by adding cold water to it as prescribed for the fabric. Place the article in the soap solution and press it with the suction washer so that if is saturated with the solution. Then work the suction washer up and down in the solution lightly pressing the article. Use a fresh soap solution if the article is very soiled. Rinse the article to remove the soiled soapy water, using warm water. Then rinse in cold or warm water as is suitable for the fabric. Clothes after the process of cleansing, get creased, and need to be straightened to look like new.

Finishing is the process used to straighten the clothes, so that the appearance is attractive and neat. The methods used for finishing in laundry are ironing, pressing, steaming, mangling and calendaring. Fabrics like cotton and linen are damped before finishing. In cases like silk and wool, where the sprinkled water does not spread evenly, these should be left half dry for finishing. Damping is done to soften the texture of the fabrics.

Rules

1. Use warm water as it spreads more quickly.

2. First damp all the hems, folds and pleats by running wet fingers over them.

3. Spread the garment on a clean table, dip the hand in water and sprinkle it lightly over the article.

4. Roll up the article and wrap it in a towel and leave it for 15 to 20 minutes.

Ironing: This process consists of running a hot iron backward and forward along with selvedge threads of the cloth with pressure. The heat of the iron and the pressure applied is controlled according to the texture and the nature of the fabric. For example, silks are not ironed with a very hot iron and a fine muslin cloth does not need much pressure to smoothen its surface. Cotton and linens are all ironed with a hot iron. All silks and art silk except velvet and crepe are ironed with a warm iron. Woolen as a rule do not need much finish and are not ironed.

Pressing: This process consists of placing a hot iron on the creased portion of the material and then lifting it up. The operation is continued till the crease disappears. It differs from ironing in that it is not a continuous running of the iron to and fro on the surface of the cloth. Pressing is used for finishing woolens and fabrics with a special texture, such as georgettes, crepes.

Steaming: This process consists of allowing the steam to pass through the surface of the cloth. Fabrics with a pile surface, such as velvet and velveteen are finished by this process. The passing of the steam through the pile of the fabric on the wrong side helps to raise and freshen the pile.

Mangling: Mangling is used only in cases of rough articles, such as jharans, tweeds, etc., where the surface is expected to be neat but not very smooth. The article immediately after washing and before drying is passed through a mangle several times and then put to dry. This process helps to straighten the threads.

Calendaring: Calendaring is used in commercial laundries to finish straight pieces of cotton and linen articles, such as table cloths, curtains and bedsheets. Drying and finishing is done in the same process. The straight pieces of articles are passed through two heated metal rollers which continuous rotate. The process dries up the moisture and the pressure, caused by the rotation, irons out the material. In washing cotton and linen care must be taken:

(i) to avoid the use of such methods and cleansing reagents as are likely to weaken the fibers,

(ii) to preserve the whiteness of the white, and the colour of the coloured articles,

(iii) to clean, stiffen, finish and to freshen the appearance of the fabric, and make it look as new as possible.

Examine the article for tears, holes and stains and mark them with a light pencil. Mend all the tears, and holes before wetting the garments.

Laundering of Cotton and Linen

Sorting: Sort the articles in the following groups. Each group is required to be steeped in separate containers of water:

(i) Coarse articles, such as jharans, aprons used in the kitchen.

(ii) Coarse articles for cleaning and dusting.

(iii) Bed linen and other personal clothes.

(iv) Table linen.

(v) Handkerchiefs.

Steeping: This process is very important in the washing of cottons and linens as it economizes time, labour and soap. Loose and soluble dirt is removed by the pedesis of the water particles.

Washing: The method employed in washing is determined by the texture of the fabric, the type of article, its colour, and the type of dirt present in it.

Boiling: All white cottons and linens are boiled. Boiling disinfects, whitens and freshens the clothes. Water used for boiling must be soft and soapy. Use soda and shredded soap in the proportion of one teaspoon of soda and one tablespoon of soap to a gallon of water to soften water. Soda alone should not be used as it may damage the fabrics. Soda must be first dissolved in a little water.

Half fill the boiler, add soda first, dissolve and then soap. Heat and agitate the water to form a lather. Open out the clothes and drop into the boiler, bring to boil, and boil for 15 minutes. Over boiling causes white clothes to become yellow.

Rinsing: After boiling, rinse the clothes in several warm waters to remove all traces of soap from the fabrics.

Stiffening and Blueing: It is done as one process. Shake a bag of blue in the prepared starch to get the desired shade. All white clothes are blued. All cottons and linens except bed-linen and underwear are starched. Articles, such as table mats, tray clothes, table napkins, etc. are heavily starched while personal clothes are given a light stiffening. Nurses' caps, men's dress shirts and collars need an extra stiffness and so they are stiffened with cold water starch. Use of a mangle is very effective for removing all the moisture.

Drying: Outdoor drying is best for all white articles as sunlight helps to bleach the cloth, quickens the drying, disinfects and freshens the clothes. They should not be left out in the sun too long but removed as soon as they are dry. Hot sun causes white clothes to become yellow.

Coloured Cotton and Linen Fabrics

Fast coloured articles gradually fade and get dulled by age and repeated washings. Factors which affect colour are long contact with moisture, excessive heat, acids and alkalies, and friction.

Stains are to be removed with water and soap as far as possible. Coloured articles must not be steeped. Wash all the articles by either suction washing or by kneading and squeezing. Rinse in 2 or 3 warm waters till all the soap is removed. The acid or vinegar need not be used for articles, of which the colour is guaranteed to be fast.

Remove moisture thoroughly before hanging the article to dry, to avoid getting dark patches on the lower side of the article. Dry the article in the shade to prevent bleaching caused by sunlight. Cotton and linens are generally starched and, thetefore, need a good finish. Most of these are finished by ironing except velveteen, which is steam-pressed.

Laundering of Wool

Wool is an animal fibre of delicate texture. The fibre is covered with overlapping scales of the gelatinous nature. Moisture, heat and alkali soften the scales of a fibre; and if friction is applied, while the fibre is in this softened state, it will cause interlocking of the scales, which will result in shrinking and felting. Alkali also spoils the texture of the fibre which becomes hard and yellow. Uneven temperature too is harmful, as it causes sudden dilation and contraction of the scales and thus, produces shrinking and felting of the fabric. Wool retains a large amount of moisture and is very heavy when wet, and if it is hung up in this state, it stretches downwards and gets out of shape.

Shake the woolen articles to remove the dust. To prevent the felting of spoiling of the shape of hand, knitted garments mark out the outline of an article before wetting it. The garment should be allowed to dry flat on the paper, as only thus will it keep its shape.

Wool does not absorb colouring matter rapidly, so fresh stains are easy to remove. If bleaching is done, use only hydrogen peroxide or sodium perborate at a moderate temperature. Javelle water should never be used on wool. For woolens, steeping is not generally used, as long immersion in water weakens the fabric. Children's clothes, which are dirty, should be steeped for ten to fifteen minutes in slightly warm water made alkaline with borax.

The woolens should be washed and rinsed in water of constant temperature which is 100°F, or luke warm water. Alkalies, except borax, damage the texture ofthe woolen. fabrics and so avoid using them. If the water is hard, add a few drops of ammonia to the water for white woolens and borax for white as well as coloured woolens. Soap solution should be used.

Prepare a permanent lather with warm water and soap flakes. If the articles are heavy use soap jelly with ammonia to make the lather. Rinse in several waters of the same temperature for the thorough removal of the soap. Use citric acid, i.e. a squeeze of lime, juice to the last rinse for white woolens and vinegar for coloured woolens. This will counteract any alkali that is left in the fabric and freshen it.

Wrap the articles in a dry cloth or towel and press between the hands if the article is small. To remove the moisture bulky articles should be spread on a flat surface and then pressed with a suction washer or with a wooden roller. Outdoor drying is not advisable as strong sunlight and intense heat affect the texture of the fabric. During drying, lift, shake and turn occasionally and pull it to its shape. All woolens are finished by pressing except the woven fabrics, such as flannel and serge which should be ironed lightly.

Laundering of Silk

Silk is another animal fiber of delicate and fine texture which needs special care in laundering. Silks are available in may qualities with different textures, such as velvet, georgette, crepes, etc. Fresh stains are preferably removed, if possible, with cold or warm water according to the nature of the stain. For old stains which are difficult to remove, use weak reagents, such as weak solutions of borax, or sodium perborate for coloured silk, and hydrogen peroxide with a few drops of ammonia for white silk. Javelle water should never be used on silks as this will damage the fiber very much.

A small proportion of borax, added to the water, will make steeping more effective. Soap flakes are suitable, so is soap fluid and reeta nut solution. Water for silk must be soft. Cleansing is done by kneading and squeezing or by suction washing. Rinse the silks in two or three warm waters to remove the soiled soap from the fabric. Add a few drops of citric acid (Nimbu ka Ras) or acetic acid to the last rinse, which should be of cold water to the sheen of the fabric.

There is a natural gum in" the silk fibre, which is stiffened by the final cold rinse, giving a light stiffness to the article. If extra stiffness is necessary, add gum water to the last rinse. Silks should be squeezed lightly by hand to remove the moisture. Heat must be avoided and so, drying of silk is not done in the sun. A hot iron will scorch the silk, whilst a cold one will drag and crease the surface of the silk instead of giving it a smooth finish. The heat of the iron should be tested on a piece of paper. If no mark is left on the paper until you have counted three, the temperature is correct for the silk.

All dark colours are ironed on the wrong side to avoid a glaze. Fast coloured silks are treated in the same way as white silks. To revive the freshness of the colour, use vinegar or citric acid in the last rinse. Never use salt to prevent the colour from bleeding.

Laundering of Rayon

Rayons are artificial fibres derived from cellulose. Rayons have no natural elasticity. Rayons are washed in the same way as silks. The soap should be neutral, and the water soft, and not above 100°F in temperature.

When articles are lifted out of water, their weight must be supported with the hands or they should be placed on a draining board. If allowed to hang in mid air, they will stretch and may tear. Squeeze the fabric between the palms of hands to remove the moisture. Rayons, should be protected from heat and so, drying in the sun should be avoided. Rayon fabrics are usually turned out into sewn garments except in saris.

Other synthetic fabrics such as polyamides - polyesters, acrylic and acetate are easy to care fabrics. They are hydrophobic fabrics; that is they do not absorb moisture readily. This contributes to speedy drying and is responsible for resistance to shrinkage and spotting. Most of them are thermoplastic; it means that only light pressing with low heat iron is necessary to restore the original appearance of a fabric.

Some rich and expensive silks, rayons and woollens lose their luster, sheen and rich texture when washed. Such fabrics are cleansed by a method called dry cleaning. Dry cleaning is really not dry, but it is cleaning with grease solvents other than the soap solution. There are two methods of dry cleaning:

1. **By means of Grease Absorbents:** There may be some dry absorbent like fuller's earth, french chalk, talcum powder, salt, bran, bread crumbs, baked flour, moong powder, powdered sulphur. One of these powder is sprinkled or rubbed into the article to be cleaned. This is then folded to allow the powder to absorb the grease. Since the grease holds the dirt the garment is now easy to clean.

2. **By means of Volatile Grease Solvents:** These chemicals are all liquids and easily penetrate the garments but do not wet them as does water, and these liquids easily' evaporate in air. Examples of grease-solvents are petrol, ether, methylated spirit, chloroform, carbon tetrachloride, tri-chloroethylene, mineral turpentine and a latest patent product of ICI known simply as Solvent.

The dry cleaning process may be performed by:

(a) The immersion of garments in a grease solvent in order to dissolve the grease.

(b) Spot cleaning by sponging dirty spot with a grease solvent

(c) Absorption of grease by powders, (i) sprinkled on dirty spots or by (ii) application of a paste made of a grease absorbent powder and a grease solvent.

Drying: Hang the articles to dry for a day in a shady place away from the sun and fire and in plenty of draught preferably outside in the open for a day at least, so that all traces of petrol and its odour disappears. As long as the petrol odour remains in the article, it should not be ironed. The article should be finished according to its type and texture.

RESOURCE MANAGEMENT | 5

Management is an essential component of family living. Each day we use management process consciously or unconsciously. As soon as a family is set up in a house and the members begin to work for common goals, the need for formulating a plan of action arises. It calls for organising and controlling the use of available human and non human resources and also delegation of responsibility (this is home management). Since management plays a significant role in shaping our lives, it is essential to understand basic concepts of managemeent in the home.

CONCEPT OF HOME MANAGEMENT

Home management is a very important factor, which contributes to the health, happiness and well being of a family. It paves way for a better growth and development of the family members. Life has become very complex because man has increased tools and has changed the tactics of living. As a result, it has become necessary for him to develop more skills in the use of available resources in order to get what he wants for himself and his family to improve his status. In other words management deals with "using what we have, to get what we want." What we have is the resources. The resources that we have may be time, money, energy, skill etc. What we want is the achievement of goals. Goals are the aims in our life. Attainment of goals give pleasure and non attainment gives dissatisfaction.

Dissatisfaction can be avoided only through the wise application of management process. The quality of management will vary depending on the managerial abilities of individuals. Management process will enable one to identify and locate available resources and use them effectively to achieve the desired goals.

STEPS IN MANAGEMENT PROCESS

Management is nothing but a process of management that takes place in a systematic way, having knowledge of the content. If there is no management there will be confusion and no proper achievement will be shown. Hence management plays a significant role. Process may be defined as comprising a series of actions that lead to the accomplishment of objectives. The four steps in management process are planning, organizing, controlling and evaluating.

1. Planning

It is mapping out courses of action in order to reach intermediate and long term goals. It is the first step in the management process. Planning covers a wide range of decisions, dealing with family activities. It deals with decision making process, i.e.—defining the problem, seeking alternatives etc. In making plans, decisions must be made as to what actions are necessary to achieve the desired objectives; why each of these actions is necessary; who is responsible for. each action; and when where and how each action will take place. To determine these things planner must search for available alternatives and then make their selection.

In a family situation where more than one person is involved in making a plan, communication is necessary. Unless there is proper communication between family member, plans will not be successful. The person who plans should organize the plan best suited for each member of the family.

2. Organizing

When two or more persons combine their efforts to establish a home, an understanding of how the work and responsibilities are to be shared is necessary. Organizing consists of dividing and grouping of activities and assigning them to individuals. It may be defined as the process of establishing the proper relationship among work, people and other resources and channeling authority and responsibility.

3. Controlling

It is the activity that aids in putting and keeping the plan in action. It involves a careful observation of performance. It is the checking of work and performance to be sure that the procedure is moving in the planned direction. It includes making changes when necessary for a plan in action. Such checking may concern the quality of work, or costs in terms of either money or time, or the feeling or the satisfaction of the people.

If suppose one or more of the family members appear to have feelings, controlling calls for flexibility (use of alternative) in thinking and planning, rather than a rigid and set pattern of action. Controlling calls for both leadership and joint action in the family. Unless there is co-operation and understanding of the members, the best results will not be achieved. Skillful direction and guidance are needed to help control the plan in operation, knowledge of what is to be done, methods and instruction for doing the task must be understood by everyone concerned with it.

There are different phases in control step—i.e. energizing, checking and adjusting:

(a) **Energizing:** It is the initiating and sustaining the action. People differ a great deal in ability to get started on their plans and to carry them through. Setting intermediate goals may be helpful in energizing action since they provide an opportunity for rapid accomplishment with its accompanying satisfaction.

(b) **Checking:** It is checking the progress of the plan, which is done automatically in many respects, e.g. checking the time in real preparation, checking the quality of product etc. It is necessary to have standards or intermediate goals at strategic points as a basis for checking. Specific devices for checking plans in action vary with resources concerned.

(c) **Adjusting:** The third phase of this control step is adjusting the plan, thus mating fresh decisions. Conditions may change e.g. a student has planned to make notes I by sitting in library; but she finds that she has less time than expected, so she will get the chapter xeroxed and read from it.

Supervision

When the carrying out of a plan is delegated to others, supervision usually becomes I important. It may be very vague and sketchy, almost non-existent, or it may be very complete and definite.

Directing

If the technical aspects of the particularly, the resulting end product are uppermost in the mind of the manager, the process is called 'directing', e.g. Home maker directing the maid to do various chores.

Guiding

If the effect of the supervision of the person's development is uppermost, the process is guiding e.g. mother guides her children to do their home work.

4. Evaluating

It is looking back over what has been done and judging the result with respect to the goals. It is to determine how good ajob has been done. Thus evaluation involves a complete review of what has already taken place with a view towards better management in the future. After proper evaluation many mistakes can be avoided and better ways devised for carrying out the plan.

In home management, the measure by which success or failure of a plan can be evaluated is the extent to which it has attained/achieved family goals and objectives. In a family each member's standard should be satisfied. It helps to improve the standard of living of the family. Evaluation can be self evaluated too.

Evaluation in a home is done by setting up questions for the individual group to answer. In regard to planning and controlling questions are related whether work was successful and what improvements can be made. If the work was unsuccessful then why? Keeping in mind the goals look into the weak points and find the solution for its success.

There are two types of informal evaiuations, the overall variety and a more detailed kind. Overall variety recognizes the general quality of the job done. Without much; analytical thinking manager may recognize ajob as 'good' in itself or as 'good' in relation to give conditions.

The more detailed type of evaluation is determining the degree of excellence of the managerial job. It is an attempt toward accuracy of judgement and consists of the separate evaluation of different parts of management.

VALUES, GOALS AND STANDARDS

Management plays an important role in shaping our lives. It enables to recognise the values, the allocation of resources to attain the family goals so as to enhance the standard of life.

Goals, values and standards are closely related concepts. Value is the base and from values stem the other two concepts - goals and standards. Values are important to the individual but vague to express in operational terms. The concept of goal is more specific. It signifies something definite towards which one works. A standard is defined as something used as a basis.

Value indicates the worth that is attached to any object, condition, principle or idea. Value is the capacity of something or somebody to satisfy the human desire. These are the ways behind our actions and the basis for setting goals.

All values are human. They are created, evaluated and enjoyed by persons. A value is always important to the person who holds it. It is desirable and satisfying. It has the ability to develop in self-

creative way. It is relatively stable but tends to change gradually.

The intensity of values vary from individual to individual. Values help an individual to direct his effort more intelligently in seeking satisfactions.

Values are of two types - Intrinsic and Instrumental. An intrinsic value is one that is important and desirable for its own sake. e.g. art. The interest in beauty is an intrinsic value. An instrumental value is the means to attain other values, e.g. Efficiency in work. Some values possess both intrinsic and instrumental worth. The human values - love, affection, health; comfort, ambition, knowledge, wisdom, play, art and religion have both intrinsic and instrumental values.

The major values classified by *Parker* are:

Love: It is the interest in relationship with people in its broad sense and its various forms are expressed as sex love, parental love, friendship and community love.

Health: It is the interest in physical and mental well-being.

Comfort: It is the interest in making life as pleasant and agreeable as possible.

Ambition: It is the interest or desire for success in life for a victorious achievement.

Knowledge and wisdom: It is the interest in truth and its use in all activities in living.

Technological interest or efficiency in work: It is the interest in the efficient making and using of things.

Play: It is the interest in beauty in all forms of expression.

Religion: It is the interest in goodness and rightness in unifying all aims and purposes in living.

Values grow out of human desire and interest. Values differ in cultures. The family has the major responsibility for fostering values among the members.

Goals

Goals are value based objectives. The goals grow out of desires, past experiences and environment.

Goals are the ends that any individual or family is willing to work for. The family's goal will help in shaping the family's life pattern and setting standards.

The formulation and attainment of individual and family goals require the knowledge, judgment and understanding the ways of using family resources. Goals should be definite and attainable. Goal-setting is a continuous process. Many goals are immediately attainable. One goal stems from another and leads to a third.

Goals can be for short term, mid term or long-term. The shortterm goals are the initial goals, which leads to the final long-term goals. The major goals that are created by the family grow out of its own environment and experience.

The major goals of home making are

1. Providing optimum physical and mental health for the members of the family.

2. Facilitating for optimum development of the individual members of the family.

3. Satisfying family relationships.

4. Recognition, acceptance and appreciation of human differences.

5. Establishing satisfactory relationship with the community and other subsystems of the society.

Standards

Standard is defined as scale or parameter used for comparison. Standards are more specific than values or goals. Standards are related to specific materials. It is influenced by external factors. Standards are set limits one will accept in working toward a goal. Standards are mental pictures of what is considered essential and necessary to make life satisfying. If achieved, leads to satisfaction, if not achieved leads to uncomfortable situation. Standards remain as part of one's pattern of living and habit.

Standards vary according to the values of the family or group. On this basis they can be classified as conventional standards and flexible standards.

Conventional Standards are fixed and arise from the values of social acceptance. In this people change to meet the standards. Conventional standards are traditional and are accepted by the community or by a social group within it. They are fixed at a given time and liable to change when condition change.

Flexible standards are developed and changed according to the individual's demand. They change to suit the human situation. But they are not widely accepted by the community.

Standard of living is the combination of many specific standards. It consists of a pattern of commodities, services and satisfactions which a person thinks essential for happy living. According to Hazel Kyrk, "standard of living is made up of the essential values to be sought. It is an attitude towards a way of regarding or of judging, a given mode of life". Standard of living determines the character of the real income of the family. The standard of living of a family encompasses not only the actual qualities and quantities of goods and services but also the ways of using these goods and services.

RESOURCES

The resources that individuals and families have at their disposal consists of the tools, assets, capabilities and the ways and means they possess. These are used in countless ways to achieve what is important to each person and to the family as a group.

These are two groups mainly:

Human resources

1. **Abilities and skills of family members both native and acquired attitude:** The opinions or feelings that activate or related action. These can be very powerful activation in helping or handling attainment of goals.

2. **Knowledge:** Possessed by each person, both factual and in terms of relationship.

3. **Energy:** Energy or the power of the members to carry on both physical and mental activities.

Non human resources

These are tangible used by the families move easily recognized, and some are sought after.

1. **Time:** Time made up of shorter or longer periods of duration, in which activities are carried on. It's limited supply, felt by some, varied from person and from family to family in activity patterns carried on in a given period.

2. **Money:** It is exchanged for commodities, services and mechanical power used by every family.

3. **Goods:** Durable, perishable, property etc.

4. **Facilities:** For which the family does not pay directly but community to which it has free access, such as parks, roads, schools, certain kinds of transportation, libraries and many other services such as police protection, markets, medical facilities, free concerts and other entertainment are all provided by the social group.

All resources have certain basic characteristics:

1. **All resources are useful:** All resources have utility which means the satisfying power. Unless we identify the uses for an item, it is not recognised as a resource and also related to the specific goal. Thus usefulness of a particuhr resource would vary for different goals. For example, money may be the most valuable resource for processing a house. But to do well in a test, intellectual ability counts most.

2. **All resources are limited:** All resources are scarce, some are more scarce than the others. If the resources were unlimited or abundant, management would be necessary. A decrease in resources usually brings an increased appreciation of the importance of management. The limits of each resource must be assessed in relation to specific goals. The limitations on resources can both the quantitative and qualitative e.g. time is the most limited resource, quantitatively, since no day can contain more than 24 hours, nor can any of these hours be saved.

Energy too is a limited resource, differing from time in that the amount of energy available varies greatly from person to person like a certain job is too heavy for one person, yet expecting another to do it.

The amount of money resource varies greatly form person to person, and for an individual in different periods of his life. Abilities too are limited. The limitations are set by inherent capacity and the training involved. The Material goods a family possess are limited by two factors; the amount of money available for their purchase and the ability and opportunity for the family members to produce the materials themselves.

3. **All resources are interrelated:** People often have to use a resource mix or combinations of resources to achieve the family goals e.g. when a young couple want to decorate their house, they use some of their tangible resources in terms of money, some of the inherited and gifted furniture as well as some of the intangible resources of innovative ideas and creative ability to paint and decorate the house. In management the interrelated use of resources in a resource mix is more important than the use of any specific one.

4. **Substitution:** Alternatives could be worked out for a single limited resource. A manager has to substitute the replaceble resources for the very scar resource in the management situation e.g. if a home maker has more time than money at her disposal, she does her own house work. On the other hand, if she has more money than time, she may hire certain tasks done or use community facilities.

DECISION MAKING

Home management, a dynamic process involves decision making. Decision making is the heart of Home management. It requires knowledge of essential information, application of knowledge in life situation and the willingness to know and to apply. So the role of decision making in management involves knowing and actually applying essential information in problem situations of day to day life.

Management is a mental process which involves a series of decision-making. The steps in decision making are:

1. Defining the problem
2. Identifying the alternative solutions
3. Analysing the alternatives
4. Selecting an alternative
5. Action in carrying out the plan and bearing responsibility for the consequences.

1. **Defining the Problem:** It involves the recognition of the problem. It needs relevant information to identify and define it first. Unless the problem is clearly defined and analysed the ultimate decision would not be effective. For e.g. Planning household activities, purchasing labour saving devices, selecting clothing for the family.

2. **Identifying the Alternatives:** Decision making will be effective only when one identifies possible alternatives. The choice of best selection of alternatives requires thorough knowledge about the availability of resources and their limitations.

3. **Analysing the Alternatives:** After identifying the alternatives, one should think of the consequences of each alternative systematically to find out the relevant one, considering the goals, values and standards.

4. **Selecting an Alternative:** After analysing the problem one should carefully select from the possible alternatives. Evaluation plays a very important role in this selection. Choosing the best from the several possible alternatives will be helpful in solving the problem.

5. **Accepting the Consequences of the Decision:** This is the ability to assess and accept the consequences of the decision for making future decision. It is the evaluational process. This experience would indicate the final outcome of the decision making. It creates self confidence in people to make effective decisions in the future.

TIME MANAGEMENT

Locating ourselves in our environment with reference to time is an important part of time management. All our activities for example going to bed, getting up in the morning, having meals, playing, etc is based on the available time. Time and energy are closely related, the management and use of one affecting the other. Time use is affected by the following factors.

1. **Stage of family life cycle:** The beginning stage is the period of establishment which starts from the date of marriage till the first baby is born, a period of approximately 0 to 4 years. The time demand will differ based on whether the home maker is employed or not. The second stage is the expanding stage where the demand for time will be more for guiding and being with children. The third stage is the contracting stage when the children leave home because of marriage or employment. The time requirement at this stage will be much lighter and they will have more time for participation in community activities etc.

2. **Environment:** The size and type of the house, the number of persons in the family, the age of the family members, work area, tools and equipment available affect the usage of time.

3. **Who perform the household task:** Whether the household tasks are performed individually or shared by the family members affect the use of time.

4. The attitude towards house work and whether the homemaker is gainfully employed also has a role in affecting time use.

ENERGY MANAGEMENT

Energy management is more difficult and complex as the energy that each person has to do various activities depend on physical and mental health. Like time the demand for energy will be less during beginning and contracting stage and more during the expanding stage.

The various efforts are needed to perform different household tasks. They are mental effort, visual effort, manual effort, torsal effort and pedal effort. Depending on the energy requirement tasks can be classified as below.

1. **Light work:** Sewing, Washing dishes, Dusting furniture, sweeping etc.
2. **Moderate work:** Kneading dough, ironing, hanging clothes.
3. **Heavy work:** Bed making, mopping floor, laundry, carrying children etc.

Energy expenditure for doing various tasks depend on the mental approach, postural strain, muscle tension, concentration in work and the skill they acquire. Fatigue is a condition where the amount of work output would be reduced. This can be classified as physiological and psychological fatigue.

The reason for fatigue could be

1. The long period of mental or physical work
2. Heavy physical work
3. Working under pressure
4. Unfamiliar work
5. Non accomplishment of work
6. Monotonous work
7. Lack of motivation
8. Dislike for work
9. Desire to stop work
10. Failure of plans

Stages of Management of Time and Energy

1. **Planning:** The first stage of management is planning. The time and activity pattern of the family should be planned taking into consideration the daily, weekly, seasonal and special tasks, and the amount of time required for various activities. The steps is making the time plan are

   Step I: This consists of listing the every day, weekly, special and recreational activities of the family

   Step II: Making a plan for routine tasks considering those work that must be done at a definite time of the day. By this one will know the block of free time available.

   Step III: Fitting the special and seasonal jobs into the free time block.

   Step IV: Deciding who will do the various tasks in the family. This can be decided through group discussion.

2. **Controlling:** Carrying out time and activity plan is the next step in managing time and energy. Change of plan may occur depending on the interruptions. Motivation plays an important role in carrying out the activity plans. Developing skill and use of work simplification techniques will reduce time and energy expenditure.

3. **Evaluating:** Evaluation should be done while making and carrying out plans as well as reviewing the results. Constant evaluation of performance and checking of accomplishments should be done to make sure that things are going on as planned.

WORK SIMPLIFICATION

It may be defined as accomplishing more work with a given. amount of time and energy, or as reducmg the amount of energy or both to accomplIsh a given amount of work. In the home the interest in work simplification stems from its effect on the home maker and other family members. A home maker may wish to free work time for other activities or simply to fit work time available to required work. She may on the other hand have a liberal supply of time, but need to conserve her energy.

It is the woman who is literally overworked or who has accumulated fatigue of the physiological type who needs immediate relief. It is helpful in arousing interest to show that work simplification can accomplish one or more of several purposes:

1. It can reduce time on a given operation.
2. It can cut down the number of motions and improve type of motions on a specific task, hence probably reducing energy costs.
3. It can reduce over-all boredom resulting from long accustomed and routine habits of work.

4. It may reduce frustration fatigue if that has arisen because of lack of effectiveness on a job.

This problem of arousing interest stems from the difficulty in and necessary time for breaking old! habits and establishing new ones, essential in adopting work simplification techniques. Intellectual interest in the new method must be stimulated and the advantage to the individual must be made clear.

Improvements in methods of work have come chiefly through laboratory research. Nevertheless, laboratory techniques are not only slow but expensive, and little money is available for house hold research. Besides formal laboratory techniques there are simpler informal pencil and paper techniques used both by industry and researchers in home tasks.

Symbols used

One of the essentials in research is an accurate vocabulary. A motion is a very complex activity and to study it requires its break down into simpler elements. The Gilbreths investigated, classified and named these elements, calling them by their own name spelt back-wards - therbligs. The term therblig can be used to classify the motions of fingers, arms, hands, or the activity of the body as a whole. Each of the 18 therbligs has its special name, symbol, abbreviation and color by which shown on a simo chart. There is a trend towards using only the initials, not the graphic symbols for therbligs. For example: Grasp is indicated either by "G" or a horse-shoe shape, and color is scarlet.

Simple pencil and paper techniques
(a) Flow Process Chart

It is a step-by-step description of a worker performing a given task in its entirety. It is an overall investigation and differs from an ordinary description of a worker's activities only in that a few symbols are used to classify the steps immediately into types.

The small circle indicates that the worker is going somewhere; the large circle indicates that she is standing still but working with her hands, the square indicates inspection with eyes and triangle indicates that nothing is happening. The advantage of using the symbols along with the description is that one may quickly count up the number of each of the types of steps. For home tasks, when it is used, flow chart may be called a 'process chart-man analysis'.

Operation Chart: It is similar to a flow process chart except that it picks up one particular step in a whole process and breaks it down into the work of each hand shown in parallel columns. The same symbols may be used with the understanding that this time the small circle means a movement of the arm, the large circle a movement of the fingers with the arm more or less satisfactory. The triangle indicates complete idleness or' both arms and fingers. It takes considerably more skill to make an operation chart than a process chart move analysis. It is practically impossible to make an accurate operation chart of 2 hands except through film analysis. Each hand can, however, be followed by a separate observer and action of both hands studied particularly for delays.

The main uses of process and operation charts are for educational and promotional purposes. They help in training investigators. They make one motion and time conscious, they sharpen one's power of observation and they help in learning the principles of effective work.

(b) Multiman chart

It is similar both to the process and simo charts, though it may be far less elaborate than the latter. It is suited to the study of an activity that is carried out simultaneously by 2 or more persons.

The symbols already given may be used. An important point to watch is delay. For example: when two persons make a bed together, each will have certain delays while the other is occupied, such an observation explains the basis of the finding that the labour time of 2 persons making a bed together is normally greater than the labour time of one person carrying out the same task.

(c) Pathway chart

The pin and string method was suggested first by Mrs. Gilbreth. It may be carried out literally by pinning string on a floor covered with a rug or other textile, thus marking the pathway of a worker carrying out a given task. Her accustomed pathway is shown with one color of string, her revised pathway after study of the process, is marked with a different color. A much easier modification of this technique is the arm chair method of using a floor plan drawn to scale and fastened to a drawing board. Thumb tacks or pins are put in where the worker turns and her pathway is measured from thread wound around the pins as she works.

Rhythm is a little-investigated aspect of work simplification, although at least one technique exists for its study. This is the cycle graph, a photographic device which registers the pathway of light of a small electric bulb attached to some portion of the body that is in action. The pattern thus formed shows rhythm if the pathways are smooth and superimposed upon one another, or lack of rhythm if pathways are separate and do not flow easily one into the other.

Dr. Marvin Mundel has given five factors that influence the character of work. They are:

1. **Change in hand and body motions:** Work can be simplified by using each part of the body properly and economically.

   This can be achieved by

   1. Keeping body parts in alignment

   2. Using muscles effectively

   3. Doing the work in rhythmic motion

   4. Developing skill in work.

2. **Change in equipment and work arrangement:** Using labour saving devices, planning work surfaces at proper height, depth and width with proper tools and adequate storage space and lighting will improve the efficiency of work.

3. **Change in production sequence:** When there are a lot of household activities to be accomplished time and energy can be saved by simplifying the work through combining the tasks and eliminating unnecessary steps.

4. **Change in finished product:** Simplification of work could be achieved by changing the standards or expectations of the finished product.

5. **Change in material:** This refers to the change in the raw ingredient to get the same final products.

HOUSING

A house is a shelter consisting of walls, floors, doors, windows, roof etc. in which human' beings live. While a home is a house, in which you and your family enjoy all the happiness, affection and love of each other, health, ease and comfort, plus entertainment, social activities and indulgence of hobbies. Various factors that influence the choice of family housing are family needs, family income, housing values and standards, leisure time activities of the family members, and supply & demand relationship of the houses.

There are various methods to acquire a house.

1. **Renting:** When the family does not want to invest in static property, does not have enough money and when the job is transferable, people go for rented house. Though some advantages like no tension of maintaining the property, sell the property and loss of value of property and easy leave the existing place of residence exists, there are certain disadvantages exist like paying rent every month, restrictions from landlord, less privacy and lack of facilities etc.

2. **Owning:** This can be achieved either by buying an existing new/old house or by building a house. If an old house has to be purchased one has to think about years of construction, cost, size and ventilation of the house, and distance from man made facilities. While for buying a new house one needs to consider the locality, condition of the house, size, cost, possibility for resale, and proximity to various community services.

Families who plan to build a house should think about four aspects—(a) -choosing a suitable location (b) obtaining plans and specifications (c) obtaining architect's services and (d) estimating the housing cost.

Site Selection

Site is the plot area where the house is to be built. One has to consider the soil type, neighbourhood standards, proximity to natural and man made facilities, and orientation. Orientation is the positioning of the house in the plot in the best manner to achieve maximum benefits of natural features like wind, sunlight and to save the house from the heavy rain strokes, direct sunrays and strongwind. More openings towards east, wide balconies, weather shades or overhead roofs over the windows and balconies should be provided to make it possible for direct sunlight to enter the house and at the same time to save the interior of the house from the strong sunrays. Never prefer the plot with irregular boundaries. Prefer the house with the freehold scheme.

Rocky soil is good for the strength but plumbing costs would be high since digging is difficult. Reclaimed soil or made soil is not good because when it absorbs water it becomes slippery and often chokes up the drainliness. Combination of rocky, sandy and garden soil is the best type of soil.

Factors affecting the planning a house

Hard and fast rules cannot be laid down for space designing because no two sites will be exactly identical. Further there will be many more factors influencing the decisions regarding space arrangement like type of house i.e. with respect to the needs of the family members, occupation and their likes and dislikes, the bye laws and the neighbourhood standards. In spite of all these, certain features govern the theory of planning a residential building.

1. **Aspect:** It refers to the positioning or arrangement of doors, windows and ventilators in all the exterior walls of the building which allows it to enjoy the utmost gifts of nature such as sunshine, breeze and pleasant view. Kitchen should have an eastern aspect so that morning sunrays would purify the air. The bed rooms should have south east or south west aspect if possible by providing balconies facing these sides. Drawing room or living room should have north east or south east aspect.

2. **Prospect:** It has got the reference to the impression that the building is likely to make on the individual viewing it from outside. By this, we mean provision of large balconies at the upper floor and attractive pillars in the verandah anhe ground floor certainly adds to the beauty of the house. The simple ways to add to the prospect may be just a small projection through one or two bay windows, and casual break here and there in the continuous walls.

3. **Roominess:** It is the opposite of crampedness. It has a reference to the impact produced by making the best use of small proportions of rooms by deriving maximum benefits from minimum dimensions of a room. If the length of the room exceeds the width of the room for 11/2 times, it produces a cramped effect. Roominess can be achieved through provision of wall cupboards, and narrow strips of passages utilised for useful purpose.

4. **Grouping:** It means the disposition of rooms in respect to their relative position towards each other e.g. sanitary services must be nearer to the bedrooms and also independently accessible from the bedrooms as well as guest and living rooms. Bathroom and WC should be away from kitchen and dining room. Living and dining room should be close by. A formal drawing room, kitchen and one set of bath and WC should be situated on the same floor.

5. **Privacy:** Privacy is of two types. External privacy means screening the entire house from the byways, streets, highways and even the neighbourhood buildings. For example on the side of the main roads, formal living room and kitchen should be planned. Internal privacy is screening the interior of each room from other rooms as well as from the main entrance. It can be achieved through proper

grouping of various rooms, proper positioning of doors in walls, mode of hanging doors and provision of small corridor and lobbies. Door should be fixed in a corner of the larger wall so that larger part of the room is screened.

6. **Circulation:** It is of two types i.e. horizontal i.e. on the same floor and vertical or from one floor to the other. Horizontal circulation can be provided through the provision of separate passage to which most of the doors of various rooms can open. While vertical circulation can be achieved from the staircase. Positioning of the staircase should be located at such place which has easy access for all the rooms.

7. **Sanitation:** Good sanitation means general cleanliness for the entire house and specifically for all utility areas. Staircases and passages should be well lighted. All decay should be kept out of the drains. All edges and corners should be rounded. Plan for large windows in kitchen and storeroom. Non-absorbent materials like glazed tiles should be provided in WCs and kitchens for flooring and skirting all round the walls. Keep the garbage bin away. Thus sanitation can be achieved through proper facilities for good ventilation, lighting and cleanliness.

8. **Ventilation:** It means not only supplying fresh air to a room but also connotes the evacuation of the vitiated air and the maintenance of a movement of air in the house. For a thorough ventilation, two large windows should be provided to opposite to each other on the walls. Functions of satisfactory ventilation are freedom from bad smell, reduction in humidity, proper supply of oxygen and a sensation of comfortable coolness to the body.

9. **Practical considerations:** It is a matter of choice, preferences based on the needs of the family members that governs the decisions regarding space allocation for the house plan. House being an immovable property may be built once for several generations, don't go for weak structure. Have the needed facilities at the ground floor for the old members.

Provision for adding a wing should be made while building in the first instance.

10. **Flexibility:** It aims at multipurpose or overlapping simultaneous uses of various rooms. It can be achieved through proper grouping, roominess and privacy. It is a common practice to use a single room to carry out number of activities at the same time by the same individual or more than one individual. Flexibility of the plan refers to avoiding the rigidity of area planning. For example combining drawing and dining area during some festive occasions by a removable partition.

11. **Furniture requirement:** It is an important consideration for taking satisfactory decisions regarding space distribution for any building. It is a three fold factor. (1) To plan the total space based on the existing furniture possessed by the owner (2) to plan the total space based on the requirements of family members and then purchase the furniture (3) possession of the furniture pieces which are not worth discarding not only acts as a guideline but also acts as a limiting factor to decide about the size and shape of various rooms. It also dictates the location of doors and windows for the entire house as well as its opening. Multipurpose, folding and portable furniture is more suitable for less space. Space should be planned in such a manner that it allows the family to arrange all the equipment, furniture and furnishings without disturbing the horizontal circulation and internal privacy of the house.

Planning of different rooms

Kitchen: It is impossible to imagine any house without a kitchen or a cooking area. Even if it is a one room house, it will have at least a small corner or specific area is utilised as a kitchen. There are some important points to be covered for the perfect kitchen plan. It should be airy, well lighted and ventilated. It should have eastern or north-eastern aspect. It should have three centres viz., storage centre(refregirator and pantry where food stuffs are placed), preparation and mixing centre (where food is prepared and dish washing is done) and cooking and servil1g centre (includes stove/cooking range and counter space for serving food). The work triangle among these three centres should not be less than 15 feet and more than 22 feet. The ideal size of the kitchen is 10'×10' or 10'×12'. There are 5 types of kitchens namely, one wall kitchen where all the three work centres are in one row. Two wall or corridor type has storage and preparation centre on one side while cooking centre is on the opposite side. If three centres on three sides it is called separate unit kitchen. In L shape kitchen, three work centres from right to left are placed on two adjacent walls. U shape kitchen has three work centres on three adjacent walls. Among all these L shape is the best type since it has optimum work triangle.

Verandah: It is provided at the main entrance to put the umbrellas, raincoats, chappals etc. It also serves the purpose of providing space for the visitors to wait and acts as a corridor. It should have minimum 1.5 mt width with southwest or north west facing.

Living room: It may be just one room which gets changed into formal drawing room and informal living room at different hours of the day for various occasions. From the flexibility point of view if the room has got more than one purpose or it has got exclusive purpose of entertaining guests the following decisions may be taken in the context of living room plan: (a) the location of the room with respect to orientation and aspect (b) grouping of the room specifically with respect to its opening towards internal side of the house (c) distance from the main entrance as well as planning and provision of hall and adjoining balconies mainly from the point of view of external privacy and safety.

Bathroom: Well ventilated bath and we should possess best quality water pipes, taps and drain pipes. The surface material for the floor and the walls must be smooth and easy to clean. The slope of the floor should be towards the drain line.

Store room: It should be situated near the kitchen with stone flooring to prevent the entry of rats and mice. Store room should be well lit and ventilated and should have rows of shelves all round the walls. Lofts over kitchen and bath room at 7 to 8 feet height for storing heavy articles ca~ be built.

Staircase: It should be situated at such a place as to be easily and independently accessible from any room. Its minimum width should be 2 to 6 feet with a headspace on top of any step should be 6'6". The rise of steps should be uniform through out and should not exceed 9". The width of the step or the tread should not be less than 9". The stair tread surface should be of non-slippery nature.

Garage: The minimum dimensions for a garage are 8'×18'. A clearance of 8" above the hood of the car is sufficient. Storage space can be provided at the loft in the garage.

INTERIOR DESIGN

Design is associated with the creation of a knife, costume, poster, bridge, political campaign etc. Design is the process of accomplishing some end. Design becomes the expression of ourselves. Design is an organized intention for any contrivance or plan with some definite purpose or function. Design is mainly of two types, i.e., structural and decorative design which have been discussed in the previous chapter. However decorative design is of four types. Naturalistic design represents the actual colours, shapes, patterns, forms of the natural objects like leaves, flowers, animals etc. Stylized designs are superior to naturalistic designs. These are also called as conventionalized designs which are formed by exaggerating, modifying or altering the naturalistic design. Unusual lines, colours or textures may be used in creating this design. For example a leaf can be shown in violet colour. Geometric designs are the safest designs for untrained consumer e.g. squares, circles, rectangles, traingles, half circles, elliptical shapes etc. The modern design is the abstract design which allows the alignments and grouping of parts of the design which have' no literal representation as such.

Aims in design are beauty, functionalism and expressiveness. Beauty is the combination of quality that is pleasing to the trained eye or ear. Expressiveness in a design indicates a definite idea or theme in it. The ideas expressed in home are repose, animation, naturalness, sophistication, intimacy, formality, warmth, coolness, delicacy, antiquity, freshness etc. Design should not only be beautiful but also to be functional. For example upholstery furniture should not only beautiful but also be durable, comfortable and give the maximum of service.

COLOUR AND COLOUR COMBINATIONS

The appeal of colour is universal. It enhances the beauty of objects and gives satisfaction to the mankind. Each colour has got its own characteristic such as irritating, charming, boring, welcoming or repelling. Because of these effects, colour affect the atmosphere of the home and we react emotionally to different colours.

Dimensions of colour

Colour has three qualities or dimensions. They are hue, value and intensity.

Hue: hue indicates the name of the colour. Examples are red, yellow, blue etc.

Value: Value indicates the lightness or darkness of a colour. The value of the colour can be changed by adding white or water to make it lighter and black or more colour to make it darker than the normal colour. A value that is lighter than the normal hue is termed as tint and a value darker than the normal hue is termed shade.

Example: Red is a normal hue. Pink is tint of red and maroon is shade of red.

Dr. Denman W. Ross has given nine degrees of value scales ranging from white to black. While is the highest of all values and no colour can be as light as white. Black is the lowest of all values and no colour can be as dark as black. When black and white are mixed, we get seven different scales of grey namely highlight, light, lowlight, middle, light dark, dark and low dark, based on the amount of black and white present in the grey colour.

Intensity: This indicates the brightness or dullness of a colour. It indicates the purity or strength of a colour.

Classification of colours

Prang colour chart: According to Prang colour chart, there are three primary colours. They are yellow, blue and red. They are called primary colours because these colours cannot be produced by mixing other colours.

When two primary colours are mixed in equal proportions, we get secondary colours.

Yellow + Blue = Green.

Blue + Red = Violet or Purple.

Red + Yellow = Orange

The primary and secondary colours together are called basic colours.

When a primary and an adjacent secondary colour is mixed an intermediate colour is produced. There are six intermediate colours.

They are

Yellow + Green = Yellow Green.

Blue + Green = Blue Green.

Blue + Violet = Blue Violet

Red + Violet = Red Violet

Red + Orange = Red Orange

Yellow + Orange = Yellow Orange.

The three primary colours, three secondary colours and six intermediate colours form the outer circle of the Prang colour chart.

When two binary colours are mixed a tertiary colour is produced.

There are three tertiary colours. They are

Green + Orange = Grey Yellow or Smoky Yellow.

Orange + Violet = Grey Red or Old brick Red.

Green + Violet = Grey Blue or Slate Blue.

When two tertiary colours are mixed a quaternary colour is produced. There are three quaternary colours.

They are

Smoky Yellow + Old Brick Red= Grey Orange or Buff.

Smoky Yellow + Slate Blue = Grey Green or Olive Green

Old Brick Red + Slate Blue = Grey Violet or Prune.

The three tertiary and three quaternary colours form the inner circle of the prang colour chart. Grey colour is in the centre of the Prang colour chart.

When we draw an imaginary vertical line in the centre of the Prang colour chart, the colours will be divided into two large groups. The colours on the right side of the prang colour chart closer to blue are cool colours and the ones on the left side, closer to red and orange are warm colours. Red and Orange are the warmest colours and Blue and Blue Green are the coolest colours.

Warm colours make the objects appear bigger and closer where as cool colours make the objects appear smaller and far away. Warm colours are cheerful and stimulating where as cool colours are calm and restful. Light values increase the size of the objects and dark values reduce the size.

Colour combination or colour harmonies

Colours should be combined effectively to create beauty, pleasure and satisfaction. They produce a sense of unity in colour combinations. Colour combination or colour harmonies can be classified into related and contrasting colour harmonies.

Related colour Harmony: They are obtained by using colours which are similar. They are classified into monochromatic and analogous colour harmony.

Monochromatic colour harmony: This is also known as one hue or one mode harmony. In this only one colour in different values and intensities is used. Example. Dark blue and light blue. In a monochromatic colour scheme, charming effects can be obtained through contrast in textures of the materials used.

Analogous colour harmony: In this colour scheme the colours which are lying adjacent to each other in the prang colour chart are used. They provide interesting variety than monochromatic harmony. The colours should be of different intensities and values.

Examples: Yellow, Yellow Green, Red, Red Orange, Orange.

Contrasting colour harmonies

Complementary colour scheme: Two colours that are directly opposite in the Prang colour chart are combined. Example: Yellow and Violet, Blue and Orange.

Double complementary colour harmony: Two adjacent colours and their opposite colours In the Prang colour chart are combined. For example: Yellow, Yellow Green, Violet and Red Violet.

Split complementary colour harmony: In this a primary or an intermediate colour and the two colours that lie on either side of its complementary colour are combined. For example: Yellow, Blue Purple and Red Purple.

Triad: In this, three colours which are at equal distance in the Prang colour chart are combined. We get four triads namely primary, secondary and two intermediate triads.

Primary Triad - Yellow, Blue and Red.

Secondary Triad - Green, Orange and Violet.

Intermediate Triad:

(a) Blue Green, Red Purple and Yellow Orange

(b) Yellow Green, Blue Purple and Red Orange.

Tetrad: This is formed by any four hues equidistant. on the Prang colour chart. Example : Green, Yellow Orange, Red and Blue Purple.

Factors to be considered while planning colour scheme

1. The expected effect in size, shape and direction of the room.

2. The mood to be created in the room. Example: Masculine, feminine, traditional, formal, etc.

3. Individual preference of the family members.

4. The activities to be carried out in each room.

5. Colours of other existing furniture and furnishings in the house.

6. Only one colour should dominate.

7. The basic colour should occupy atleast 60-70% of the whole colour scheme. Second hue should be used in lesser quantity and if a third colour is used, it should be used in least quantity.

8. Follow 'Law of areas' that is, larger the area lighter the colour and smaller the area brighter the colour.

9. The current trends and fashions.

FURNITURE FOR THE HOUSE

Furniture are pieces intended for comfort, rest and relaxation, storage or articles of beauty. Furniture in all houses, are indispensable and they provide for a harmonious living. While selecting furniture the following points are to be borne in mind.

1. Furniture used should be in proportion to the size of the room.

2. The design should be simple, plain, well constructed and provide comfort to the user.

3. The furniture we select should be easy to maintain.

4. The furniture should not occupy too much space.

5. It should be light weighted.

6. Children's furniture should be of adjustable height (legs).

7. The furniture should be movable.

8. The furniture should be functional and not too decorative.

9. The furniture should stand firmly.

General Rules

1. Select, a centre of interest and subordinate all other interests to it.

2. Observe balance in arrangement. Formal balance gives dignified, restful effect, but too much of formal balance in a room will give a monotonous appearance.

3. Retain good proportion while arranging. Place all large pieces on large wall area and small pieces on small wall area.

4. Avoid using too many furniture in a room.

5. Scatter upholstered pieces among wooden pieces.

6. Avoid letting furniture hide the walls. But at the same time avoid filling too much of the centre floor area. Keep the traffic lines in the room very clear while arranging. Arrange all furniture with purpose and function in mind, grouping those, which are needed for a particular activity in one place.

In the distribution of furniture, the housewife should exercise three policies: elimination, re-arrangement, and concealment. If one can afford, broken and unwanted furniture may be discarded and fresh ones replaced. Furniture in a room may be reorganised so as to achieve satisfaction. Unsightly and jarring object must be concealed by the use of slipcovers. Defective and unattractive furniture can be concealed by the use of good attractive covers.

Furniture Needed in Different Rooms

Drawing Room: One comfortable sofa and few chairs. Teapoy which is a bit lower than the seat of the sofa, television, video cassette recorder, radio and record player cabinets to keep record albums.

Dining Room: Dining table and chairs, folding chair, if needed a trolley.

Bed Room: A double bed, bedside table and a lamp, dressing table, bed time table with lamp, place for suitcases, chairs.

Children's Room: A study table, a bed, book shelf.

Guest Room: Sofas which can be converted to bed. Dressing table, bed side table with lamp, place for suitcases, chairs.

Kitchen: Built in storage space (appliances), stools, shelves, plate rack.

FLOOR DECORATIONS

The various types of floor decorations are

1. **Kolam:** Kolam is a free hand drawing of various designs. It can be either dotted or in various designs. For drawing kolams, either white stone or chalk powder, enamel paint, white or Coloured salt, sand or powders and solutions prepared by mixing ice flour and water is used. Red mud solution is used as painting to give added brightness. In rural

areas, people spray cowdung mixed with water as base on floors before putting Kolam.

2. **Rangoli:** Coloured dry powder which are usually made from kolam powders are used. They are mixed with either sand or salt.

3. **Alpana:** Alpana is a traditional art where the design is painted with white paint. Usually zinc oxide and gum are mixed to keep it for a longer duration.

4. **Flower Carpet:** Different coloured flowers, petals and leaves are arranged over the design. Wet sand may be evenly spread beneath the flower carpet to have a raised effect.

MONEY MANAGEMENT

Money plays an important role in the life of man as an instrument through which he can satisfy his physical, material and mental needs. The income and expenditure pattern of the family decides the family's standard of living and its place in the society. It also decides the economic well-being of the family and the nation.

FAMILY INCOME

Family income may be defined as money or purchasing power earned by family members during a specific period of time and goods and services received or created in that time by the family eg. goods like vegetables from kitchen garden, services like doing household chores, teaching children etc.

Expenditure

Happiness of the family is secured by income use or expenditure. Expenditure provides the satisfaction of life for the members of the family. All expenditure for the household may be divided into needs and wants. The needs are those which are necessary for maintaining a healthy, efficient household which a family must take care of and there are emergencies and special demands arising occasionally.

The regular monthly items of expenditure for most families include food, clothing, shelter, education, health, house keeping, recreation. Part of the income may be set aside in the form of savings for special needs or emergencies such as marriage, education, pleasure trips or sickness and old age.

The various factors that affect one's expenditure are:

1. Income of the family.

2. Size and composition of the family.

3. Age and occupation of the family members.

4. Education.

5. Location of the house.

6. Health status of the family members.

7. Interests and abilities of the members.

8. The availability of the goods.

9. The price of goods.

10. The customs of the family.

11. The personal likes and dislikes.

12. The general consumption pattern.

13. The saving pattern of the family in the future.

BUDGETING

The common planning device for the use of money is the budget. It is a carefully prepared spending plan based on the actual family income. It is a plan based on previous experience, present needs and future expectations. A budget is always prepared for a fixed period of time generally for a month.

Importance of Budgeting

1. Budget acts as an intelligent guide to spending.

2. It enables a family to have an over all view of their income.

3. Budgeting facilitates adjusting irregular income to regular expenditure.

4. Budgeting helps people to discuss their needs and set their own priorities on them.

5. It helps one to cut unnecessary expenditure.

6. It helps one to be free from debts.

7. It helps one to live within one's income.

8. It encourages conscious decision making which may help in including long term goals in the Budget.

9. It relieves the family members from worries of future.

10. It forces one to decide what one wants most out of life.

11. It provides for future saving.

Budget is a guide to realistic spending aimed at avoiding over expenditure. Its success depends upon its being simple, realistic, flexible and suited to the family or individual for whom it is made. Control of the plan in action is impossible without a written plan. A written plan can serve as an excellent record for future planning. A mental plan though it may serve the effort of noting down, may not help in controlling expenditure. Important needs maybe overlooked.

Steps in Preparing the Budget for a Family

(a) List commodities and services needed by the family members throughout the budget period.

(b) Estimate the cost of desired items. Total each classification and estimate the total for the budget. Past records are helpful in this connection (Bills, cheques, receipts etc.).

(c) Estimate and total expected income from all sources for the budget period.

(d) Set aside a definite sum as emergency fund as well as for goal oriented savings and insurance.

(e) Bring expected income and expenditure in balance.

(f) Check the plan if it is realistic.

The list of Budget Items

It is necessary to list the chief budget items to make sure that each item is attended to in the expenditure plan while portioning the income. Each family may have their own way of listing the items.

ACCOUNT KEEPING

The only best way to determine whether the family income is being well spent or not, is by keeping accounts. While the budget is a plan for future spending, account keeping is a record of past spending. A household account is a record of expenditures actually incurred by the family in the course of a day, or a month. It will include the income earned by the family, the expenditure incurred, and the amount spent on each item of expenditure.

Generally accounts help to

1. Show where the money goes actually.

2. Check the amount spent on each item according to the budget.

3. Check the adequacy of allotting the income over the items.

4. Give basis for a better planning of expenditure in future.

5. Change our way of life either by reducing the consumption of certain costly food items, or taking up extra job etc.

HOUSEHOLD EQUIPMENT-SELECTION AND CARE

Kitchen utensils and equipment can be kept and used for a long time with proper care and careful handling. Equipment of various types is used in Indian homes, made of various materials such as silver, aluminium, stainless steel, brass, iron, glass, china clay and so on.

Aluminium

Aluminium utensils generally used in Indian homes are made by two forms. Stamped utensils are made from sheet of aluminium that have been rolled to the required thickness under great pressure e.g.measuring cups, spoons, strainers, graters etc. Cast utensils are formed by pouring molten metal ususally aluminium or iron in a mild cast utensils have a plain edge at the top and the handle or shank to which the handle is attached being cast in one with the pan. These articles can be cleaned with hot water and soap. Ash can be used for cleaning them. Do not use salt or alkali such as soda, as they darken and destroy aluminium.

In case the aluminium article is stained those stains can be cleaned with apple peelings boiled in water, and can be polished by rubbing with whiting. If greasy, these vessels should be steeped in hot water, and may be washed with hot soapy water, using steel wool or coconut fiber or cleaned with tamarind or lime. Stains and smoky deposits may be removed with steel wool or coconut fiber, using vim. If inside of the vessel is stained badly, water to which a little vinegar is added should be boiled in it for about half an hour. This will loosen the stains. After removal of stains, they should be rinsed with cold water and dried with a wet cloth.

Stainless steel

Steel is lighter in weight than iron and can be forged, rolled, drawn or stamped. Hard steel which has 1 % carbon is used for knives, ragers, where sharp cutting edges are required. While soft steel contains 0.1 % of carbon, used for making various types of utensils.

Where as in stainless steel some of the carbon has been replaced by chromium and nickel. It is mainly used for built in cooking surfaces, wall ovens, sinks, counter tops, appliances, flat ware etc. If it is greasy, do not use pumice stone on steel, but rub with powder. Bath brick is generally used on a knife board. It may also be cleaned with soap nut powder and finally rinsed with clean water and dried with a wet cloth.

Stainless steel can be cleaned in the same manner as aluminium i.e. of greasy stainless steel vessels should be steeped in hot water or in cold water. They may be washed with hot soapy water using steel wool or coconut fiber or with hay. Stains and smoke deposit may be removed with steel wool or coconut fiber using vim. If the inside of the vessel is stained badly little vinegar is added and should be boiled in it for about 1/2 an hour. This will loosen the stains. After removal of stains they should be rinsed with cold water and dried with wet cloth.

Iron

Iron is obtainable in two forms cast and sheet. Sheet iron is frequently warps if subjected to high heat while cast iron is heavy and rather brittle, will corrode. The rust formed on damp iron is red iron oxide.

While cleaning these utensils first the greese should be removed with waste paper and the vessel to be scrubbed well with steel wool and wood ash in hot soap water. Then it should be rinsed in cold water and allowed to dry. A small amount of greese applied to the surface of the vessel will prevent it from rusting. Utensils used mainly for cooking purposes and placed directly on the fiber collect a cot of soot at the bottom. Care should be taken to remove this. In some Indian homes a mild coat of wood ash or cow dung ash mixed with a little water is applied to the bottom of the vessel. This facilitates the easy removal of soot.

Galvanized Iron

It is used for sinks and pails. Wash galvanized iron as you would wash cast iron. Rub a few drops of oil over the surface to prevent rust where the galvanized coating has worn off. Rust is a reddish powdery substance, which forms on Iron when iron is allowed to remain damp. It is caused by the surface of the iron combining with the O_2 in the air forming a new substance called iron oxide. O_2 also combines easily with other substances and forms oxides.

The main parts of cooking stove consist of iron and steel. After cooking, wipe off, the grease of remains of food on the stove with a news paper. Wash with hot soap-suds and wipe again with clean news paper. Occasionally rub the stove with a cloth just moistened with kerosene. A special blacking can be applied with a brush for cleaning stoves but it is more troublesome to keep stoves clean by this method. Cleaning with news paper instead of cloth saves much trouble in washing cloth dirtied by soot and grease. A small hard bristled brush is best for cleaning out the corners of iron cooking utensils. Small mops are also useful.

Copper

It is used for electric wiring and seldom used for cooking utensils except as a plating or for the bottom of stainless steel. Vinegar and salt can be used to remove the tarnish on copper utensils.

Brass

It is an alloy of copper and zinc and more resistant to corrosion. It is used largely for decorative pieces rather than for cooking utensils. Copper and brass tarnish in the presence of carbon dioxide and form verdigris, which is a poisonous carbonates. If metal is badly tarnished wash it with a soda solution.

For ordinary cleaning of the brass and bronze tamarind should be applied with a little water and rubbed well. Fine brick powder may also be used with coconut fibre. The article may then be rinsed thoroughly in clean water and dried. This metal ware can be cleaned with limejuice or vinegar and a fine powder.

Stains on vessels can be removed by applying a cut piece of lime and salt. After drying polish them with brasso or any soft powder and a soft cloth. Brass fittings such as doorknobs, handles, water taps should be polished with the brasso polish after the cleaning. Too much polish should not be used, as it will make the things sticky and less shining. In case of brass ornaments, they should be first washed with hot soapy water. The hidden parts of the ornaments should be cleaned with toothbrush. After this the ornaments should be washed with plain water, dried and rubbed with a clean, soft cloth finally they should be polished with brasso.

Bronze and gun metal

It is an alloy of copper and tin. In olden days it was used for cooking utensils but now it is used for decorative purpose. Gun metal is an alloy of copper and silicen or copper and zinc. Generally it is used for the autoclave inner turnings.

Silver

Silver can be used as cutlery, teasets, cold drink sets and decoratioll pieces in houses. They are all delicate articles and get easily scratched by rough handling. Hot soapy water should be used for washing them. Use of salt on the silver articles can remove egg stains. A paste made out of whiting and water can also be used for cleaning silver articles. Use of diluted NH_3 or methylated spirit is also good for silver articles. Silver articles can also be cleaned by putting the articles in hot water containing little soda. Electroplated articles made of white metal coated with silver need special care because of the use of few metals. No metal polish should be used on such articles. Don't use acid on silver. Silver tarnishes in the presence of sulphur and forms sulphur sulfide. It should be polished with a leather known as 'chomois leather' or by 'silvo'.

Glass

It is used especially for windows, sliding doors, drinking glasses etc. Glass has low conductivity but absorbs heat well. If milk stained, cold water should be used to rinse off the grease and prevent it from sticking to the glass. Then it should be washed with warm water and soap, rinsed in cold water and dried. Once a week venigar should be added to the washing water to brighten the glass. If the glass ware is dirty or greasy, hot soapy water is wquired for washing and hot water for rinsing. Glassware must be rubbed dry and polished with a soft cloth. Finally the glass should be polished with a piece of smooth linen or tissue paper. Glass cleaner is used to remove the stains.

Pyroceram

It is non porous ceramic material mainly used for the top of the range, sinks, oven utensils etc. It provides smooth surface. This surface should be thoroughly cleaned with fine scouring powder like vim. If it is greasy, a little soda may be put and boiled water poured on it to clean.

Plastics

These are light in weight but strong, colourful, resistance to moisture and good insulators of heat and electricity, and easy to clean. These are of two types.

Thermo plastics are softened by heat but harden again when cooled, and this change may be repeated a number of times without alteration in the physical properties.

Thermo plastics: This group includes polyethylene, polystyrene nylon, vinyl, acrylics and flouroplastics.

Polyethylene is used in bottles for milk, bleaches and detergents, squeeze bottles for cosmetics, semirigid mixing and refrigerator bowls, juice containers, coffee can lids, dish pans, food storage bags & in sheet form for economical table cloths and good wraps.

Like polyethylene, large quantities of polysterene are being used in packaging applications. Disposable drink cups, cottage cheese containers and foamed meat trays are common place.

Nylon is used for gears in sewing machines, for bearings in egg beaters, for the roller parts in drawers and sliding shelves in refrigerators, and cabinets and for other parts of pumps.

Vinyl comes in both flexible and rigid varieties. Refrigerator gasketing, floor, place mats, upholstery material are familiar uses of the flexible types.

Acrylic is used in lighting fixtures because of its high transparency, good diffusion characterestics.

Fluoro plastics are basically nontoxic and essentially free of odourand taste. They are not affected by water or by normal concentrations of household chemicals.

Thermosetting Plastics: In this group full melamine, phenolics, polyesters, urea and polymides.

Melamine, obtainable in a wide variety of translucent and opaque colours is made into dinnerware, mixing bowls and is used for laminated counter tops.

Phenolics are opaque and dark in colour, usually brown or black. They are used for light plugs and switches, appliance bases, washing machine, agitators and telephones. Polyester is used for appliance housings and light weight laundry tubs.

Polymides are used as exterior coatings on cooking utensils. Urea is manufactured into buttons, cosmetic jar tops, electric plugs and picnic ware. Members of this group are resistant to heat, moisture and scratches.

Plastics are easily cleaned with a damp cloth, or by washing in luke warm water with mild soap or detergent. Abrasive household cleaners, steel wood or sand paper will scratch the surface and should not be used. Wraps or bags should never be placed in an oven because they will melt.

Finishes

There are two methods of finishing the surface of materials-applied and mechanical-depending on the corrosive properties of the base metal.

Applied finishes: Metal surfaces are often finished or coated to give a more attractive appearance, to protect the metal from corrosion or to improve its effectiveness for certain uses. The coatmg may be metallic such as chromium, tin or zinc, non-metallic such as porcelain or synthetic enamel. The metallic finishes are applied by electrolytic deposition or dipping in molten metal; non metallic ones are by dipping or spraying.

Nickel is often alloyed with chromium to make wire; and with steel and chromium to produce stainless steel. Nickel alloyed with copper is called monel metal is used for sinks and counter tops.

Chromium has an attractive silvery colour and is kept in good condition simply by wiping little a damp cloth and polishing with a dry one. Chromium plated handles and trims are used on ranges, refrigerators etc.

Tin: This is also used in the manufacturing of utensils but it is used as a protective covering for metals.

Galvanized ware (zinc)

Galvanizing is a process of coating a base metal with zinc in order to protect it from rusting. Common base metals are iron and steel. It is mostly adopted to flat ware and utensils in which the strains are slight, and used for pails, wash boards, lids for fruit jars and other articles that come into contact with moisture. Zinc coated material is known as galvanised iron or steel.

Non Metallic applied finishes

Porcelain enamel, synthetic enamel, teflon and polyamides are non metallic finishes which are frequently used in household equipment.

Porcelain Enamel: It is a glass like substance in organic in nature, which is fused to the surface of metal. It has smooth, hard surface which is easy to clean. It has greater resistance to temperature, food acids and alkalies. Titanium porcelain is particularly stain resistant and has a high degree of capacity. Porcelain enamel is used in every home ranges, refrigerator food liners and crisper pans, washers (including tops, tubs and some cabinets) dryer tops and tubs, dish, washer interiors, water heater linings, sinks, bath tubs, cook ware etc.

Synthetic Enamel: It is commonly baked enamel and is used under various trade names as the exterior finish on washers, dryers, refrigerators, freezers, and on kitchen cabinets. It is never used for the inside tub finish of washers, dryers or refrigerator liners and never for the coating on baking utensils. It will gradually wear off, too on cabinet doors at the spots where fingers frequently come into contact with it.

Paint also is a non-metallic finish. It changes color and will dip, rub off and become marred, it needs therefore frequent renewal.

Teflon: This coating is now being used for the interiors of cooking utensils. Teflon is a trade mark for the non-stick fluro carbon resin finish. It does not react chemically with food, water or detergents. It is applied as a coating to provide a surface so smooth that other materials will not adhere to it, making the surface easy to clean. Teflon is widely used on inside surfaces of skillets, sauce pans, baking utensils and many small electrical appliances. It is being used by some range manufacturers as a coating on even linings range griddles and on the inside of range hoods. Spatulas, stirring spoons, measuring spoons, blades of electric and hand beater, rolling pins and other food preparation tools have been coated with teflon.

Polyamide: It is a synthetic material, which is chemically related to nylon. It is applied as a shiny coating on the outside but not the bottoms of cook ware. It is unaffected by detergent, food and water.

Silicons: These are intermediate things between inorganic and organic substances. They have some of the characteristics of glass. As a finish they are used on the surface of waffle grids, baking pans and ice cube trays. A smooth permanent coating is formed which keeps food from sticking.

Mechanical Finishes

A mechanical finish is the finish of the metal itself, not something applied on the outside. It is usually a polish, made with a brushing tool or a satin type and occasionally a pebbled or hammered finish.

Polishing and Buffing: It is one type of mechanical finish. The sides of a sauce pan may be highly polished for an attractive appearance and bottom is given a satin finish for better heat absorption. All baking sheets are highly polished to slow up heat absorption on the bottom of the food and to prevent over browning.

Anodizing: An electrolytic process which produces a chemical change on the; surface of the metal may also be used. The oxide film is porous and absorbs colour readily. Coloured anodized finish is used for the colours of one line of same pans.

CARE, CHOICE AND USE OF HOME APPLIANCES

1. Choose the appliance of suitable size and purpose according to the requirement.

2. Information is always given with every appliance stating the voltage or its wattage or the amount of current it takes. Always follow the instructions carefully.

3. Never use an appliance once higher voltage outside the range for which it is made nor too lower voltage.

4. All appliances must be properly earthed.

5. Never adjust the appliance when the current is on. It is safe to turn off the main switch near the motor and do the needed repair.

6. Avoid handling electrical appliances with damp hands.

7. The wires, cords should be properly insulated and should be shock proof.

1. Electric Blender

It is otherwise known as mixie which usually combines the work of a blender, a mixer, a grinder and a juice extractor.

1. It is used for grinding chutneys, preparing dry and wet masalas.

2. It is used for churning butter milk and mashing fruits.

3. It is used for extracting fruit juice, grating and slicing vegetables.

Care

1. The container should be immediately cleaned with soap water after use.

2. The container must never be removed or fitted on the mixie base while the motor is running.

3. Plastic spatula should be used to stir and remove the contents from the jar.

4. The external surfaces of the machine may be kept clean with a damp cloth and covered when not in use.

2. Washing Machine

The purpose of a washing machine is to remove soil (dirt) from the clothes. It consists of a drum in which dirty clothes, water and detergent are filled. These are agitated by means of a rotating plastic impeller called agitator. Some models have a spin dryer attached. The rinsed clothes are rotated in an empty drum while hot air blows through them. They may be taken out almost dry and ready for ironing. Automatic and semi-automatic washers are now available in the market.

Care

1. After the clothes have been removed from the washer, the lid should be kept open until the washer cools to prevent a musty odour.

2. Apart from the routine care, the outer surface of the washing machine should be wiped with a wet cloth.

3. Wet Grinder

Wet grinder works on electricity with the principle of diminishing manual work. It reduces time and energy. Electrically operated wet grinders for both commercial establishment and homes are now available in the market. Though expensive, these take the drudgery out of such chores. The commonest types used for wet grinding are

1. Ordinary model

2. Tilting model

3. Table top model

Uses

Wet grinder is a mechanical device used for grinding large quantities of chutneys or preparing the batter for idli, dosa and vadas.

Care

1. Overloading of wet-grinder should be avoided to prevent overheating of motor.

2. It should not be used in a low-voltage situation. Low-voltage may cause the motor to run slowly and eventually overheat it.

3. It should be thoroughly cleaned and dried after use to prevent bad odour.

4. The equipment should be covered when not in use.

5. The equipment should be used according to the manufacturer's direction.

4. Vacuum Cleaner

Vacuum cleaners are the home care appliances that aid in maintaining high standards of cleanliness and sanitation. The three basic principles involved in vacuum cleaning are suction, sweeping and agitation.

The primary functions of an electric cleaner are

1. To remove surface dirt from the walls, ceiling, floor and furniture.

2. To remove the embedded dirt and grit from floor coverings such as rugs and carpets.

3. The long flexible hosepipe and several attachments enable one to blow off the dirt and dust from the windows and spray water to clean the doors and window glasspanes.

Care

The vaccuum cleaner must be cared for efficient use and long life.

1. Thread and hair may wrap round the cleaning brush. It is important to remove the items from the ends of the brush, so that they do not impair its freedom of movement.

2. The bag must be emptied often to maintain its cleaning power. A fuller bag requires increased force to push air through it, so there is less suction for picking up dirt.

5. Range

The range is an appliance used for food preparation. It consists of surface units or gas burner and an oven. Heat for majority of the ranges used in the homes today is produced from either gas or electricity.

Use

Cooking range performs surface cooking, baking, roasting and broiling operations.

Care

1. The extension surface of the range should be cleaned regularly with a clean cloth that has been wrung out in hot soapy water to remove grease splatters that might not be seen.

2. Oven cleaning is much easier if done frequently. Food spills should be wiped as soon as the oven cools down.

3. Electric range is finished in porcelain enamel. It is not advisable to wash the porcelain enamel on a hot range because it tends to cause the enamel to crack.

4. Acid foods spilled on the enamel surface stain it and remove the gloss. So it should be avoided.

6. Toasters

The primary function of an electric toaster is to toast sliced bread. Different types of toasters are available in the market, namely automatic, semi-automatic and non- automatic.

The automatic toaster is faster, requires less attention and eliminates some manual operations.

Care

1. Apart from wiping the outside with a damp cloth the toaster may be inverted and gently tapped to get rid of the burnt bread crumbs lodged inside it.

2. Forks should never be used to remove the bread slice as they may damage the heating element as well as give an electric shock if the toaster is connected to the main.

3. The toaster should be placed on a heat-resistant non-conducting asbestos sheets.

7. Electric Gysers

Electric Gysers are quite popular in modern houses both in kitchen and bathroom. Gysers are fixed on to the wall so that they do not occupy space.

Use

It is used for heating water for bathing and washing purposes.

Care

The electric supply of the house should be properly earthed to avoid short circuit.

8. Immersion Rod

It is used for heating water in the homes where gysers are not in use. It consists, of a heating element made of a high resistance alloy. When current passes through it, it gets heated to a high temperature and in turn is used to heat water.

Care

1. Unless it is dipped into the water, it must never be switched on.

2. The minimum water level at which it is safe for use is marked on it. This instruction should be followed.

9. Solar Cookers

The advancement of modern science has made available many techniques for using the different potentials of energy and utilizing them for increasing fuel needs. Many cooking devices utilizing the solar energy have been developed at present. One such is solar oven that has received considerable attention. The reflector solar devices have taken many sizes, shapes and materials of construction. The solar cooker properly designed can deliver temperature as high as 450°C. In a tropical country like India, the wide use of solar ovens should be enthusised with proper results to suit urban and rural or high and low income families.

The solar cookers are used to boil rice and dhal, bake biscuits and roast groundnut. The solar heaters are used for the provision of hot water for domestic uses. Solar heated water may be sufficient for bathing, washing and cooking needs of the family.

10. Microwave Oven

It is an Electronic oven designed for cooking most foods usually cooked in gas and electric range including foods commonly cooked on surface units. It is also used to thaw frozen foods, to heat leftovers, to warm the baby's bottle.

Microwaves themselves are the sources of energy and not the heat. Microwave cooking appliances heat only by radiation. In electronic ranges the microwaves penetrate the food, setting the food molecule in motion, an action that generates heat within the food and brings about the cooking results. The process is very rapid, two to ten times faster than the conventional methods depending upon the amount of food. In the conventional methods of cookery, heat is applied to the outside of the food. Pyrex glass and ceramic cookware (Corning ware) are used as dish materials.

11. Pressure Cooker

The pressure cooker is so designed that food is cooked approximately at 120°C, and the steam pressure of 15 1b. per sq.metre is approximately maintained.

Care

1. The cooker must be cleaned with warm soapy water or a cleaning agent after use.

2. The rubber gasket needs to be checked periodically for cuts and cracks and replaced.

3. The weight, valve and safety valve need to be checked to ensure safe operation.

4. The pan and lid must be wiped dry and put away after use.

12. Beaters

They are used to incorporate air into a mixture to develop a fine texture and to blend ingredients. Hand beaters may be of two types.

1. **Whisk Beater:** It is effective in incorporating large amount of air and gives maximum volume of mixture. It require one hand for operation. It consist of a series of several small wires brought together at the top to form handle.

2. **Rotatory Type:** The rotary beater, is a tool with blades that rotate as a hand wheel is turned. It generally requires two hands for operation-one for support and the other for turning the wheel.

Care

Beaters of either type should be cleaned and dried thoroughly after use.

13. Graters

Graters are extensively used as kitchen utensils. Graters may be of various shapes-flat, cylindrical or square. Graters are available with various sizes of holes which are either punched or drilled.

Use

The drilled holes are round or oval in shape, produce slices of food and fairly a large volume of food.

Care

After use it must be thoroughly cleaned, dried and stored properly.

14. Refrigerator

Refrigerator is a device that maintains the temperature at 0°C (32°F) or above and humidity which influence the quality of food stored in the freezer.

Use

1. It helps to preserve food stuffs so that they maintain their natural, physical appearance and nutritive value.

2. It helps to keep things cool.

3. It has made possible the enjoyment of many foods throughout the year.

4. Daily shopping is no longer necessary. It saves steps, energy and time.

Care

1. The refrigerator should not be over crowded.

2. Frequent opening of the refrigerator should be avoided.

3. Hot vessels should be cooled before being placed in the refrigerator.

4. Regular inspection of stored food and the removal before spoilage is required to keep the refrigerator clean.

5. Defrosting should be done periodically. This may be done by shutting off the current or by opening the fridge door. Defrosting is advised before the deposit is too thick.

6. It should be placed in a cool place about 15 to 30 cm away from the wall to permit heat escape.

7. Avoid using sharp instruments to remove ice in ice trays or in scraping off frost.

CONSUMER PROTECTION

Due to mass production, new products are constantly introduced in the market. Consumers find it difficult to determine the uses for which they are fitted and to select them wisely because advertisement, attractive packaging, display and mass media are extensively used by manufacturers to push goods on consumers. Not all producers and sellers are honest. The desire for profit lead some manufacturers to cheat consumers by offering adulterated and poor quality products in the market. In short consumers in India are worst sufferers of the economic exploitations and unfair trade practices. It is therefore necessary for consumers to educate themselves about their rights and seek protection from exploitation with the help of government and voluntary organisations.

Legislations

In India there are a number of laws enacted to protect consumer's interest directly. Some of the important laws are mentioned below.

The prevention of Food Adulteration Act (PFA)

In 1954 the Indian parliament enacted a law called" The Prevention of Food Adulteration Act" It came into force from 1st June 1995. The P.F.A lays down minimum standard requirements for all categories of food. Any food stuff that does not come up to the minimum standards specified by the PFA rules is considered adulterated.

The Agmark Act 1937

The 'Agmark' is a trade mark of quality levels of agricultural commodities set up by the Directorate of marketing and Inspection of the Government of India. 'Agmark' seal can be seen on food stuff such as edible oils, butter, ghee, eggs, cereals, pulses, oil seeds, legumes, etc. This helps the consumer in selecting foods and offers him protection with regard to quality.

I.S.I. (1947)

This is a certification mark of the Bureau of Indian Standards (BIS) which was earlier called as the Indian Standard Institution (I.S.I.). Indian standards cover food items such as vegetables, fruit and meat products, spices, and condiment, processed foods, cereal and soya products, candies, beverages, print paper, etc. For the consumers, certification marks ensures that the product is cheap, safe and pure.

Drugs and Cosmetics Act - 1940

This Act was passed to protect consumers from drugs and cosmetics of substandard quality by preventing them from being manufactured and marketed. It lays down that no person or firm can stock, sell or distribute drugs unless they have a proper license issued by the state government for the purpose. Under this law it is mandatory that every dealer must issue a cash memo for the drug sold to the consumer.

Essential Commodities Act, 1955

Under the provision of the Act, the central and state government have been empowered to regulate the production, supply, distribution, and processing essential commodities such as cattle fodder, coal, iron, steel, paper, cotton and woolen textile, petroleum, petroleum products, drugs, foods, raw jute and cotton. It provides punishment on any hoarder, black marketer and profiteer. The offenders can be imprisoned for 3 – 5 years.

The Standards of weights and measures Act 1976

The act provides for the:

1. Establishment of an international system of units (metric) for weighing and measuring.

2. Formulation of specifications for weights, measures and equipments used for weighing and measuring.

3. Approval of models of equipment before they are manufactured.

Weights and measureb without seal or verification stamp are not genuine under any circumstances.

COPRA–1986

The enactment of 'Consumer Protection Act' 1986 is a milestone in the consumer movement. This law gives a consumer the right to get compensation for any loss suffered in accordance with the negligence of the manufacturers.

HUMAN DEVELOPMENT | 6

Development of a human being from a zygote to a full grown adult is a subject that has fascinated people over generations. Not only is this knowledge useful as a tool for understanding self, but also for guiding the growth of children. This knowledge of how children grow and develop from birth onwards will help in understanding the developmental process of children. It will also be helpful in recognising areas where the growth or development of a child is not normal or slower than it ought to be.

STAGES IN THE LIFE SPAN

Human development can be better understood if we focus on its different stages while relating to the whole. The human life span can be divided into the following stages:

Table: Stages of life span

S.No.	Stages of life	Age
1.	Prenatal period	conception to birth
2.	Period of the neonate	birth to one month
3.	Infancy	1 month to 2 years
4.	Early childhood	2 to 6 years
5.	Middle childhood	6 to 11 years
6.	Adolescence	11/12 to 18/19 years
7.	Early Adulthood	18/19 to 40 years
8.	Middle age	40 to 60 years
9.	Old age	60 and above

In the stages listed above, the first one refers to development before birth and the next four can be clubed together to denote 'Childhood'. After childhood it is adolescence followed by adulthood which covers the next two stages i.e., 7 & 8. The last one left is old age. Hence basically there are four stages of development after the birth which are–

1. Childhood
2. Adolescence
3. Adulthood
4. Old age

PATTERNS OF DEVELOPMENT

Development essentially means change as a result of the complex interactions between many processes - biological, social and cognitive.

1. **Biological processes** involve changes that are physical in nature. Our genetic heritage, growth of body organs, acquisition of motor skills, hormonal changes at puberty, all reflect the role of biological processes in development.

2. **Cognitive processes** involve changes in the thinking, intelligence and language of the child. Perception, attention, understanding, problem solving, memorizing, imagination, all reflect the cognitive processes in children's development.

3. **Social processes** involve the changes in the child's relationship with other people, emotions and personality. The first smile of an infant, the development of attachment between the mother and child, children learning to share, to assert, to take turns, to play with others, all reflect the social processes in development.

All these processes are intricately interwoven which means they constantly influence each other. The cognitive processes promote socio-emotional processes and the biological processes influence cognitive processes. For example, a sick child (biological process) is irritable and cries frequently (socio-emotional). If unable to attend school regularly, the child lags behind in studies (cognitive processes). Constant irritability also influences the relationship with others (social processes).

GROWTH AND DEVELOPMENT IN EARLY CHILDHOOD (0-5 YEARS)

Growth and development are complementary processes. Growth indicates the quantitative changes in the body, that is height and weight, while development refers to both the qualitative and quantitative changes, for example language acquisition. Development can be defined as a 'progressive series of orderly, coherent changes'.

> **Growth:** Quantitative change
>
> **Development:** Quantitative and qualitative change

All development takes place according to certain principles some of which are as follows:

1. All growth and development follow an orderly sequence. A child can sit only when the muscles of the back are ready to support the body.

2. Each child normally passes through a number of stages, each with its own essential characteristics.

3. There are individual differences in development. Every child grows at his own pace.

4. Though the human being develops as a unified whole, each part of the body develops at different rates. Basically there are two sequences in the rate of development.

    (a) Cephalocaudal i.e. development proceeds from head to toe. The head and brain develops first, then the torso, the neck etc.

    (b) Proximodistal i.e. development proceeds from centre to extremeties. The child first gains control over the spine, then arms, then fingers.

5. Development is essentially the result of the interaction between maturation and learning. While maturation is the 'unfolding of characteristics potentially present in the individual's genetic endowment', learning refers to the "relatively" enduring changes that come about as a result of experience and practise.

FACTORS AFFECTING GROWTH AND DEVELOPMENT

(i) **Heredity:** It is the process by which the features and characteristics are passed from parents to the child before the child is born. Thus features like the colour of the skin and eyes, the height, body build, intellect and talents, etc., are all fixed and no one can change them beyond a limit.

(ii) **Prenatal environment:** This is the environment of the foetus in the womb. If the mother gets poor nutrition, is emotionally upset or smokes, drinks, or takes some medicine or suffers from certain diseases, the growth of the child can be adversely affected.

(iii) **Nutrition:** Proper nutrition is essential for the healthy development of the child. A malnourished child's growth may be retarded or slow.

(iv) **Intelligence:** Higher intelligence is associated with faster development while lower intelligence is associated with retardation in various aspects of development.

(v) **Emotional climate of home:** If there is a lot of discord/fights at home or the child is not given enough love and attention or there is physical/mental abuse of the child, then the child's development is adversely affected.

(vi) **Health of the child:** If the child frequently falls sick, suffers from some disorder, is disabled or has disturbed endocrine functioning, the development is likely to suffer.

(vii) **Level of stimulation:** The amount of stimulation the environment provides to the child i.e., the opportunities for exploration of environment, opportunities of interaction with other people, etc., all influence the rate of development.

(viii) **Socio-economic status:** It also influences the development by deciding the kind of nutrition, stimulation, facilities, opportunities, genetic endowment the child gets.

(ix) **Sex:** All children follow the same sequence of development. However, certain skills are faster in girls than in boys and some other skills are faster in boys than girls. For example, language acquisition is faster in girls and skills like jumping catching, throwing are faster in boys. Sex is also a factor that decides the potential of a child in physical development - boys grow up to be taller, heavier and more muscular than girls.

PHYSICAL DEVELOPMENT

Physical development includes (i) an increase in height and weight, (ii) changes in body proportion and (iii) development of teeth, bones and muscles.

(i) Increase in Height and Weight

A newborn baby weights about 2 to 3.5 kg at birth and loses about 150-200gms in just 3 to 4 days. After that the baby grows rapidly and doubles the weight by 6 months. The birth weight become 3 times by 1 year.

The length of the baby at birth is about 40 to 50cm and in one year it becomes 1 ½ times of the lenght at birth. Thereafter it increases as shown in the table below.

Table: Reference body weight and height of Children and Adolesents according to NCHS

Age (years)	BOYS		GIRLS	
	Height (cm)	Weight (kg)	Height (cm)	Weight (kg)
0	50.5	3.3	49.9	3.2
1/4 (3m)	61.1	6.0	60.2	5.4
1/2 (6m)	67.8	7.8	66.6	7.2
3/4 (9m)	72.3	9.2	71.1	8.6
1.0	76.1	10.2	75.0	9.5

Age (years)	BOYS		GIRLS	
	Height (cm)	Weight (kg)	Height (cm)	Weight (kg)
1.5	82.4	11.5	80.9	10.8
2.0	85.6	12.3	84.5	11.8
3.0	94.9	14.6	93.9	14.1
4.0	102.9	16.7	101.6	16.0
5.0	109.9	18.7	108.4	17.7
6.0	116.1	20.7	114.6	19.5
7.0	121.7	22.9	120.6	21.8
8.0	127.0	25.3	126.4	24.8
9.0	132.2	28.1	132.2	28.5
10.0	137.5	31.4	138.3	32.5
11+	140	32.2	142	33.7
12+	147	37.0	148	38.7
13+	153	40.9	155	44.0
14+	160	47.0	159	48.0
15+	166	52.6	161	51.4
16+	171	58.0	162	53.0
17+	175	62.7	163	54.0
18+	177	65.0	164	54.4

(ii) Changes in Body Proportion

The head of the new-born is 1/4th the size of the body. As the child grows, the body becomes more proportionate as you can see from the illustration given below.

Milestones of physical development

A baby develops from the head to toes. The neck and shoulder muscles must be strong before she can sit, the trunk must be strong before she can stand. The time clock for development depends more on what is inherited than on environment but a baby who spends more time in pram will not learn to crawl as soon as a baby sitting on the floor surrounded by interesting-looking objects.

1. **Six weeks:** smiles at mother; eyes stare at a ring on a string and follow the mother.

2. **Three months:** turns head towards sound, head bobs down on mother's shoulder.

3. **Six months:** head steady and back straight when held on shoulder; sits with support of cushions; stretches arms to be lifted up.

As the newborn grows rapidly, control is first gained over muscles in the trunk and back, then in the arms and lastly in the extremities or the fingers.

(iii) Development of Teeth, Bones and Muscles

(a) **Teeth:** A normal healthy child first erupts the lower front teeth known as central incisor between 5-6 months, followed by upper incisor at 7 months. The next teeth to erupt are upper side-teeth (canines) in the 8th month followed by lower canines between 9th to 10th month. By the time a child is 3 years old he/she has 20 teeth. They are called milk teeth, because they are replaced by permanent teeth in middle childhood.

(ii) **Bones and Muscles:** When a child is born the bones are soft and contain more cartilage tissues. As the child grows, calcium gets deposited in the bones. The process of deposition of calcium in the bones is called ossification and is a continuous process. That is the reason, when children fall, they rarely fracture their bones. Children's bones are covered with fat and muscles. In the early years the fat deposit is more than the muscles. As they grow, it gets replaced by muscles.

MILESTONES OF MOTOR DEVELOPMENT

Age	Motor Development
0-2 months	Kicks aimlessly, stretches hand and feet, closed fist.
2-4 months	Follows a moving person with eyes, stares at a bright object, lifts chest short distance when placed on abdomen, holds head. Rolls from back to the side. Begins to grasp toy in hand.
4-6 months	Holds head steady when carried. Holds toys and reaches for objects. Raises hands to be lifted. Lifts head and shoulder and rolls over. Lifts self by hands or forearms when lying on the stomach. Sits up when propped.
6-8 months	Can hold head and sit erect without support. Bangs spoons or pats floors. Can pick up objects from floor, table. Can hold a toy in each hand. Has learnt to use the thumb to grip things.
8-10 months	Begins to crawl, can pull self up to stand by holding on to furniture. Holds small objects like buttons, coins between thumb and finger. Can hold, bite and chew objects.
10-12 months	Stands with slight support. Walk with support. Can push light objects. Picks up small and big objects and examines them.
1-2 years	Walks without support. Drinks from a cup. Can handle a spoon. Plays with push and pull toys. Can climbing stairs and come down as well. Scribbles. Eats by self.
2-3 years	Plays tirelessly. Can feed himself well. Bowel and bladder control is acquired. Can brush hair and teeth. Can take out and put back toys from cupboards. Follows simple instructions.
3-5 years	Can button and unbutton dress, can dress without help. Can attend to personal needs like toilet, washing. Ready for school.

SOCIO–EMOTIONAL DEVELOPMENT

At birth a child is neither social nor unsocial but by 3 months he/she smiles and responds to friendly overtues. By 5-6 months the child can discriminate between a stranger and familiar person. Cooperates in simple games by 1 year and becomes shy in presence of strangers by 1½ years. Loves the company of same age persons by 2 years. The child starts throwing temper tantrums and resents the arrival of the new baby in the family. The fear of separation from the family members becomes significant. Loves to copy the action of his parents.

Around 3 years of age, displays affection towards parents and starts cooperative play. Has imaginary friends, practices sex role activity. May enter pre-nursery. During 4-5 years of age, prefers to play with other children and becomes competitive.

LANGUAGE DEVELOPMENT

At birth a child cries to tell about his/her woes and needs. Slowly the crying becomes more peculiar and the mother can distinguish between hunger, discomfort and pain cries.

Around 3 months, the child starts cooing, i.e. makes happy gurgling sounds when pleased or picked. Around 6 to 7 months, cooing is converted to babbling sounds, which is a repetition of syllables like Ma - Ma, Ba - Ba, etc. By nine months, a child can speak words. One word is used at a time to convey a whole sentence like 'doll' means 'I want a doll'. By one year, the child can combine two words. By 2 years 2 to 3 word sentences are spoken easily.

By the age of 5 years, a child has a vocabulary of about 500 words. This vocabulary then grows rapidly.

FEATURES OF COGNITIVE DEVELOPMENT

Some of the features of cognitive development seen in a child from birth upto five years are:

- Realises that the world exists even if he/she cannot see it (object permanence)
- Unable to see the perspective of others (egocentric)
- Unable to think logically
- Believes all things (living and non-living) to be possessing life and feelings
- Indulges in fantasy and make-belief play
- Easily confused by surface appearances
- Has uneven attention
- Has limited memory
- Confused about causal relationships
- Acquires basic concepts of colour, shape, size, number, days etc.
- Has high level of curiosity

TAKING CARE OF CHILDREN

A new born is helpless, delicate and tender and the mother needs to take special care so that the child grows up to be healthy and strong. Every child should get proper food, ample sleep and rest, regular bathing, suitable clothing and needs to be immunized against diseases.

1. **Feeding:** The first yellow secretion from the breast when the child is born is called colostrum. It has protective antibodies which provide immunity against certain diseases.

   Breast milk is easily and quickly digested. It has ideal composition and temperature. It provides emotional satisfaction to the mother and security to the child. Hence, all new-borns should be breastfed.

   Once the child is 3 to 4 months old, mother's milk is not sufficient to meet the nutritional needs. Hence the child has to be slowly weaned from milk to liquid to semi-solid to solid diet. This introduction of top feeding is called weaning. In the beginning fruit juice, clear soups of vegetables and dals are given, followed by mashed dals, fruits and vegetables, soups and kheers. One year old child can chew raw vegetables, chappatis, fruits, etc. However, weaning has to be done gradually.

2. **Rest and Sleep:** Rest is required for growth and development. It makes the child strong and healthy. The rest period varies from child to child, but on an average the sleeping pattern of children is as follows -

Age	Hour of Sleep
0-2 months	20 to 22 hours per day
2-6 months	16 to 18 hours per day
6-12 months	12 hours per day (and 1-2 hours afternoon/morning nap)
1-2 years	12 hours at night and a nap in the afternoon.
2-5 years	8 to 10 hours including a nap in the after-noon.

3. **Bathing:** All children should be bathed regularly to get into the habit of regular bathing, preferably at the same time each day. Before bathing, massaging should be done. Baby should be bathed with water at a temperature of about 85.00F. In summers, babies should be given a bath twice a day and in winters once a day or on alternate days.

4. **Suitable Clothing:** A child's garments should be comfortable, soft, of absorbent material like cotton, simple in design, bright in colour, and easy to wash. They should not have too many frills, trimmings and buttons, draw-strings, and ribbons.

As children outgrow the size quickly, clothes should never be too many or too expensive. Nappies or diapers are the most essential clothing for a baby, hence it should be soft, light weight, absorbent and quick drying.

5. **Immunization:** Right from birth all children should be immunized regularly against communicable diseases as it increases their body résistance.

Immunization Schedule
(against vaccine preventable diseases)

FOR WHOM	WHAT	WHEN	WHY
Pregnant Women	T.T	Early in Pregnancy One month after the first shot	Protects against Tetanus
Infants (Below 1 year)	BCG (Bacillus Calmette-Guerin Vaccine)	At birth	Protects against Tuberculosis
	Oral Polio Vaccine (0)		Protects against Polio
	DPT-1		Protects against Diphtheria, Pertusis (whooping cough) and Tetanus
	Oral Polio Vaccine (1)		Protects against Polio
	DPT-2	At 10 weeks	Protects against Diphtheria, Pertusis (whooping cough) and Tetanus
	Oral Polio Vaccine (2)		Protects against Polio
	DPT-3	At 14 weeks	Protects against Diphtheria, Pertusis (whooping cough) and Tetanus
	Oral Polio Vaccine (3)	Protects against Polio	
	Measles	At 9 months	Protects against Measles Chicken-pox Protects against Chickenpox
Children	MMR	At 15 months	Protects against Measles, (Above 1 year) Mumps and Rubella
	DPT Booster	At 16-24 months	Protects against Diphtheria, Pertusis (whooping cough) and Tetanus
	Oral Polio Vaccine Booster		Oral Polio Vaccine

FOR WHOM WHAT		WHEN	WHY
	DT	At 5-6 years	Protects against Diphtheria and Tetanus
	TT	At 10 years	Protects against Tetanus
	TT	At 16 years	Protects against Tetanus

BEHAVIORAL PROBLEMS IN CHILDREN

Young children often demonstrate behaviours which are inappropriate. For example, a child may be in a habit of hitting everybody else, breaking things, abusing/telling lies, etc. These are behaviours which not only harm children physically but also make them unpopular with other children. There can be many reasons why children develop these behaviours. Some are listed here:

- When children live in an environment which forbids any self-expression they pick up behaviours which are unacceptable.

- When parents and teachers expect too much from children and they are not able to keep upto expectations, they show unacceptable behaviour.

- Often children learn that unacceptable behaviours are tools to get what they want. For example, the child learns that when he hits his younger siblings parents attend to him or when he cries and rolls on the floor he gets the toy he wants.

- When family environment is disturbed, children start showing unacceptable behaviour, eg., when parents quarrel with each other, they hit each other or when their mothers and grandmothers do not get along with each other.

- When there is a crisis in the child's life. Children show unacceptable behaviours on birth of another sibling, the death of a beloved member of the family.

- Children may also develop unacceptable behaviours because physically they are not able to cope up. This happens when they have had a long illness or when they fall sick too frequently.

The caregivers at the playcentre have to be alert and understanding. whenever there is a child who shows unacceptable behaviour they must act immediately. Since, very often the cause of the behaviour originates from home they must ask for cooperation of the parents, understand the problem and develop a strategy which helps to cure the problem. Punishing and scolding or ridiculing will not help. Some of the common problem behaviours are described in the following table together with a description of what adults normally do but they should not do and what they should do.

Common Behaviour Problems Observed Among Young Children

Behaviour	Meaning	Do not	Do
(a) Hurts other children	- Angary, feeling troubled	- Punish or hurt - Make the child feel bad	- Divert attention - Separate other children quietly - Help the child feel loved by giving other outlets for feelings.
(b) Destroys things	- Feeling of help-lessness - Jealousy - Boredom - Seeking attention	- Scold, shout, punish, spank or hit	- Keep precious things out of reach - Provide place for play - Offer low-cost substitutes - Divert and involve the child in other activities

Behaviour	Meaning	Do not	Do
(c) Sucks the thumb	- Need for sucking, love, comfort and - Tiredness - Hunger - Dissatisfaction - Boredom	- Punish or scold - tie fingers or smear them with bitter medicine	- Provide sucking satisfaction - Offer love affection and assurance - Involve in pleasurable and interesting activity - Provide things needed for the child
(d) Wets the bed	- The child is not ready for training - Fear - Insecurity	- Threaten or punish - Insist on prior information - Tell you do not love the child	- Accept the child as he/she is - Expect accidental bed-wetting - Help and encourage the child to become confident
(e) Tells lies	- Fear of punishment - Exaggeration - Imagination - Attention seeking	- Preach or punish or reject - Make him apologize - Get upset	- Understand the reason - Give the needed attention - Provide opportunity for enriching the imagination - Tell the truth
(f) Refuses to eat	- Is not hungry - Feels unwell - Dislikes particular food - Forced to do the act	- Force or punish - Make a scene - Reward, threaten	- Be calm - Introduce new foods along with the favourite
(g) Fears	- Reviews painful experience - Needs parent's closeness - Feels guilty or unloved	- Force, seek reason for fear, shame or threaten	- Reassure and comfort - Make the environment a happy one. - Encourage efforts. - Avoid fearful experiences
(h) Steals	- Ignorance of property rights - Unsatisfied needs - Irritation - Hostile feelings	- Scold, make feel bad, punish or reject - Cut off love - Humiliate before others	- Let the child own things and get a sense of ownership - Be kind, understanding and not too strict. - Provide creative outlets - Help make real friends

GROWTH AND DEVELOPMENT DURING MIDDLE CHILDHOOD (6-11 YEARS)

PHYSICAL DEVELOPMENT

Change in Body Proportions

The head of the newborn is 1/4th the size of the body and that of a 6-8 year old is about 1/6th of the body and by adulthood it will become 1/8th of the body. In other words, the head becomes smaller in proportion to the rest of the body as one grows. In middle childhood along with gross muscles, fine muscles develop rapidly.

Development of Teeth, Bones and Muscles

(i) **Teeth:** By the time a child is 3 years old, the child has 20 teeth and these are the milk teeth. But by the time the child is in middle childhood, he/she has 28 teeth and these are all permanent teeth. An adult has 32 teeth.

(ii) **Bones:** By middle childhood, all the bones in the body are formed and henceforth, these continue to grow in size and strength. Bones become brittle when there is too much calcium in them and they break easily. During middle childhood, there is sufficient calcium in the bones to make them strong. This is one reason why the activity level in middle childhood is high. Strong bones provide better anchorage to the muscles.

(iii) **Muscles and Fat:** All bones are covered with fat and muscles. Girls have more fat around their bones than muscles. At seven to eight years, girls start to gain more fat than muscles on their arms, legs and trunk, whereas boys have more of muscles than fat. This is why they have more strength. Boys can generally run longer distances, jump higher, etc.

MOTOR DEVELOPMENT

The body has two types of muscles, namely, the large muscles such as those of the arms, legs, back, etc., and the small or fine muscles such as those in the fingers, toes, etc. Muscular activity is possible because of their contraction and flexion (relaxation). Different muscles placed in different parts and some in same parts of the body perform and control different movements. Some part of this control is automatic while some part is learnt. Movement due to muscular control which is learnt is called muscular co-ordination.

Muscular co-ordination is of two types : fine and gross. The movement of the fine (small) muscles is called fine muscular coordination while the movement of large muscles is called gross muscular coordination. Activities such as running, balancing, skipping climbing, involve mostly the coordination of large muscles.

Sensitive Period

Sensitive period is the time when one can learn a specific activity most effectively.

Around the sensitive period, the body is ready to learn a particular activity or skill most efficiently. If the child is given practice and encouragement at this time to learn that activity or skill, the child will learn it best. Children in the age group of 6-11 years learn maximum number of different activities. They play different types of games. What does this information indicate ? That many of the muscles are maturing at this stage.

The following chart shows the motor development or certain activities and skills from 6 years to 10 years.

Age	Run, Kick Throw Ball	Balance	Skip, Hop and Jump
6 yrs.	Can throw a ball	Can balance on one foot for very short while	Can skip with two legs.
7 yrs.	Can throw a ball at an estimated distance	Can balance on one foot for short while.	Can hop and jump in small squares
8 yrs.	Can throw a small ball at an estimated distance	Can balance on one foot for a short time.	Can skip and play games with alternate hopping rhythm.
9 yrs.	Can throw a small to even larger distances, runs with	Can balance and hop on one foot coordinated movements	Jump as high as oneself. for long periods.
10 yrs.	Can judge and stop a small ball	Can balance and hop on one foot for long periods	Can run and jump hurdles at same time

LANGUAGE DEVELOPMENT

By middle childhood (6-11 years) a child's basic command over language is complete. The child has a vocabulary of about 14,000 to 30,000 words. The ability to use language well and to communicate well develops at this age. By now, the child also understands that one word can have more than one meaning. Children like to crack jokes where the same word or similar words have the same or similar meanings.

Children of six years to eleven years begin to understand the formation of sentences better. Not only do they know that the same word can have different meanings they also know that words with the same pronunciation can have different spellings and thus different meaning. For example, CORN can mean the cereal or the hard, painful growth on the skin. HERE and HEAR or WHOLE and HOLE have not only different meanings but also different spellings. They enjoy using metaphors and tongue twisters.

Besides the metaphors and tongue twisters that the children enjoy, they also develop a sense of humour. Much of the children's humour at this age is centered around the subtle meaning of language. Children love jokes which may appear rather silly to adults.

SOCIO–EMOTIONAL DEVELOPMENT

Social development involves not only learning to behave in a socially approved manner but also developing the ability to get along with others. And, Emotional development means gaining control over one's emotions and learning to express them in socially approved ways.

The common thing that emerges from both the definitions is "learning to behave in socially approved ways." By middle childhood all major emotions are present in the child. Between 6-11 years of age children learn to gain more control over emotions. They learn to select and express emotions in more socially approved ways. Emotional development occurs simultaneously and almost as a part of social development. Hence, we refer to it as socio emotional development of children.

Since social development refers to a child's ability to adjust to the social surroundings i.e., home, playmates, school, etc. This means that certain people like parents, playmates of the same age group, teachers at school, influence the social development. In the following sections we shall learn about how they actually influence the social development.

(i) Parents

Middle childhood is the stage where children develop self confidence and acquire self-esteem. Confident parents provide better opportunity to children to be confident. Parents who accept their children "as they are" and love them, help the child to develop self-confidence. Such parents lay down clear rules for the children. They praise their children for the good things they do and usually do not punish them for their wrong doings. If the child does anything wrong, they try to explain why it is wrong. In other words, they adopt a democratic method of disciplining the children.

(ii) Peer Group

Peer group refers to the playmates of the same age group. Peer group plays an important role in helping fellow mates develop socio-emotional skills. For example, children come to know from each other that all parents have high expectations from their children. If one child falters, she knows that others also do/can falter. In other words, peer group offers a platform for children to compare.

From the peer group, children also come to know that all parents guide, dictate and scold. They learn that no child gets a free hand in doing whatever she/he wishes to do. This may make an individual child very angry and rebellious but by talking to the peer group, she realizes that she is not only one who feels like this. All children get angry with their parents but the peer group helps the children to cope effectively with this anger and not become rebellious against parents. Thus, peer group provides comfort and emotional security that adults cannot. Children learn from their peers to keep parents happy and thus, master the skill of getting along in society.

Peer group also teaches children to become independent.

In short, we can say that peer group:

- helps to see how one compares with others of same age;
- provides emotional security and comfort that an adult cannot;
- helps the child learn how to get along in society;
- helps children to become independent of their parents.

(iii) School

School also plays an important role in the socio-emotional development of children. Teachers encourage students to do well. When they praise the children for things done well and scold them for bad/poor performance, they are helping children to develop. For example, everyone can not be good at sports or at drawing or at needle work. Every child cannot stand first in class. But every child is good at doing something or the other. Teachers praise and encourage children to do better in whatever task they are good at. Remember, self confidence is essential for learning skills needed to become a useful adult.

Cognitive Development

Cognitive development refers to the way a child thinks, reasons and solves problems.

The period 6-11 years is a major turning point in cognitive development. Now the child learns to think in a more logical way.

GROWTH AND DEVELOPMENT DURING ADULESCENCE

DEFINING ADOLESCENCE

Adolescence is the period of development between childhood and adulthood. A boy or girl enters adolescence as a child and emerges as a man or woman, expected to be ready to assume an adult role in thesociety. For everybody, the years 11 to 18 are the most eventful. During these years there is rapid physical and sexual growth and maturation. It is very difficult to say exactly when adolescence starts. However, onset of puberty is generally accepted as the beginning of adolescence. The period around 11 or 12 years of age is the onset of puberty which usually lasts for 2 years. During these years there is a spurt in physical growth and appearance of sex characteristics. The first sign of puberty in girls is menstruation and in boys, nocturnal emission (ejaculation of semen during sleep).

The physical changes that take place during adolescence are as follows:

Girls	Boys
1. A girl gains about 8cms in height between 11 to 13½ years of age.	1. On an average, boys grow about 20 cms in height between 13 to 15 years of age.
2. Develop more fatty and subcutaneous tissue giving rise to rounded contours.	2. Develop a lot of muscles, enabling them to do heavy physical work.
3. The shoulders are slender while hips become broader and rounded.	3. Boys develop broader and stronger shoulders while their hips remain slender.
4. Hair growth in the arm-pits and pubic area.	4. Hair on the body becomes darker and curlier. Hair appears in the arimpits and pubic area. Facial hair appears at side of the mouth, lips, cheeks and then the sides of the face.
5. The voice becomes more shrill and adult like.	5. The voice breaks, i.e., becomes squeaky and matures. This happens because the larynx enlarges and vocal cord lengthens. Adam's apple becomes prominent.

Girls	Boys
6. Appearance of the breast-bud.	6. Increase in the size of the penis.
7. Onset of menarche or first menstrual cycle. First few cycles may be irregular and sometimes painful.	7. First nocturnal emission occurs nearly a year after the penis starts growing. The seminal fluid may not contain sperms at puberty.

Although the overall sequence of physical and sexual growth and maturity are comparable for boys and girls, girls attain their adult height, weight and ability to bear children, two years earlier than boys.

EARLY AND LATE MATURATION

Some adolescents undergo the physical changes described above, earlier than others. This has a specific influence on the psychological aspects of their development.

It is generally seen that the early maturing girls feel very conscious and odd about their bodies and they think why is it happening to them ? Since they look grown up, adults expect them to behave more responsibly. Late maturing girls look younger and are not expected to measure up to adult standards of behaviour. Therefore they are more relaxed. However, they do not get attention from boys.

Early maturing boys are more confident as compared to girls. Because of their greater physical strength and well developed bodies they are chosen leaders. They are satisfied with themselves. At the same time, adult expectations from them are high. Late maturing boys feel inferior because of lack of physical growth and they keep thinking whether they will ever become big and strong like their friends.

Usually these feelings are temporary and as adolescents grow they get over these feelings as well. Parents need to talk to adolescents and explain to them the physical changes that take place in the body. They should also give them sex education.

SOCIO-EMOTIONAL DEVELOPMENT OF ADOLESCENTS

Adolescents have mood swings in the early years. They cry and laugh easily, they are moody and irritable because they do not understand about all the changes that are taking place in their bodies. But as the years pass the hormonal activity within them settles down. With this their vulerability also disappears.

Socially, they like to be with the peer group most of the time. This group has its own culture, values, language, dress style, music and other likes and dislikes. Comforming to the group norms is an important objective of all adolescents. This is the reason adolescents have many friends. Anyone who cannot make friends goes into depression which can have dangerous consequences.

LANGUAGE DEVELOPMENT

By the end of middle childhood the child has a vocabulary of about 4000 to 5000 words. With greater use of the vocabulary already learnt, the adolescents' language becomes fluent and complex. They are able to add many more words to the vocabulary and also use them for forming complex sentences. All this helps them to communicate fluently.

A characteristic feature of the language development during adolescence is the use of 'slang' and 'short forms' for words. Slang can be called a word used to represent a set of words or an idea. For example, chicks is a slang word for pretty young girls while 'bindaas' means carefree attitude.

Another feature is the beginning of the use of stage short forms or abbreviations e.g. Connaught Place becomes C.P. and Greater Kailash becomes G.K. For many people these characteristic features of the language continue in their adult lives as well.

COGNITIVE DEVELOPMENT

Before a child enters adolescence, he/she needs to see things to be able to understand the relationship between them. During adolescence all that changes. The adolescent's thinking becomes abstract. The adolescent can imagine situations and events. For example on being told that A is bigger than B, and B is bigger than C, a 15 year old can draw the conclusion that A is bigger than C. A child who has not entered adolescence, would have to see the objects A, B and C before she can come to a conclusion.

The adolescent is able to think contrary to fact ideas. For example, if an adolescent is asked to tell the advantages of "if we all could fly", the adolescent can think of answers like- "There would be no need for vehicles". With this imaginary and contrary to fact ideas, the adolescent is able to understand similies, abstract jokes with meaning which have to be inferred. These abilities enable the adolescent to take decisions by thinking of all the possible alternatives for the solution to a problem. Thus we can say that the adolescent's thinking becomes more mature and systematic.

ADOLESCENTS NEED SEX EDUCATION

By the end of adolescence the adolescent is sexually mature and should be prepared for marriage and family life. Therefore, the adolescent needs to be educated about his/her sexual development and needs to adjust to these changes. The adult sexual behaviour of an adolescent will be determined by the attitudes he/she acquires about sex. The parents and school environment can play a very important role in the acquisition of these attitudes. This education is also called 'education for reproductive health'.

During this time, the adolescent's preoccupation with sex is very natural. The appearance of secondary sex characteristics and the activity of hormones in the body raises many questions in his/her mind. He/she depends on information from the peer group and from printed material. The kind of information the peer group gives is not always correct and contains a lot of misconceptions and fallacies. Similarly, the printed material if available is not always of good quality and can be very misleading. It can confuse the

adolescents rather than do any good. Therefore, parents can play the role of informed adults who can handle questions about sex. Majority of parents feel very awkward and do not know how to handle the questions adolescents ask. It is important that parents develop a wholesome relationship with their wards so that they do not feel any hesitation in asking questions and the parents should not hesitate in giving the right answer to the question asked.

ROLE OF PARENTS

During this period, the adolescents want independence from their parents and yet they are dependent on them for their needs. They do not like to be told 'Do this' and 'Don't do this'. Parents still want to control them while the adolescents want freedom and this leads to a tussle between the parents and adolescents. Here, the parents have to decide how much control they should exercise on their adolescent children, how much freedom is to be given, in which area they can let the adolescent have his/her say and in which they need to put their foot down. In short, the parents have to work out a congenial and workable disciplinary technique.

Let us discuss some parenting styles and their influence:

(1) Parents who give more freedom to the adolescent as he or she grows and at the same time take interest and responsibility for adolescent's decisions, encourage the adolescent to become more independent and responsible.

(2) Parents who are very strict and who play the role of an authority figure, i.e., who do not let the adolescent take any decision on her own, seriously hamper the adolescent's ability to be independent.

(3) On the other hand if parents are indifferent, i.e., who leave the adoles cents with their problems and do not interact with them, have children who grow up with indifferent attitudes.

Parents who encourage the adolescent to participate in family matters, value their opinion and take more interest in their activities, have children who are more confident. Thus, we can say that the parent-adolescent relationship should be based on mutual respect and love.

ROLE OF PEERS

During adolescence, most often between the ages of 14 to 16, there is a gradual shift from parents to peer group (same agemates). The changing family structure i.e. extended family (grandparents, parents and children) breaking and giving rise to nuclear family, makes the peer group very important. In nuclear families, the adolescents do not have anybody to talk to about their problems. This is because the parents are busy earning a living and there is no one else at home.

During adolescence the peer group becomes more important because of the following reasons:

(i) Everybody is going through the same conflicts and problems.

(ii) The general feeling is that the peers understand them more than their parents.

(iii) It is during adolescence, that the individual learns how to interact with members of the opposite sex. The peer group provides this opportunity for interaction.

(iv) All adolescents feel it is very important to talk, walk, speak, dress and generally behave like their peer group does. This is often called the "peer culture". Can you give an example? Yes, one example could be wearing of one earring by the boys. Another could be cutting hair too close or growing them too long.

Many people feel that "peer culture" is a way for the adolescents to feel different from their parents. They have their own code language and dress code.

It is important that the parents let the adolescent be a member of the peer group, but they need to keep an eye on their activities, as these activities might unknowingly be anti-social in nature, for example, forming of gangs and indulging in street violence.

However, it is not always true that parents and peer group are absolutely opposite to each other.

Many a time, peer group can reinforce parental values, if it is of the same socio-economic status and educational level as the adolescent's family.

ROLE OF SCHOOL AND TEACHERS

School is a major institution, other than the family, which is responsible for teaching a number of social as well as academic skills to the adolescence. Whether or not an adolescent does well in studies depends to a large extent on the school environment and teachers.

If the school discipline is not very harsh and the student's point of view is respected, the adolescent is more likely to enjoy academic work. When the teachers are properly trained, warm and enthusiastic and recognize the hidden talents of the students, they bring out the best in the adolescent which makes them feel very good about themselves.

On the other hand, poorly trained, incompetent teachers with large classes, a lot of work load, rigid curriculum and regulations can have a negative impact on the students. This does not give enough opportunity to the adolescents to solve the questions and satisfy the thoughts that come to their mind. As a result, they may lose all interest in studies and are not motivated enough to do well. Many of them may even drop out of school.

Parent's active interest and their feelings and attitudes about the school and teachers can also influence how the adolescents feel about school and teachers. The adolescents may regard the school and teachers the way the parents do.

Apart from playing the important role of teaching academic and social skills, the school can play a very important role in bridging the "generation gap" between the parents and the adolescents. The teacher occupies a central position between the two, if the teacher is liked by the students, they are more likely to listen to the teacher than their parents. The teacher can use this opportunity to explain to the adolescents the parents', or rather the adult's point of view in a friendly manner.

Peers in school can play another important role, as far as academics or studies are concerned.

Since it is very important for the adolescents to be a part of the peer group, if the peer group lays a lot of stress on studies, the adolescent would also study hard to be a part of her/his group.

ADOLESCENTS, TOO, HAVE PROBLEMS

During adolescence, physical changes take place very fast. Development takes place in other areas as well. The expectations of parents and other adults change. All this confuses the adolescent very much. With parents and peer support, most adolescents emerge out of this period as mature individuals but some may develop disorders in their behavior. Let us talk about them in brief.

(1) **Eating Disorders:** Some early maturing adolescents may feel that they are becoming too fat and may stop eating required quantities of food. Others may think that nobody loves them and in order to get attention they start overeating and grow fat. Some others become very sensitive and they vomit when they are scolded or when they are tense.

(2) **Suicidal Tendencies:** Many adolescents are unable to form friendships with their peer group. They do not trust parents either. In such situations, they might feel very lonely and think nobody loves them. This can lead to suicidal tendencies, which might just be to get attention or may be serious attempts.

(3) **Peer Pressure:** To prove to their friends that they are 'macho' (strong and grown up), the adolescents may indulge in alcoholism, smoking and may even take drugs under peer pressure. All these problems usually occur because the adolescent or 'young adult' is very sensitive during this period and the slightest neglect from friends and family is perceived as a dire situation. These problems can easily be handled by understanding parents and caring friends.

(4) **Personal Problems:** Adolescents have number of personal problems related to their looks - too fat or too thin, too tall or short. They are worried about the shape of the nose, their own clothing sense, etc.

(5) **Social Problems:** They do not like to participate in social and family functions. Adolescents hesitate in the company of opposite sex for the fear of being ridiculed and judged.

(6) **Biological Problems:** Biological problems of adolescence are complicated for both boys and girls, but more for girls. Girls find it more difficult to share their problems with others. They do not know how to seek information about changes in their body.

They develop a sense of fear towards consulting medical and health professionals regarding their problems. There is no proper education on problems of health, particularly reproductive health among adolescents. Religious rituals and superstitions wrongly prescribe a number of unhygienic practices that affect the girls psychologically during puberty and menstruation in particular. There is a serious need to provide appropriate knowledge and counselling services for the adolescents.

(7) **Teenage Pregnancy:** In India, adolescents in large numbers are still married even before they are fully physcially developed. Pregnancy and motherhood, therefore, also occur before the reproductive maturity is attained. Teenage pregnancy, whether within marriage or outside it, is often unplanned and leads to serious mental and physical health, social and economic consequences. Pregnancy at an early age can result in severe damage to the reproductive tract because of difficult child birth. Babies born to adolescent mothers are generally under weight, are more likely to die at birth or in infancy. Early childbearing also results in psychological strain on the young mother and curtails her educational and employment opportunities. Adolescent pregnancies often result in societal disapproval and include shame, guilt, embarrassment and fear. To avoid these, one may end up seeking help from an unqualified

person who may use improper methods to terminate the pregnancy.

It is useful to know about the means and methods of avoiding an unwanted pregnancy. Advice on these matters can be obtained from any qualified medical or nursing personnel in your neighbourhood.

ADULTHOOD

Different cultures have different ages at which children reach the adult status or the age of legal maturity. Generally, they reach this status when their puberty growth is complete and when their sex organs have developed to the point where they are capable of procreation.

SUBDIVISIONS OF ADULTHOOD

Early Adulthood: Early adulthood extends from age eighteen to approximately age forty, when the physical and psychological changes, which accompany the beginning of the loss of reproductive capacity appear.

Middle Adulthood (Middle Age): Middle adulthood, or middle age, begins at forty and extends to age sixty, when both physical and psychological decline become apparent in the average person.

Late Adulthood (Old Age): Late adulthood - senescence, or old age – begins at sixty and extends to death. While physical and psychological decline speed up at this time, modern medical techniques, as well as careful attention to clothing and grooming enable many men and women to look, act, and feel much as they did when they were younger.

CHARACTERISTICS OF EARLY ADULTHOOD

This is a period of adjustment to new patterns of life and new social expectations. The young adult has to take roles such as that of spouse, parent and bread winner and to develop new attitudes, interests and values in keeping with these new roles. Some of the outstanding characteristics are;

1. Early Adulthood is the *"settling - down age"*. This is the period when young men and women are trying out different life patterns in terms of jobs and different individuals to share their life. Once individuals decide upon the pattern of life they believe will meet their needs, they develop pattern of behavior, attitudes and values which will tend to be characteristically theirs for the ramaining of their lives.

2. Early Adulthood is the *"Reproductive Age"* - parenthood is one of the most important roles in the lives of most young adults.

3. Early Adulthood is a *"Problem Age"* - young adults need to cope up with all adjustments within their work and with partner and larger circle of friends and relatives. Expectations are too high and to meet demand make it even more difficult.

4. Early Adulthood is a period of *"Emotional Tension"* - what young adult's worry about which leads to emotional tension will depend upon their work load at their work place, at home and in the social circle and also how much success or failure they are experiencing in meeting these problems.

5. Early Adulthood is a period of *"Social Isolation"* - with the end of formal education and the entrance into adult life pattern of work and marriage, the association with peer groups is slowly weaned. This is when they experience social isolation.

6. Early Adulthood is a *"time of Commitment"* - As young adults change their role from student and dependent (characteristic of adolescence) to that of independent adults, they establish new pattern of living, new responsibilities and take up new commitments for themselves and their partners.

Young adults with high level of education, good health support and guidance from partner and family members, high ambitions and realistic goals, ability to accept success or failure gracefully, ability and willingness to communicate with others, respect for others and active participation in prestigious community affairs will easily climb up the ladder to successful economic and social status.

Poor health or physical defects can be hazardous to personal and social adjustments but these can always be overcome with the support one gets from the family and friends.

A lot of adjustments need to be made by young adults, the most important being - adjustment to marriage, to parenthood, and to the expanded family circle.

There are chances of singlehood also but how women feel about unmarried life and adjustment to singlehood differs from that of men. For men stress is less than single women.

REASONS WHY YOUNG ADULTS REMAIN SINGLE

- An unattractive or sex-inappropriate appearance.
- An incapacitating physical defect or prolonged illness
- Lack of success in the search for a mate
- Unwillingness to assume the responsibilities of marriage and parenthood
- A desire to pursue a career that requires working long and irregular hours or much travelling
- Residence in a community where the sex ratio is unbalanced
- Lack of opportunity to meet eligible members of the opposite sex
- Responsibilities for aging parents or younger siblings
- Disillusionment as a result of unhappy earlier family experiences or unhappy marital experiences of friends
- Sexual availability without marriage
- An exciting lifestyle
- Opportunity to rise in the vocational ladder
- Freedom to change and experiment in work and lifestyle
- Belief that social mobility is easier when single than married

- Strong and satisfying friendships with members of the same sex
- Homosexuality

DIVORCE

Divorce is the culmination of poor marital adjustment and comes when husband and wife have been unable to find any other satisfactory solution to their problem. Many unhappy marriages do not end in divorce because of religious, moral, economic or other reasons and many marriages end up in separation, either legal or informal, and desertion.

The traumatic effect of divorce is usually greater than that of death because of the bitterness and emotional tension preceding it and because of the social attitude towards divorce. This has a major impact on the children.

Success of adjustment to Adulthood can be measured in terms of three criteria – *achievement, satisfaction and personal adjustment*. Adults usually reach the peak of their carrier and family life by the time they are in their late thirties. The degree to which adults are successful in adjusting to the important problems they face in adult life will determine the degree of their satisfaction.

MIDDLE AGE

Middle age is generally considered to extend from age forty to age sixty. The onset is marked by physical and mental changes. Some of the most important characteristics are.

Characteristics

1. **Middle age is a dreaded age** – It is recognized that, next to old age, it is the most dreaded point in the total life span and the one, adults will not admit that they have reached until the calendar and the mirror force them to do so. Some of the reasons are, the mental and physical deterioration, cessation of the reproductive life, restrictions in finance and independence.

2. **Middle age is a time of transition** – transition always means adjustment to new interest, new

values, new pattern of behaviour, physical changes, changed roles etc., The most important adjustment is with death of a spouse. Of course adjustment with the problems of aging parents is always there.

3. **Middle age is a time of stress** – while major adjustment's to work, home, social life are made, this will lead to stress. Women have stress during the period of menopause.

4. **Middle age is a time of achievement** – middle age should be a time not only for financial and social success but also for authority and prestige. They usually reach their peak after which they rest to enjoy the benefits of their hard work.

5. **Middle age is a time of evaluation** – evaluation of their achievement and accomplishments in terms of money, social status, family size, their earlier aspiration, plans for future life etc., is carried out.

6. **Middle age is the time of the empty nest** – the time when the children no longer want to live under the parental roof. This period is much more traumatic for women than men. This leads to boredom especially if one has given up the job and other activities.

Adjustment in Physical Changes

One of the most difficult adjustment middle age men and women must make is to change the appearance. They must recognize that their body is not functioning as adequately as it formerly did and may even be 'wearing out' of in certain vital areas. This reproductive capacity is coming to an end and losing some of their sex drive and sexual attractiveness.

Women may experience a sudden cessation of menstruation. Many women gain weight during menopause mainly around the abdomen and hips. They also experience personality changes, become depressed and hostile. Among men, there is a gradual decline in gonadal activity leading to decline in sexual desire and sex organ functioning.

Good social adjustments in middle age is important. They should give up the "rocking chair"

philosophy which many middle age people follow. They should not think they have to remain inactive and give up many of their normal activities and desires. Instead they need to develop skills to keep them engaged in economic and social activities, take up responsibilities in the family like looking after grand children and giving a moral support to the members of the family.

Adjustmental hazards are more to single women than single men. Adjustment to loss of a spouse presents many adjustment problems for the middle aged man or woman. This will lead to disruption in the pattern of living.

They also have to adjust to approaching old age and retirement. The success with which men and women adjust to middle age can be assured by their achievements, emotional status, effects of physical and psychological changes or personality and the degree of satisfaction of happiness the middle aged person experiences.

OLD AGE

Old age is the closing period in the life span. Age sixty is usually considered the dividing line between middle and old age. Chronological age is a poor criteria to use in marking off the beginning of old age because there are such marked differences among individuals in the age and better aging actually begins. Because of better living conditions health care, most men and women today do not show the mental and physical signs of aging until early seventies. The characteristics of old age are far more likely to lead to poor adjustment than to good and to unhappiness rather than to happiness. That is why old age is even more dreaded than middle age.

Characteristics of Old Age

1. Old age is a period of decline – decline comes partly from physical and partly from psychological factors. There is change in body cells due to the aging process. Unfavorable attitude towards one self and life in general can lead to decline or become depressed and disorganized. Motivation plays a very important role in decline.

2. There are individual differences in the effects of aging. People age differently because they have different hereditary endowment, different socio economic and educational backgrounds and different patterns of living. The general rule is physical aging precedes mental aging.

3. Old age is judged by different criteria – age is judged in terms of physical appearance and activities. One who has white hair is labeled as old. There are many who try to cover up their aging symptoms to create illusion that they are not yet old.

4. There are many stereotypes of old people – let it be the folklore, the media, poetry, fiction, jokes or different forms of humor or scientific studies, all portray the aged as those who are worn out physically and mentally, unproductive, accident – prone, hard to live, days of usefulness are over, should be pushed aside to make way for younger people.

Poor adjustment is characteristic of old age – Because of the unfavorable social attitudes towards the elderly that are reflected in the way the social group treat them, it is not surprising that many elderly people develop unfavourable self-concepts. These tend to be expressed in maladjusting behavior of different degree of severity.

Common Changes in Appearance during Old Age

Head Region

- The nose elongates
- The mouth changes its shape as a result of tooth loss or the necessity of wearing dentures.
- The eyes seem dull and lusterless and often have a waterly look.
- A double or triple chin develops.
- The cheeks become pendulous, wrinkled, and baggy.
- The skin becomes wrinkled and dry, and dark spots, moles, or warts may appear.
- The hair on the head becomes thin and turns grey or white, and tough, bristly hair appears in the nose, ears, and eyebrows.

Trunk Region

- The shoulders stoop and thus seem smaller
- The abdomen bulges and droops
- The hips seem flabbier and broader than they did earlier.
- The waistline broadens, giving the trunk a sack like appearance.
- The woman's breasts become flabby and droop.

Limbs

- The upper arm becomes flabby and heavy, while the lower arm seems to shrink in diameter.
- The legs become flabby and the veins prominent, especially around the ankles.
- The hands become scrawny, and the veins on the back of the hand are prominent.
- The feet become larger as a result of sagging muscles, and corns, bunions, and collouses often appear.
- The nails of the hands and feet become thick, tough, and brittle.

Changes in Physiological functions

Changes in Physiological functions include decline in the ability to see, hear, marked changes in taste, sense of smell becomes less, and also that of sensitivity to pain. Elderly people tire quickly and require a longer time to recover from fatigue, changes in skilled movements especially handwriting, slow in learning new skills and quite often tend to become awkward and clumsy. Recall is affected. Old people tend to have poor recent memories but better remote memories.

Quite often due to lack of income or low economic status they become dependent and have to compromise on many of their hobbies, interests, activities etc.

Common physical hazards

Include disease and physical handicaps like circulatory, metabolic and mental disorders. Heart diseases, rheumatism, arthritis, visual and hearing impairment, etc., are also common. Due to psychological and physiological disorder and economic reasons, malnutrition in old age is common.

Physical and Psychological needs in living arrangements for the elderly

Physical needs

- The house temperature should be comparatively even from floor to ceiling because poor circulation makes the elderly especially sensitive to chilling.
- Elderly people need large windows to ensure plenty of light because of the gradual impairment of vision.
- Provisions should be made for safety. If the elderly should have to climb few steps, floors should be unwaxed or covered with wallto-wall carpeting, and danger areas should be lighted at all times.
- There should be adequate space for indoor and outdoor recreation, a conditon best met in multiple-housing developments or in institutions.
- Noise should be controlled, especially during the night. This can be done by locating sleeping quarters in a quiet part of a house or an apartment.
- Elderly people should have labour-saving devices, especially for cooking, dishwashing, and cleaning.
- The living quarters should be on one floor to avoid possible falls on steps.

Psychological Needs

- Elderly people should have at least one small room of their own so that they can have some privacy.
- Living arrangements should include space for sedentary recreation, such as reading and television watching.
- There should be provision for storage of cherished possessions.

- Elderly people should live close to stores and community organizations so that they can be independent in their activities.
- Elderly people should be near relatives and friends so that frequent contacts are possible.
- Provisions should be made for recreation and amusement, especially during the very hot/cold months when going outdoor is difficult and being housebound becomes monotonous and boring.
- Provision should be made for transportation to shopping areas, places of amusement, hairdressers, and churches/temples.

Some important conditions contributing to happiness in old age

- A favourable attitude toward old age developed as a result of earlier pleasurable contacts with elderly people.
- Happy memories of childhood and adulthood.
- Freedom to pursue a desired lifestyle without outside interference.
- A realistic attitude toward, and acceptance of, the physical and psychological changes that aging inevitably brings.
- Acceptance of self and present living conditions even if these fall below expectations.
- An opportunity to establish a satisfying, socially acceptable pattern of life.
- Continued participation in interesting and meaningful activities.
- Acceptance by and respect from the social group.
- A feeling of satisfaction with present status and past achievements.
- Satisfaction with marital status and sex life.
- Reasonably good health without chronic health problems.
- Enjoyment of recreational activities with relatives and friends.
- Productive activities whether in housework or volunteer services.
- A financial situation adequate to meet needs and wants.

SPECIAL NEEDS OF DISADVANTAGED CHILDREN

All children are 'unique' yet similar to one another in most aspects of growth. However, some children are very different from their age-mates that they 'stand out'. The obvious 'standing out' creates problems during the growing periods. Such children have to deal with the normal/usual problems of growth along with all those difficulties that may arise because of being different.

The child's ability to cope with these problems is limited. The child is unable to deal with the social and emotional problems. This has marked effect on the child's personal and social development. Such a child needs special attention during the formative years so as to be able to grow to the full potential.

According to psychologists a Normal Child can be defined "as one who is physically, socially, mentally, intellectually and morally adjusted and is in harmony with one-self and his/her surrounding environment." Such a child is able to conform to the norms of the particular society.

Baker, a well-known psychologist defines the Disabled Child as "one who deviates from what is supposed to be an average in physical, mental, emotional and social characteristics to such an extent that the child requires special educational services to help develop to the maximum capacity."

Categories of Disabled / Disadvantaged Children

The disabled children can be broadly grouped into three categories. These are:

(a) Physically handicapped children

(b) Mentally disadvantaged children.

(c) Socially maladjusted children.

Causes of Disability among Children

The various causes of physical disability are as follows:

(a) Heredity

(b) Unfavourable prenatal environment

(c) Injury during child birth

(d) Accident during early childhood causing orthopaedic problems.

(e) Surgery requiring the amputation of the diseased part.

(f) Mental and emotional problems in early childhood result in stammering, and speech defects.

(g) Ear infections and injuries resulting in hearing defects.

(h) Psychological, emotional problems and feeling of neglect result in behavioural problems. Such children are not able to keep up with the desired social norms and hence are at disadvantage.

(i) Imaginary defects called 'Phantom handicaps' occur when small children imagine they are handicapped and demand to be excused from doing things they don't want to do.

Types of Disabilities / Handicaps

Handicaps result in physical, neurological and social maladjustment and defects.

A. Physical Defects

(a) **Eyes.** Blind and partially sighted

(b) **Ears.** Deaf and hard of hearing

(c) Missing limb/weak limb

(d) **Physical abnormalities** such as webbed fingers, hunch back, sixth finger/toe, malformed ear, harelip, cleft palates, face and body birth marks.

(e) **Defective speech.** It results in stammering that affects child's personality.

(f) **Chronical defects.** The defects that exist year after year are generally referred to as chronical defects i.e. congenital heart diseases, rheumatism and muscular atrophys.

B. Neurological Defects

These are caused by disorders of the central nervous system e.g. cerebral palsy, epilepsy and schizophrenia. Cerebral palsy results in paralysis/motion disorder of limbs due to brain malfunction. Sudden uncontrollable attacks (seizures) resulting in loss of consciousness and muscle control are common among epileptic patients.

These defects can be corrected/ improved to a great extent when detected and treated in time. Medical, surgical and scientific advancement is providing tremendous improvements to cope with the different handicaps.

C. Social Maladjustment Defect

Socially maladjusted children do not conform to the acceptable social norms of the society. The children can be indulging in anti-social activities leading to juvenile delinquency and other related problems. Socially disadvantaged child is a deprived child deprived of love, proper guidance and general social security.

When is the Child Considered Disabled/ Disadvantaged

A Child is considered disadvantaged:

(a) When he/she cannot make the maximum use of one or several of the senses e.g. blind child, deaf and mute child.

(b) When he/she is not able to adjust well in the society one lives in. Such a child will exhibit behavioural problems.

Kauffa defines children with behavioural disorders as "those who chronically and markedly respond to their environment in socially unacceptable/personally unsatisfied ways but who can be taught more socially acceptable and personally gratifying behaviour.

(c) Do you know that a child who is able to make sharper use of senses e.g. exceptional/ bright child can also be disadvantaged.

Blindness

Vision is a critical tool that children use in obtaining information about the world in which they live. Impairment of vision can lead to partial or total blindness. The children without vision will need special materials and attention to develop fully.

Very often a blind child is not able to compete with the normal one. As a result these children may remain physically and economically dependent to a certain extent.

Causes of Blindness

Visual impairment can be caused by the following factors:

A. **Congenital Blindness:** It refers to a child being born blind. Genetic impairment results in the malformation of vital organs like eyes during the foetal development. Such children learn about their environment through the senses of touch and hearing.

B. **Acquired Blindness:** In this case the child is not born blind. The child may lose eyesight on account of some accident. The resulting eye-defect is called acquired or adventitious blindness.

C. **Nutritional Blindness:** It is the result of prolonged absence of vitamin-A rich foods in the diet. Deficiency of vitamin-A causes dryness of eyes, (xerophthalmia) and impaired vision in dimlight (night blindness). Poor state of epithelial tissues coupled with resulting eye infections causes serious damage to the eyes.

D. **Delayed Remedial Treatment:** Poverty, ignorance and superstitions are responsible for delayed medical treatment. Lack of proper medical facilities also add to eye related problems. India's blind population forms a major chunk of world's total.

Characteristic of a Partially blind child

A partially blind child is clumpsy, awkward and cautious in his/her movements. Their eyes may be red, watery, swollen, itching and sensitive to light. Child may complain of headache, nausea and blurring of vision. Child may have squint and appear 'cross-eyed'. Poor vision makes the child irritable, self- centered and preoccupied.

Child has fewer opportunities to learn to get along with different social groups. This results in social adjustment problems.

The children become rebellious and aggressive for they have to rely on others to do things for them. This often leads to frustration and inferiority complex among them.

Special needs of a blind child

It is important to render all possible help and attention to the blind child to enable him/her to be independent, self-reliant and economically viable. Physical, social and emotional needs have to be attended with special attention to yield satisfying results.

Deafness

New born infants are able to respond to the sound by startling and blinking of eyes. As they grow they recognize their parents' voices and enjoy their own cooing and gurgling sounds. Listening leads to language development. Latter the children learn to attach meanings to sound.

Children born with hearing impairment are unable to learn for they have not heard the sound to which they can attach meanings. This result in communication barrier.

Deaf and Hard of Hearing

A **Deaf child** is one who has lost the sense of hearing before learning the language. This means that the child is born without the ability to hear. Such children are often mute and silent.

Hard of hearing on the other hand is a defect that is acquired later in life. The child experiences varying degrees of hearing loss.

Characteristics of a Deaf Child

The child may be dumb besides being deaf.

The speech defects are common among children with hearing impairment.

They have difficulty in learning language/vocabulary. It is an enormous challenge to learn to communicate in a language one cannot hear.

Consequently these children are low in intelligence because they are incapable of using available opportunities.

Such children have suspicious minds because of lack of coordination between vision and hearing. This also results in their inability to make friends.

A deaf child is often indifferent and stubborn.

Sensitivity to hearing impairment among children leads to frustrations and inferiority complex.

The resultant poor communication causes tremendous socializing problems.

Special needs of a Deaf Child

Hearing defects cause a lot of problems ranging from language and vocabulary to comprehension and communication.

Physical Needs can be effectively taken care of by providing physical comfort to enable these children to improve their listening skills. Parents can help the child to locate sounds i.e, running of water to the tap or ringing of bell to the door. Intelligent parents can use playway techniques to help child recognize the sound e.g. hiding a musical toy and encouraging the child to look for it.

The child is helped to discriminate the sounds e.g. difference between father's and mother's voice, singing and crying etc.

The next step is the recognition of speech sounds. It is directly influenced by child's ability to use vision and other senses.

Need to Love and be Loved is as important for these children as it is for the blind. Love and affection provide emotional security besides the much needed encouragement for better learning.

Educational Needs involve child's ability to understand the languages. They learn to communicate through visual and manual means.

Oral Method or Lip-Reading is a special way of educating deaf children to identify sounds by watching the lip movement. It is slow method involving a lot of patience for the learner as well as the educator.

Manual Method or Sign Language helps the child to communicate with gestures, cues and finger-spellings.

Need to be Independent is of utmost importance to the deaf child. It reduces his/her dependency on parents, and siblings. The ability to be independent makes them important components of the society they live in. Invention of hearing aids have provided the much need relief to the deaf.

PHYSIOLOGY 7

INTRODUCTION TO HUMAN PHYSIOLOGY

Physiology is the study of different organ systems and the functions of the human body. As small children we begin to wonder what enables people to move, how it is possible for them to talk, how they can see the world and feel the objects around them, what happens to the food they eat, how they derive from food the energy needed for exercise and other types of bodily activity, by what process they reproduce so that life goes on. All these and other human activities make up life. Physiology attempts to explain them.

Various organs and systems of the human body

They are the skeletal system, muscular system, nervous system, circulatory system, respiratory system, the gastrointestinal system, excretory system and the reproductive system.

Skeletal system includes the bones of the skull, face, vertebral column, ribs and sternum, shoulder girdle and pelvic girdle.

Muscular system consists of various muscles that are attached to the bones with the tendons. Muscles move the limbs and other parts of the body in directions allowed by the ligaments.

Nervous system is composed of the brain, the spinal cord and the peripheral nerves that extend throughout the body. The nervous system controls many of the bodily activities, especially that of the muscles.

The nervous system is composed of two portions -the sensory portion and the motor portion. The sensory portion relays information to the brain through the senses of sight, hearing, smell, taste and feel. Motor portion relays information from the brain to the muscles to react accordingly.

Circulatory system is composed mainly of the heart and blood vessels. The blood acts as a transport system for carrying substances.

The circulatory system carries nutrients to the tissues and carries waste products away from the tissues. A special accessory circulatory system known as the lymphatic system takes care of dead tissues and dead bacteria.

Respiratory system consists of the air passages and the lungs. Air moves in and out of lungs by contraction and relaxation of the respiratory muscles. The exchange of gases namely O_2 and CO_2 takes place via the lungs.

Gastrointestinal system begins from the mouth where food after being swallowed enters the stomach, then the small intestine and the large intestine, finally to be excreted as feces through the anus. During the passage of food through the gastrointestinal tract, food is digested and nutrients are absorbed.

Excretory system comprises of the kidneys which help in removing unwanted substances from the blood. Kidneys also regulate concentrations of ions such as sodium and chloride, potassium, magnesium and many other substances.

Reproductive systems of the male and female are essential to provide for life's reproduction. The female provides the egg (ovum) which has to be fertilized by a sperm from the male, from which a new human being develops.

Thus it should be obvious that no single part of the human body can live by itself. The human animal is a sensing, thinking and motile organism which can adapt itself to its surroundings. In the framework of the organs and tissues, there are about 75 trillion individual cells, each one of which is a living structure. The next chapter will describe the structure and function of the cell that makes the human body possible.

CELL

All organisms are composed of cells. The cell is the structural basis of life. Organisms may be made up of one or more cells. If the organisms are made up of a single cell, they are called unicellular organisms, e.g. amoeba, chalamydomonas, bacteria, and many fungi; while the organisms made up of a few cells (e.g. some algae and fungi) to several million cells are called multicellular organisms.

Robert Hooke in 1665, was the first to identify cells. In the early 19th century, Matthias Schleiden, Theodor Schwan, and others recognized the universal occurence and importance of cells and formulated a comprehensive cell theory in 1838-39 which states that:

(i) The cell is the smallest unit of living matter capable of assimilation, respiration, growth and reproduction; and

(ii) The cell can live independently and reproduce its own kind (in other words, all cells come from pre-existing cells).

Max Schutze (1861) proposed that living matter of an organism is protoplasm and the cell is simply an accumulation of protoplasm limited by an outer membrane and containing a nucleus.

Types of Cells

The living organisms have two types of cells.

● **Prokaryotic Cells:** These are the cells without definite nucleus, i.e. nucleus is not bound by a nuclear membrane. It is called nucleoid *e.g.* bacteria, Blue-Green Algae. (Cyanobac-teria) PPLO, etc.

● **Eukaryotic Cells :** These have a definitely organised nucleus with a definite nuclear membrane which surrounds the genetic material and it has membrane bound cell organelle such as mitochondria, lysosomes, chloroplasts etc., *e.g.* animal cells, plant cells, fungi, algae, etc.

Structure of a Cell

A mature cell has the following three important parts: Protoplasm, Vacuoles, Cell wall.

I. Protoplasm

All the components of a cell internal to the cell membrane are constitute protoplasm. The portion of protoplasm without the nucleus is called cytoplasm.

Protoplasm is regarded as the physical basis of life. It contains a number of specialized structures called the *cell organelles* and chemical compounds known as *cell inclusions.*

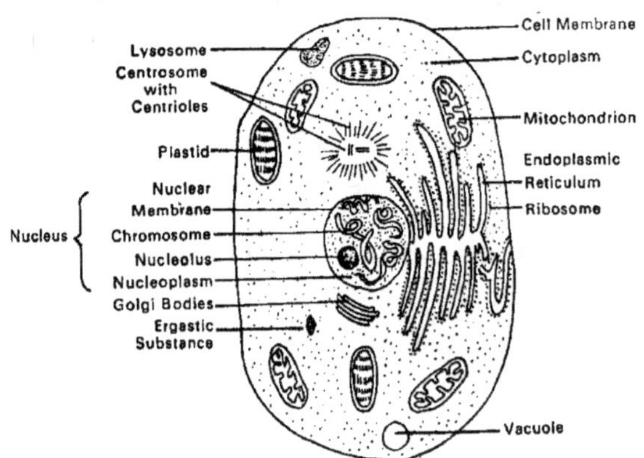

A Diagram of Cell

Physical Properties

1. Living protoplasm is a colourless, semi-transparent matter with lustrous appearance.

2. It is fluid to slight viscosus in constitution.

3. It is elastic in nature.

4. Living protoplasm shows a streaming movement, generally in a circular way called *cyclosis.*

5. It remains alive between 0-60°C and at higher temperature, it dies and coalgulates into solid mass.

6. It has got high affinity for water, remains saturated.

Structures and Functions of Different Parts of Protoplasm

Protoplasm has two main parts:-

(1) Cytoplasm

(2) Nucleus

Cytoplasm

Cytoplasm is the part of protoplasm which surrounds the nucleus and itself is surrounded by dead cell wall. It can be divided into the following parts: (a) Plasmalemma (b) Tonoplast, (c) Cytosol (the liquid substance of protoplasm) (d) Cell organelles (e) Microbodies.

The plasmalemma, tonoplast or plasmamembrane are bilipid structures. The plasmamembrane or plasmalemma encloses the cytoplasm while the tonoplast encloses the vacuoles.

- **Plasma or Cell Membrane :** It is the outer covering of each cell, which separates its contents from the surounding medium. It is a living, ultra thin, porous, semi-permeable membrane. It provides the mechanical support and external protection to the protoplasm. It acts as a efficient barrier to exterior environment and allows selective permeability to necessary materials to and from the cell.

- **Cell Organelles:** The cytoplasm contains specialised structures called organelles.

They are discrete, double membrane bound, well-organized protoplasmic structures in which many of the metabolic processes of the cells occur *e.g.* chloroplasts, mitochondria, dictyosome, etc.

Cells have two types of matters: (*i*) *metabolically active cell organelles*, and (*ii*) *metabolically inactive cell inclusions*. **Metabolically active cell organelles** are Plastids, Mitochondria, Endoplasmic reticulum, Ribosomes, Golgi bodies, Centrosomes, Flagellum and Cilium, Lysosomes, Spherosomes, Microbodies etc., and **metabolically inactive cell inclusions** are of three types - (a) *Reserve materials* such as carbohydrates, nitrogenous matter, fats and oils etc. (b) *Secretory products*; these are colouring matter, enzymes, nectar, etc. (c) *Excretory products* such as alkalloids, glucosides, tannins, latex, essential oils, resins, gums, mineral crystals, organic acids, etc.

(i) Metabolically Active Cell Organelles

Plastids

It is a bodies of varying shapes found only in plant cells. It is semi-autonomous organelles surrounded by double membrane envelope. Plastids synthesize fats, proteins, and starch. They vary in number in different cells. There are at least three different kinds of plastids - *leucoplasts, chromoplasts, and chloroplasts*. The **Leucoplasts** are colourless organelles, occur in sex cells, storage cells, roots and underground stems. They form starch grains. The **Chromoplasts** is carrying pigments which imparts colour to plants. The **Chloroplasts** contain chlorophyll. It is the green substance that converts carbon dioxide and water into sugar in presence of sunlight. It also imparts green colour to the plant. The Chloroplast is made up of two membranes - the inner and the outer membrane. These membrane expanded into flat, baggy structures called *thylakoids*. Several of which pile up and form a functional unit called *granum* (plural - grana). A *chloroplast* contains several such grana which are interconnected. It contains *chlorophyll* and other photosynthetic pigments to trap the sunlight. The matrix of the chloroplast is known as *stroma*. The grana and stroma contain several enzymes necessary for photosynthesis.

Mitochondria

These are double membrane, rod-like or spherical, extremely small organelles. The outer membrane of a mitochondria is smooth whereas the inner membranes show many infoldings called cristae. Mitochondria are the sites of energy release (in the form of ATP) for all the cellular purposes and hence are also known as the 'power houses' of the cell.

Endoplasmic Reticulum (ER)

It is a highly convoluted infoldings of the cell membrane in the cytoplasm. ER is in continuation with the nuclear membrane. The outer surface of the ER is either smooth or rough due to the absence or presence of ribosomes on its surface. These are called as Smooth Endoplasmic Reticulum (SER) or rough endoplasmic reticulum (RER) respectively. The ER is probably involved in the vital processes of metabolism.

Ribosomes

The ribosomes are granular masses which are either associated with the endoplasmic reticulum, or dispersed freely in the cytoplasm. They contain RNA and are the sites of protein synthesis in the cell.

Ribosomes are sub-microscopic, polypeptide manufacturings naked nucleoproteins. Robinson and Brown (1953) discovered ribosome in plant cells and Palade (1955) discovered it in animal cells.

Golgi Bodies

The Golgi apparatus consists of an irregular network or rod-like globular or granular bodies in animal cells. It is often concentrated around the nucleus and associated with endoplasmic reticulum. Large number of golgi bodies occurs in gland and nerve cells, but less number of golgi bodies occurs in muscle cells. For the given type of cell, golgi bodies are uniform in shape. The chief function of golgi bodies in gland cells is to collect protein secretions from the endoplasmic reticulum and pass them outside the cell. Golgi bodies add carbohydrates to these secretions to stiffen them into material called zymogen granules. The golgi apparatus in plants is known as *dictysome*.

Golgi apparatus is present in all eukaryotic cells except RBC and sieve tube elements. It is also absent in prokaryotes and sperm cells of seedless embryophytes.

Centrosomes

The Centrosome, found in most of the animals cells is a rather dense area of protoplasm, lies close to the nucleus. The Centrosome containing two cylindrical structure are called centrioles. Each Centrioles is surrounded by pericentriolar material. They play an important part in cell division, species lacking them include amoebae, unicellular red algae, pines and the flowering plants.

Cilia and Flagella

Cilia and flagella are specialized surface structures which help in movements of the cell. When these surface structure are very short and numerous, they are termed as **cilia** and when these structure are longer and fewer, they are termed as **flagella**.

Lysosomes

Lysosomes are vacuole-like bodies that secrete enzymes to digest food substances. Lysosomes are also involved in various other functions like, in defence against bacteria and viruses, in destroying old and worn out organelles and often resulting in the death of the cells. Because of this last role, they are referred to as *suicide bags* of the cells.

The Lysosomal membrane is impermeable to the digestive enzymes stored within it capable of withstanding their digestive action against macromolecules within the cells.

Spherosomes

Spherosomes are single membrane bound small spherical organelles which synthesise and store fat. They are present in cytoplasmic matrix.

Lomasosomes

They are vesicular and membranous structures usually present between cell wall and plasmalemma of plant cells. Their definite function is not known but probably they help in cell wall elaboration. They are mainly found in fungi and were termed so by Moore and McAlear.

Microbodies

They are single membrane bound small cell organelles which take part in oxidation reactions other than those of respiration. Microbodies often possess a crystalline core and granular matrix. They are two types: *peroxisomes* and *glyoxisomes*.

- **Peroxisomes :** These microbodies have enzymes for peroxide biosynthesis. They occur in most of the animals and plants but are more common in photosynthetic cells.

- **Glyocisomes / Glyoxysomes :** These microbodies occur only in fat of plant cells where they take part in oxidation of fats and perform glyoxylate cycle. Glyoxisomes possess catalase.

(ii) Metabolically Inactive Cell Inclusions

In the process of metabolic activation of the cell, several non-living substances are produced in it. They are also called organic bodies. They may be present in soluble or insoluble state and are organic or inorganic in nature. They can be divided into following categories.

- **Reserve Materials :** The reserve food material includes starch grains, glycogen granules, protein granules, aleuroplasts and oil droplets etc. The carbohydrate is present commonly in form of glucose and fructose. The two common monosaccharides found in the plant are mannose and galactose. The sucrose or cane sugar is a disaccharide. The most widespread trisaccharide in plant is raffinose.

- Secondary Products : They include mucous, gums, annins resins, alkaloids, late etc.

Nucleus

It is the central component of cell which control and regulate all activities of cell. There are generally one nucleus per cell, though some cells possess two or more nucleus. The nucleus is usually round and confining a watery fluid, the *nucleoplasm*, bounded by two porous membranes (nuclear membrane) that are often continuous with the endoplasmic reticulum. The nucleoplasm contains the substance called *chromatin*, which carries the genes, or determiners of heredity. Besides this, one or several spherical bodies called nucleoli are enmeshed in the chromatin network. The chromatid is composed of nucleoproteins - a combinations of proteins and nucleic acids - DNA (deoxyribonucleic acid) and RNA (ribonucleic acid). Thus, chromatin bears the genetic information units - the genes. The various cellular activities are controlled by the nucleus through its chromosomes.

Chromosomes

It is a rod-shaped structure visible under the light microscope during the cell division. Each chromo-some is made up of chromatin material. Some portions of chromatin take a darker stain during interphase. This region is called heterochromatin.

Chromosomes are 0.5 to 30μm in length and 0.2 to 3μm in diameter. Major exceptions include several insects whose giant chromosomes may reach a length of nearly 300mm and a width of 10μm.

Vacuoles

These are non-cytoplasmic areas present inside the cytoplasm. They are supposed to be greatly expanded endoplasmic recticulum. The vacuoles of plant cells are bound by a single, semi-permeable membrane called tonoplast, whereas the vacuoles of animals cells are bounded by a lipo proteinaceous membrane.

Cell Wall

The cell wall is the second layer of the cell envelope below the glycocalyx. This layer determines the shape of the cell and provides a kind of strong structural support to prevent the bacterium from bursting or collapsing in a hypotonic solution.

Plant cells are characterized by the presence of a rigid cell wall on the basis of which they can be differentiated from animal cells. In many cases it is an extension of outer membrane. This wall may be absent in some lower plants and cells taking part in reproduction. It protects the cell from unfavourbale conditions, separates one cell from the other, provides strength and definite shape to the cell. Thus the cell wall constitutes a kind of exoskeleton.

CELL DIVISION

To divide and duplicate is one of the fundamental properties of cells. In fact, the growth and development of all organisms are dependent upon the enlargement and division of their cells.

Plants and animals are usually composed of millions of cells when they are fully grown, yet they all begin life from only one cell: a fertilized egg cell or zygote. The zygote divides to produce 'daughter' cells which eventually become specialized into all the body tissues.

There are two major types of cell division *mitosis* and *meiosis*. Each of these is divided into two events—nuclear division (Karyokinesis) which is followed by the division of the cytoplasm (Cytokinesis).

Mitosis

In cells with nuclei, an important step in cell division is the division of the nucleus. The nucleus (except in sex cell) divides by the process called mitosis. Mitosis occurs in four successive stages; prophase, metaphase, anaphase, and telophase. There are no sharp dividing lines separating the various stages, and the events of each stage vary somewhat in different organism. The four stages are preceded by a resting stage, called interphase.

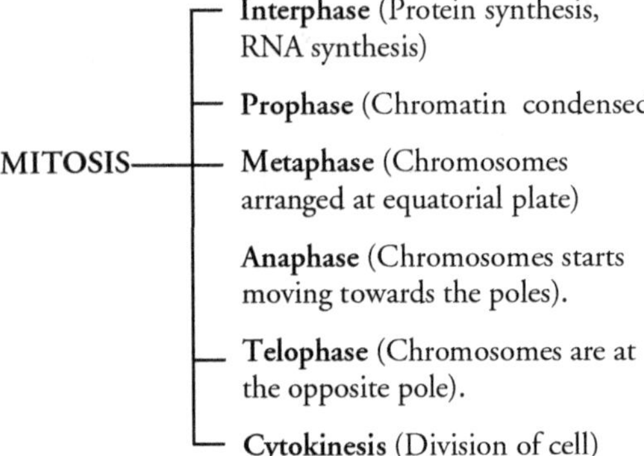

Interphase

The cell is engaged in metabolic activity and prepare for mitosis (the next four phases that lead up to and include nuclear division). Chromosomes are not clearly discerned in the nucleus, although a dark spot called the nucleolus may be visible. The cell may contain a pair of centrioles (or microtubule organizing centres in plants) both of which are organizational sites for microtubules.

Prophase

Chromatin in the nucleus begins to condense and becomes visible in the light microscope as chromosomes. Then nucleolus disappears. Centrioles begin moving to opposite ends of the cell and fibres extend from the centromeres. Some fibres cross the cell to form the mitotic spindle.

Prometaphase

The nuclear membrane dissolves, marking the beginning of prometaphase. Proteins attach to the centromeres creating the kinetochores. Microtubules attach at the kinetochroes and the chromosomes begin moving.

Metaphase

Spindle fibres align the chromosomes along the middle of the cell nucleus. This line is referred to as the metaphase plate. This organization helps to ensure that in the next phase, when the chromosomes are separated, each new nucleus will receive one copy of each chromosome.

Anaphase

The paired chromosomes separate at the kinetochores and move to opposite sides of the cell. Motion results from a combination of kinetochore movements along the spindle microtubules and through the physical interaction of polar microtubules.

Telophase

Chromatids arrive at opposite poles of cell, and new membranes form around the daughter nuclei. The chromosomes disperse and are no longer visible under the light microscope. The spindle fibres disperse, and cytokinesis or the partitioning of the cell may also begin during this stage.

Cytokinesis

In animal cells, cytokinesis results when a fibre ring composed of a protein called actin around the centre of the cell contracts pinching the cell into two daughter cells, each with one nucleus. In plant cells, the rigid wall requires that a cell plate be synthesized between the two daughter cells.

Mitosis is important for growth and multiplication of cells. It ensures that the two daughter cells inherit the same number of chromosomes, and hence the same characteristics as the parent cell. It plays a significant role in wound healing, regeneration of damaged parts (as in tail of lizard) and the replacement of cells lost during normal wear and tear (e.g., skin surface). It may give rise to tumour or cancerous growth if the process goes out of control.

MEIOSIS

It occurs in cells that produce gametes in sexually reproducing organisms. In these organisms, the fusion of an egg and a sperm cell produces a zygote, which develops into a new organism.

Most of the cells of an organism are diploid (2n). They contain pairs of similar chromosomes, known as homologous pairs. One member of each pair was inherited from the mother by the egg cell and one from the father by the sperm cell. Each species has a characteristic number of chromosomes. Human cells, for example, have a diploid number of 46 or 23 pairs of chromosomes.

The essence of meiosis is that it produces gametes that are haploid (n) that is, they have only half the number of chromosomes found in the other cells of the parent organism.

RESPIRATORY SYSTEM

All living organisms respire. In fact, respiration is one of the basic characteristics of living organisms so that if an object does not respire, it is considered non-living. For example, a rock, a piece of wood, a pen or pencil, a car or a motor cycle are all non-living because none of them respires. On the other hand, an insect, lizard, cat, dog, man, and a rose plant, or even a bacterium that can be seen only through a microscope, are all living and, therefore, respire. This is so because all living organisms and their component tissues and organs (in case of multicellular organisms) are involved in diverse activities all the time. For all these activities, energy is required which is made available through the process of respiration. The energy is made available in the form of ATP *(Adenosine triphosphate)*, referred to as the *energy currency of the cell,* which is synthesised during the breakdown (oxidation) of the food substances consumed by the organisms. Not only this, respiration is also the source of *cabon-skeletons* (small organic molecules) that are required for the synthesis, of other complex biomolecules that make up the body of the organism.

AEROBIC AND ANAEROBIC RESPIRATION

Respiration which uses oxygen is called *aerobic respiration*. Which respiration takes place in absence of oxygen it is called *anaerobic respiration*. Very little energy is released during anaerobic respiration because glucose is not completely broken down into carbon dioxide and water, it is changed into alcohol or lactic acid.

Fermentation. The *fermentation* (from the Latin meaning 'to boil') is the partial break down of glucose under anaerobic condition to yield ethanol and CO_2. This is carried out by microorganisms (yeast).

RESPIRATION IN ANIMALS

Single-celled organisms have no organs for respiration: they simply exchange carbon dioxide and oxygen across their cell membranes. Higher animals, however have special respiratory mechanisms. Insects have a network of tubes (tracheae) that open to the outside and bring oxygen into the body. Fish and several aquatic invertebrates have gills, which permit the exchange of gases with the surrounding water; a pumping mechanism then carries the oxygenated blood through the animal's body. Some fishes and amphibians use their thin, moist, vascular skin for respiratory exchange. Land-dwelling vertebrates have lungs that vary in complexity. The lungs are inflated by various types of pumping mechanisms, which cause oxygen to enter in response to a change in air pressure. Oxygen is transported throughout the body by bonding with haemoglobin pigments in red blood cells. Haemoglobin also acts to carry carbon dioxide from body tissues back to the lungs where it is exhaled.

HUMAN RESPIRATORY SYSTEM

In human beings lungs are the respiratory organs (pulmonary respiration). Lungs communicate with the atmospheric air through nostrils, pharynx (throat), larynx (voice- box), trachea (windpipe), bronchi and bronchioles. These bronchioles terminate into millions of tiny sacs like structures called alveoli. The thin walls of alveoli are lined with a network of blood capillaries. Alveoli have a far larger surface area than the total skin surface and consequently provide for greater respiratory exchanges.

Lungs are located in the thorax cavity. Diaphragm and the intercostal muscles, help in contraction and expansion of the lungs during breathing.

Respiratory gases are exchanged between the alveolar air and the blood in alveolar capillaries.

Most of the oxygen entering the blood combines with haemoglobin to form oxyhaemoglobin and is thus transported by RBC. The high pO_2 and low pCO_2 in the alveoli haemoglobin takes up large volumes of oxygen in the lungs. On reaching the tissue capillaries, oxyhaemoglobin dissociates to release oxygen; the low pO_2 and high pCO_2 in the tissue enhances this release of oxygen. This oxygen released in the tissue is then utilised in breakdown of food, releasing energy and waste products – CO_2 and H_2O.

THE SKELETAL AND MUSCULAR SYSTEM

A *skeleton* is a part of an animal which provides support for the rest of the body. Nearly every species of multi-cellular animal has a skeleton. Most are made of hard material *e.g.* bone, cartilage, chitin. They are either *exoskeletons* on the outside of the body (*Example:* insect skeletons) or *endoskeletons* inside the body (*Example:* vertebrate skeletons). Some animals have a hydrostatic skeleton which consists of fluid under pressure *e.g.* earthworm.

Bone is a very hard material, found only in vertebrates. It is made up of living cells, calcium phosphate (a mineral salt), and collagen (a protein). ***Cartilage*** is a second skeletal tissue of vertebrates. It is more plastic and resilient than bone, but not so hard. These properties make it a suitable covering for surfaces where bones meet (articular surfaces) at movable joints.

Chitin is the hard substance of which insect exoskeletons are made. It is a type of polysaccharide.

Functions of Skeleton

The skeleton helps to give body its shape, and provides a frame from which organs are suspended. The skeleton surrounds and protects soft parts of the body, *e.g.* in vertebrates, the skull protects the brain. In most animals the skeleton provides a system of levers which can be moved, and attachments for the muscles which move them.

The Vertebrate Skeleton

All vertebrate skeletons are built on the same general plan which includes the following:

(i) *An axial skeleton*, made up of the skull and vertebral column

(ii) *An appendicular skeleton*, made up of the limb girdles and limbs or paired fins in fish.

The skull consists of a thick cranium which protects the brain cavities to house the eyes, ears, and olfactory organs; an immovable upper jaw; and a movable lower jaw. The vertebral column (backbone or spine) is made up of small bones called vertebrae. A rat has 46-50 and humans have 33 *vertebrae*. The vertebrae form a hollow tube (the neural canal) which contains and protects the spinal cord.

The *limb girdles* comprise the *pectoral gridle* (shoulder gridle), to which the fore-limbs are attached, and the *pelvic gridle* (hip gridle) to which the hind-limbs are attached.

Total bones in human endoskeleton are 206 (number of bones in newly born baby is 306).

MOVEMENT IN ANIMALS

In higher animals, the skeletal muscle cause the movement and locomotion of the body by contracting. At least two muscles are needed to move a joint. One called the ***flexor muscle,*** contracts and bends a joint. On the opposite side of the joint there is an ***extensor muscle.*** This straightens the joint. Since flexer and extensor muscles pull a joint in opposite directions they are said to form an *antagonistic system.*

Muscles are attached to bones by tough, inelastic fibres called *tendons.* Tendons have two main functions :

(i) They protect muscle cells from wear, because they, are not the muscle cells pass over the movable ends of the bones and,

(ii) They concentrate the pull of the muscle into a small area.

The pectoral girdle is attached to the vertebral column by tendons, which gives it some mobility. It acts as a shock absorber in vertebrates which spring (*Example*, leopards) or hop (*Example*, frogs).

The bones of the pelvic girdle are fused to each other and to the sacrum (the fused sacral vertebrae). The whole makes up a very strong structure through which is transmitted the backward thrust of the hind-legs against the ground.

Joints

Joints occur wherever two or more bones touch. Some *joints are immovable* and are called *fixed joints,* Example–those in the skull. Some *joints are slightly movable*, example vertebrae can move slightly against the discs of cartilage in between them and other *joints are freely movable* called *synovial* joints, example the limb joints. The bones of freely movable joints are held in place and yet allowed to move freely by bands of fibres called *ligaments.*

In *hinge joints*, movement occurs in one plane only *e.g.* the knee and the elbow joints. In *ball-and-socket joints*, movement occurs in three planes *e.g.* the hip, the shoulder. In *pivot joints* one bone twists against another. A pivot joint occurs where a peg on the axis vertebra fits into a socket in the atlas vertebra. In a *sliding or gliding joint* the surfaces which rub together are flat *e.g.* the vertebrae joint.

Muscular System

Muscles, the tissues attached to bones, are composed of fibres. They are capable of contracting and relaxing to effect body movement. There are about 630 important muscles in human body, which normally account for 40 per cent of the weight. There are about 100 joints and 10,000 km of blood vessels in the human body. Water constitutes about 70 per cent of human body tissues.

Largest muscle: The bulkiest muscle in the body is *gluteus maximus* or buttock muscles.

Longest muscle: Sartorius (tailor's muscle) is the longest muscle in the body. It has its origin in the upper part of the hip bone, crosses obliquely over the upper portion of the thigh, passes behind the femur and is attached to the tibia in the leg.

Smallest muscle: The smallest muscle in the human body is the *stapedius,* which controls the stapes, an auditory ossicle in the middle ear. It is less than 1/20 of an inch and 0.127 cm long. The ear also contains one of the few tissues, which has no blood supply.

DISORDERS OF THE SKELETAL SYSTEM

This is divided into the following types:

  I. Skeletal disorders

  II. Types of Fractures

  III. Postural Deformities.

I. Skeletal disorders (their causes and effects)

(a) **Arthritis** (Inflammation of one or more joints) : Over 200 diseases may cause arthritis, including osteoarthritis, rheumatoid arthritis, gout, tuberculosis, and other infections. *Effects :* Swelling, warmth, redness of the overlying skin, pain, restriction of motion.

(b) **Osteo Arthritis** (Degenerative joint disease) : Osteo-arthritis is due to wear of the articulatory cartilage, and may lead to secondary changes in the underlying bone. It may be primary, or it may occur secondarily to abnormal load to the joint or damage to the cartilage from inflammation or trauma. *Effects :* The joints are painful and stiff with restricted movement. Osteoarthritis is recognized on X-ray by narrowing of the joint space (due to loss of cartilage) and the presence of osteophytes, osteosclerosis, and cysts in the bone.

(c) **Rheumatoid Arthritis** (The second common form of arthritis, after osteo arthritis) : Rheumatoid Arthritis is a disease of the synovial lining of joints. The joints are initially painful, swollen, and stiff and are usually affected symmetrically. *Effects :* As the disease progresses the ligaments supporting the joints are damaged and there is erosion of the bone, leading to deformity of the joints. Tendon sheaths can be affected, leading to tendon rupture.

(d) **Bone Cancer** : Bone cancer may occur as a secondary cancer form, for example, prostate cancer. *Effects :* Damage to stem cells (the cause of leukaemia).

(e) **Gout** : Gout is caused by a defect in uric acid balance in the metabolism - resulting in an excess of the acid and its salts (urates) which then accumulate in the bloodstream and joints, respectively. *Effects :* Gout can result in attacks of acute gouty arthritis, chronic destruction of the joints, and deposits of urates (tophi) in the skin and cartilage especially of the ears. The excess urates also damage the kidneys, in which stones may form.

(f) **Osteoporosis** (Loss of bone tissue) : Infection, injury and synovitis can cause localized osteoporosis of adjacent bone. Generalised osteoporosis is common in the elderly, and in women often follows the menopause. It is also a feature of Cushing's disease and prolonged steroid therapy. *Effects :* Bones that are brittle and liable to fracture.

(g) **Rickets** (Childhood disease) : Rickets is a childhood condition caused by insufficient vitamin D and Calcium. *Effects :* Bow legs.

II. Types of Fractures (their causes)

(a) **Simple** : A clean break of the bone with little or no break in the overlying skin.

(b) **Greenstick :** An incomplete break of the bone in which part of the outer shell (cortex) remains intact.

This occurs particularly in children, who have more flexible bones than adults.

(c) **Compound** (also known as "Open") : A broken bone that pierces the overlying skin.

(d) **Cominuted :** A fracture in which the bone is broken into more than two pieces. A crushing force is usually responsible and there is extensive injury to surrounding soft tissues is common.

(e) **Impacted :** A fracture in which the bones involved are driven into each other.

(f) **Complicated :** A broken bone that also involves damage to other organs - in addition to broken Bone(s) and possibly also broken skin. An example is a broken rib that punctures a lung.

NERVOUS SYSTEM

The nervous system, is an organized group of cells specialized for the conduction of a stimulus impulse from a sensory receptor through a nerve cell network to the site at which the response occurs.

The nervous system enables a multi-cellular animals to respond to changes in their external and internal environment. Nerve tissue is composed primarily of cells called *neurons.*

A typical vertebrate neuron consists of dendrites, a cell body, and an axon. The dendrites generate nerve impulses in response to stimulation from a sense receptor or from another neuron and carry impulses towards the cell body, which contains the cell's nucleus. The axon carries an impulse transmitted to it by the cell body to another neuron or to an effector muscle or gland. There are three general types of neurons: *sensory,* which relay information from the senses; *motor,* which carry impulses to effectors; and association, which transmit impulses between sensory and motor neurons. A *synapse* is the junction between two neurons.

In mammals these neurons comprise two types of nervous systems : (1) *Central nervous system* including the brain and spinal cord; and (2) *Peripheral nervous system* consisting of nerve cells and fibres which link the brain and spinal cord with other parts of the body.

CENTRAL NERVOUS SYSTEM

(i) Brain

In man it is located in the skull called *cranium.*

The cerebrum of brain is divided into two hemisphere : the *left cerebral hemisphere* and *the right cerebral hemisphere.* Each hemisphere is divided into four lobes

(a) Frontal lobes   (b) Temporal lobes

(c) Parietal lobes   (d) Occipital lobes

Each lobes is named after the bone of skull under which the part of brain lying.

(ii) Spinal Cord

It is a long narrow tubular structure that extends from the brain to the bottom edge of the first lumbar vertebra. It is covered by the same meninges as the brain and is housed in the neural canal within the vertebral column.

Dorsal and ventral grooves divide the cord into the right and left halves. Running through the centre of the spinal cord is the central canal which is filled with cerebrospinal fluid. A cross-section of the spinal cord reveals an outer region of white matter and inner region of grey matter. The spinal cord has a two fold function: it conducts impulses to and from the brain, and acts as a reflex centre.

PERIPHERAL NERVOUS SYSTEM

The Peripheral Nervous System (PNS) connect the body with central nervous system. The nerve fibres of PNS are two types

(a) **Afferent (Sensory) fibres :** It transmits impulse from tissues or organs to CNS.

(b) **Efferent (Motor) fibres :** It transmits impulse from the CNS to perpheral tissues or organs.

PNS can be divided into :

(a) **Somatic Neural System :** It transmits impulse from CNS to skeletal muscles.

(b) **Autonomic Neural System :** It transmits impulse from CNS to involuntary organs and smooth muscles of body. This system can be divided into two types :

(i) Sympathetic neural system

(ii) Parasympathetic neural system

The *parasympathetic system* slowdown the heart beat, diverting blood from the muscles to the stomach, and intestine, contracting the pupil of the eyes etc. The *sympathetic system* speed up heartbeat, enlarge pupils, supply additional blood to muscles.

The peripheral nervous system have following nerves.

(a) Spinal Nerves are those nerves that emerge from the spinal cord. There are 31 pairs of spinal nerves, all of which are mixed nerves (nerve consisting of both sensory and motor neurons). Each spinal nerve originates in two roots-dorsal root containing sensory neurons and a ventral root containing motor neurons which join together to form the spinal nerve.

(b) Cranial Nerves are those nerves that emerge from the brain. There are twelve pairs of them - some are sensory, some are motor and some are mixed nerves.

Reflex Action

A reflex action is defined as an involuntary action in response to an external or an internal stimulus. It is an inborn automatic response to a stimulus, and is the functional unit of the nervous system.

Reflex actions involving the spinal cord are called *spinal reflexes* and those involving the brain are called *cranial reflexes.*

CIRCULATORY SYSTEM

Circulation is the process by which nutrients, respiratory gases, and metabolic products are transported throughout a living organism.

In unicellular and small multicellular organisms, simple diffusion is often sufficient to transport oxygen and carbon dioxide. The streaming movement of the cell cytoplasm is called *cyclosis,* it is sufficient to conduct larger molecules like sugars, fats, proteins to different parts of the cell. In more complex organisms, however, specialized systems have been developed to provide adequate circulation to all tissues.

In *simple multicellular organisms* like sponges and coelenterates (e.g. jellyfish and hydras) water circulates from the surrounding medium through channels in their bodies. Cells in contact with the water take up food and oxygen directly from it.

In *the flatworm*, which has true circulatory system, a fluid carrying nutrients bathes the animal tissues while moving passively through the spaces between its component cells. Oxygen is taken up directly from the environment at the animal's surface.

The *earthworm*, has a well developed circulatory system. It consists of a network of blood vessel which is in contact with almost all cells of the body.

The insects such as *cockroach* have an *open circulatory system*. The blood pumped by a many chambered heart, passes through a closed vessel, the aorta, only for a part of its circulation. For the rest it flows through the body cavity, the *haemocoel* and tissue spaces.

All vertebrates have *true circulatory system* which has *closed circulation*. In a closed system, blood remains within a network of vessels. It is carried away from the heart through the arteries. Capillaries and veins return the blood back to the heart.

The lung-fishes have a dual circulation consisting of the *systemic circulation,* which carries oxygenated blood to the body tissues and returns deoxygenrated blood to the heart, and *pulmonary circulation,* which pumps deoxygenated blood to the air bladder and returns oxygenated blood to the heart.

Adult amphibians have a dual circulation. The heart is not completely partitioned in amphibians. There is some mixing of pulmonary and systemic circulation occurs in heart. In amphibian exchange of oxygen and carbon dioxide occurs through their moist skin as well as through their lungs, respiratory exchange takes place in both the pulmonary and systemic circulation. As a result, there is less need to avoid mixing of the blood in the heart.

Reptiles have lungs for respiratory exchange and therefore have a more complete separation of the pulmonary and systemic circulation than is found in amphibians. In both birds and mammals there is a complete separation of both ventricle and atrium into a two-sided heart.

In man the heart beats about 72 times per minute. The total volume of blood in the human system is about 5 litres. Approximately 5 litres of blood is pumped out by the heart every minute.

HUMAN BLOOD

Blood is the circulatory fluid of the circulatory system. It is a specialized connective tissue which performs the following vital functions :

(a) In respiration, transport of oxygen from the lungs to the tissues and of carbondioxide from the tissues to the lungs.

(b) In nutrition, transport of absorbed food substances to the cells;

(c) In excretion, transport of metabolic wastes to the kidneys, skin and intestine for their removal;

(d) In regulation of metabolism, transport of hormones from their site of production to that of their action;

(e) In other regulatory mechanisms, maintenance of body temperature, osmo-regulation, and acid-base balance;

(f) In clotting of blood.

Blood and its Composition

Blood is a red sticky fluid, slightly alkaline in nature. It is composed of a fluid portion, the *plasma* (50-55% of the volume) and three types of corpuscles (45-50% of the blood volume) namely *erythrocytes* (red blood corpuscles, RBC), *leucocytes* (white blood corpuscles or WBC) and *blood platelets*. The corpuscles are embedded in the plasma.

Plasma

Plasma is light yellow fluid with 90-92% water, 6-9% proteins and 1% of dissolved substances. Plasma acts in blood clotting and in defence of the body against diseases.

RBC

RBC or red blood cells or erythrocytes number about 5 million per cu mm of blood in man. RBC cells are *devoid of nuclei*. RBC mainly consist of *haemoglobin,* a pigment which transports oxygen. These cells are formed in the bone marrow. Their average life span is 110 to 120 days. Worn out cells are destroyed by the spleen.

HUMAN BLOOD CHEMISTRY

1. **Water** — 90-92%
2. **Proteins** (Albumen, Globulin, Properdin, Prothrombin, Fibrinogen) — 6-8%
3. **Inorganic Salts** (Cations are Na, K, Mg, Ca, Fe and Mn. Anions are chloride, bicarbonate and phosphate) — 1-2%
4. **Others** (i) **Food Materials** (Glucose, Amino Acids, Fatty Acids, Triglycerides) — 1-2%
  (ii) **Waste Materials** (Urea, Uric Acid and Creatinine)
  (iii) **Regulatory Substances** (Hormones, Vitamins, Enzymes)
  (iv) **Anticoagulants** (Heparin)
  (v) **Cholesterol**
  (vi) **Antibodies**
  (vii) **Dissolved Gases** (O_2, CO_2, N_2)
5. **pH** — 7.4

WBC

WBC or white blood cells or leucocytes, are larger, fewer-about 5 to 9 thousand cells per cu mm of blood and contain one nucleus each. They are irregular shaped cells. They are of five different types namely—neutrophils, lympocytes, basophils, eosinophils and monocytes. Their major function is to provide immunity to the body. The WBCs have a life span of less than 2 weeks and they are produced in the red bone marrow. An overproduction of WBCs results into a disease called *leukemia.*

Platelets

Platelets or thrombocytes are small spherical bodies numbering about 300,000 per cu mm of blood. They play an important role in the formation of a solid plug called clot at the site of injury to a blood vessel, so as to prevent further loss of blood. Blood platelets are enucleated. They live for only a few hours.

Blood Clotting

In case of injury the blood loss occurs. To prevent this loss, animals have evolved an elaborate mechanism which results in the clotting or coagulation of blood. During this process a series of chemical reactions take place resulting in the formation of a clot that plugs a broken vessel.

When injury occurs, the damaged tissues and blood platelets release a substance called *thromboplastin.* On exposure to air the platelets disintegrate. In the presence of *calcium ions* thromboplastin converts the inactive enzyme *prothrombin* (present in the plasma) to an active enzyme, *thrombin.* Thrombin finally converts the soluble *fibrinogen* of plasma into insoluble fibres of *fibrin.* The fibrin entangles the blood cells and microbes to form a clot.

Human blood escaping from the body normally clots within 3 to 4 minutes. The blood does not clot within the blood vessels because of the presence of an enzyme, *antihrombin* (heparin).

Blood Groups

The four types of blood are called blood groups, and are known by the letters A, B, AB and O. Before the blood transfusion can take place it is necessary to make sure that the donor's and recipient's blood will mix together without agglutination. Blood groups which mix without agglutination are said to be compatible.

Blood compatibility depends upon chemicals called agglutinogen or antigens on the surface of the red cells, and chemicals called agglutinin or antibodies in the plasma. There are two types of antigens: A and B; and two types of antibodies: anti-A and anti-B.

Blood group A has A antigen on its red cells and anti-B antibody in its plasma.

Blood group B has B antigen on its red cells and anti-A antibody in its plasma.

Blood group AB has A and B antigens on its red cells and no antibodies in its plasma.

Blood group O has no antigens on its red cells but has both anti-A and anti-B antibodies in its plasma.

Blood Transfusion

Anti-A plasma agglutinates A red cells, and anti-B plasma agglutinates B red cells. So these combinations of plasma and red cell are incompatible as far as blood transfusion is concerned.

These facts have given rise to a rule for blood transfusions: the donor's red cells must be compatible with the recipient's plasma. Thus blood can be safely transfused as follows:

Blood Group	Transfused or donated to persons with blood groups	Receive blood from Persons with blood groups
A	A and AB	A and O
B	B and AB	B and O
A B	AB only	All groups
O	All groups	O only

People with Group O blood are called universal donors. Their red cells have no antigens and so cannot be agglutinated by blood of any other group. People with Group AB are called universal recipients. Their plasma has no antibodies therefore it does not agglutinate blood from the other groups.

Rh Factor

About 85% of humans have an antigen on their red cells called the Rhesus factor. People with the Rhesus factors are called Rhesus positive (Rh$^+$) and those without it are called Rhesus negative (Rh$^-$).

Rh$^-$ patients can receive one transfusion of Rh$^+$ blood without harm because their plasma does not have an antibody to react with the incoming red cells. Subsequent transfusion, however, may be dangerous because Rh$^+$ blood stimulates the body of the Rh$^-$ recipient into producing a plasma antibody which agglutinates Rh$^+$ blood. Such recipients are then said to be sensitized to Rh$^+$ blood and will agglutinate any which is transfused into them. Rh$^-$ blood can be transfused into Rh$^+$ people any number of times without harm.

A Rh$^+$ father and Rh$^-$ mother could have a Rh$^+$ child. During pregnancy the developing child's red cells may enter the mother's blood, perhaps through a fault in the placenta. The mother's body will then produce an antibody which destroys Rh$^+$ cells. This anti-body will not harm her first child but if she has a second Rh$^+$ child and its red cells enter her blood, she will produce more antibody and there is a danger that this will reach the embryo, destroy its red cells, a condition known as *erythroblastosis foetalis* which may cause serious blood disorders or death.

This danger can now be avoided. A Rh$^-$ mother with a new born Rh$^+$ child can be injected with chemicals which stop her body producing the Rhesus antibody.

Heart

Heart is the pumping station of the system. Its average weight is about 340 grams in men and 255 grams in women. Normally it lies somewhat to the left in the chest. Completely enclosing the heart is a double sac—the *pericardium.*

A wall, called the *septum,* divides the heart into a left half and a right half which thus prevents the mixing of deoxygenated and oxygenated blood of the heart. Each half, in turn, is divided into an upper chamber—the *auricle,* or *atrium* and a lower chamber- the *ventricle.* The auricles receive blood from the veins. The ventricles pump blood into the arteries.

There is an opening, between the auricle and the corresponding ventricle on each side of the heart. The two openings are guarded by **auriculoventricular valves** (AV), made up of thin, membranous flaps. The valve between the right auricle and right ventricle has three flaps. It is called the **tricuspid valve.** There are only two flaps in the valve between the left auricle and left ventricle. This is called the bicuspid valve. It is also known as the mitral valve.

The left and right ventricles pump blood respectively into the aorta and the pulmonary artery, both openings being guarded by semi-lunar valves to prevent back-flow of blood from the arteries to the ventricles. Aorta or the big artery carries the oxygenated blood to every part of the body. ***The pulmonary artery, carries deoxygenated blood to the lungs.***

Each pumping action of the heart or *cardiac cycle* consists of events in the heart repeated cyclically during each heart beat. Contraction and relaxation of cardiac chambers (auricles or ventricles) are respectively called *Systole* and *diastole*. When the atrium contracts, the ventricle is still in diastole and the blood collected in the atrium is pumped into the relaxing ventricle. Then the atrium starts relaxing and the ventricle starts its systole. The AV valve immediately closes producing the first heart sound '*lubb*' and prevents the back-flow of blood from the contracting ventricle to the relaxing atrium. The rise of pressure in the contracting ventricle pushes the semilunar valves to open and blood is ejected from the ventricle to the great artery. Simultaneously, the atrium is in diastole and blood continues flowing into it from the great veins. When the ventricle ends its systole and starts relaxing (ventricular diastole), the artia are also continuing their diastole. This conditioin is called joint diastole. With the onset of ventricular diastole, the semilunar valves close sharply to prevent back-flow of blood from the great artery into the ventricle. This produces the second heart sound '*dup*'. With the ventricle in diastole, the AV valve opens again and the blood again starts flowing from the atrium to the ventricle.

Blood Circulation

Humans and all other mammals have a double circulatory system : the **pulmonary circulation** and the **systemic circulation**.

The blood vessels associated with the liver and kidney are as follows : The liver receives its blood supply through the hepatic artery, a small branch of the aorta. Blood from the intestine is also brought to the liver where excess of certain nutrients is converted into suitable forms for storage. The blood vessel that carries the blood from the intestine to the liver is called the *hepatic portal vein* (A vein that begins and ends in capillaries is called a portal vein). Blood from the liver is carried by the hepatic vein that joins the inferior vena cava.

Renal arteries arising from the dorsal aorta supply the blood to the kidneys and renal veins that join the inferior vena cava carry the blood away from the kidneys.

Blood Vessels

The blood vessels constitute the pipelines through which the blood from the heart is carried to the different parts of the body and again brought back to it. There are three distinct types of blood vessels:

- **Arteries :** Carry oxygenated blood away from the heart except the pulmonary artery which carries deoxygenated blood from the heart to lungs for oxygenation.
- **Veins :** Carry the deoxygenated blood from the tissues to the heart except the pulmonary veins which carry oxygenated blood from the lungs to the heart.
- **Capillaries :** Between the arteries and the veins are a network of capillaries. An exchange of materials between the blood and the cells of the tissues takes place through these thin walls of the capillaries.

Heart Beat

They arise in a small bundle of tissues, called the *sinoauricular node,* or *sino-atrial node* (SA node) which is located in the upper part of the right auricle. The impulses sent out by this node is called a *wave of excitation.* This spreads through the right and left auricles, causing their muscles fibres to contract. The wave of excitation reaches a second node-the auriculo-ventricular, or atrio-ventricular, node-in the upper part of the wall between the two ventricles. The impulses are then relayed by way of a bundle of tissues to a fibre network, known as the *Purkinje system.* This network transmits the impulses to the muscle fibres of the ventricle and causes them to contract, releasing blood to the arteries. The SA node is called the *pacemaker* of the heart because it originates the cardiac impulse and, consequently, determines the rate of heart beats.

Blood Pressure

As blood is ejected from the left ventricle into the aorta, there is an increase in blood pressure—that is, the pressure of the blood upon the walls of the blood vessels. After the ventricle has started to relax, the pressure falls. The highest point in the pressure range is called the *systolic pressure.* The lowest point in the pressure is called the *diastolic* pressure.

In the young adult, the average systolic pressure is 120 mm. Hg. The average diastolic pressure is 80 mm. Hg. Any systolic pressure over 140 or diastolic pressure over 100 is considered abnormal. This condition is called *hypertension, or high blood pressure.* In some persons, the blood pressure is lower than normal. Such persons are said to have low blood pressure, or hypotension.

EXCRETORY SYSTEM

Excretion is the process by which an organism gets rid of the waste products of its metabolism. Most waste products become toxic, if allowed to accumulate in an organism, and may fatal from organism. Therefore every living thing has some means of getting rid of its waste products. These mechanisms may also be used to get rid of other unwanted substances such as superfluous water, and salts, so as to aid in osmoregulation.

Waste Products

Urine is composed of water (95%), urea (2%) uric acid (0.05%). Amount of urine secreted per day is 1.5 to 2 litres. Protein metabolism results in nitrogenous wastes such as ammonia, urea and uric acid. While the carbon dioxide is eliminated by the respiratory system, the nitrogenous materials are taken care of by the specialized excretory organs.

The mechanisms that evolved to carry out excretory functions differ greatly in various organisms and environments. An animal living in a desert must be able to conserve water in its body, while a freshwater fish needs the capacity to rid itself of large amounts of water.

In flatworms, *flame cells* constitute the excretory system. The *nephridia* constitutes the excretory organs of invertebrates like annelids (segmented worms).

The excretory organ of molluscs is the *renal gland.* In insects disposal is through a bunch of long tubules called *Malphigian tubules.*

Birds, like reptiles and insects, excrete uric acid into a continuation of the alimentary canal. Some marine birds have, in addition, salt glands (modified tear glands) which remove excess salt from their bodies and discharge the concentrated solution through the nostrils.

Amphibians store large quantities of dilute urine in a large *bladder* which acts as a water reserve when the animal is on land.

Freshwater fish must overcome the problem posed by water entering the body through osmosis and salts leaching out. To compensate, they produce large volumes of dilute urine and take in salts from the water through specialized cells in their gills. Nitrogenous wastes, for the most part, are diffused as ammonia through the skin. Marine fish, on the other hand, lose water through the skin and take in salt by osmosis.

HUMAN EXCRETORY SYSTEM

The human excretory or urinary system is typical of that of all mammals. It consists of two *kidneys* where urine is produced by filtration, secretion, and reabsorption; the *ureter tubes* that transport the urine; the *bladder* where the urine is stored; and the *Urethra* through which the urine is voided.

In humans, kidneys are paired bean-shaped organs about five inches long. Located in the abdominal cavity, one on either side of the vertebral column. The concave portion lies nearest the backbone and is deeply cleft by the hilus through which arteries, veins, nerves, and lymphatics enter the kidney sinus. A cross-section of the kidneys show them to be made up of a darker *outer cortex* and *inner medulla* composed of rough cones with apex projecting into the sinus.

The functional units of kidney are called *nephrons,* which are about a 1,000,000 in each kidney. Each nephron has *Bowman's capsule* at one end (a double-walled cup) and the rest part of the nephron is differentiated into a coiled *proximal convoluted tubule, a* 'U' *shaped tin Henle's loops,* and a *distal convoluted tubule.*

Urine formation begins in Bowman's capsule which encloses a dense cluster of microscopic blood vessels, the *glomerulus.* Under the driving force of blood pressure, plasma filters from the blood. Proteins and about 80 per cent of the water are held back in this process. The filtrate passes through the inner wall of the capsule and moves into the tubule.

The proximal tubule passes from Bowman's capsule in the renal cortex into the medula and makes a U-turn (Henle's loop). The distal convoluted tubule then re-enters the cortex and joins with several other distal tubules to form a collecting tubule, which carries the urine to the renal pelvis and the ureters. The ureters move the urine to the bladder in peristaltic waves.

The two ureters (10-12 inches long) enter the hollow muscular bladder where urine collects until it is voided through the urethra in urination (or micturition). The urethra differs in males and females. In human males it is about eight inches long and is also the channel for semen in ejaculation. In women it is only one and two inches long and carries only urine.

THE SKIN

The skin is an organ that provides protective covering to the body. It weighs 9 Ibs, is 0.5 to 5 mm thick and has an area of about 18 sq feet. It consists of two parts: (A) **Epidermis and** (B) **Dermis.**

A. Epidermis

Epidermis is a dry stratified squamous epithelium, 0.1 mm thick. On palm and sole it is 0.8 to 1.4 mm thick respectively. It consists of four layers:

1. **Stratum corneum** consists of several layers of closely packed cornified and fused cells. Cytoplasm is lost to a dry and fibrous protein called keratin.

2. **Stratum lucidum** is a clear translucent glossy layer of 3 to 5 cells deep. It is present only in the thick epidermis of palm and sole.

3. **Stratum granulosum's** component cells, in 3 to 5 layers, are flattened and diamond-shaped. Cytoplasm is packed with granules of keratohyalin.

4. **Stratum germinativum** consists of several layers. Basal cells are columnar and dark staining. Next higher cells are spiny or prickle cells forming a spiny layer. Mitoses occur in basal and prickle cells. Daughter cells reach the surface in 4 to 14 weeks to replace the peeled off skin.

Pigmentation

The colour the skin itself is yellow due to the presence of carotene. Blood, showing through gives reddish colour. Fine granules of melanin present in basal cells are responsible for yellow or brown colour.

(B) Dermis

It consists of two papillary and reticular layers of mostly collagenous and elastic fibres. Papillary layer has ridges and papillae protruding into epidermis. While some papillae contain tactile sensory corpuscles, other contain only blood vessels. Reticular layer forms the main fibrous bed of dermis.

A subcutaneous layer, not considered to be part of the skin, blends into the dermis. This layer formed of fat lobules is called panniculus adiposus.

The hair comprise elastic, tapering horny threads. Hair length varies from 1 mm to 5 feet. It consists of a free shaft and a root that embeds in the skin. Hairs are not perpendicular but slope at an angle. A tubular hair follicle, partly epidermal and partly dermal, encloses the root. Towards its deep end the follicle is expanded into a hair bulb. The base of the bulb is pierced by a prominent connective tissue papilla.

Associated with a follicle are sebaceous glands and erector muscles. A sebaceous gland is usually located in the angle between hair follicle and erector muscle. Its short duct empties into the follicle. These are holocrine glands in which secretory cells are lost with the oily secretion keeping the hair supple and soft. The oily secretion comprises a mixture of fat, cellular debris and keratin. The erector muscle of a hair inserts into the dermal root sheath, slightly above its mid level. On contraction, the muscle lifts the hair as in the event of cold or fright.

Sweat glands occur throughout the skin except on the nail-bed, ear drum, glans penis and margin of the lip. A sweat gland consists of a secretory coiled tubule that lies mostly in the subcutaneous layer. Its narrow duct raises through the dermis to the epidermis by a tortuous course. Its opening called sweat pore, is a minute pit on the epidermal surface. These are merocrine glands as they do not suffer cytoplasmic loss.

Functional correlations : Besides protection, the skin has excretion as one of its less important functions. The skin regulates the body temperature through the evaporation of water from the sweat glands. During summer, when the environmental temperature exceeds man's normal body temperature (98.6°F), the sweat glands bathe the skin surface with sweat. As this moisture evaporates, it cools the surface of the body to lower its temperature. In man, the perspiration or sweat includes besides water, certain body salts, Na+, K+, Ca++, Mg++ and Cl- in particular, and some nitrogenous matter such as urea and protein. Loss of salts through the body through excessive perspiration can be the cause of sun stroke than is the heat itself. Workers in factories who spend most of the time in temperatures at or above 100°F, must take extra salt to replenish these minerals lost through sweat. It helps avoid muscular cramps. Fear and anxiety also cause perspiration to flow.

There are also nerve endings (receptors) in the deeper layers of the skin that are sensitive to touch, cold, heat, pressure and pain.

LUNGS

The lungs are a pair of spongy organs consisting of elastic tissues situated in the chest cavity and separated from each other by the heart and other contents of the mediastinum. The right lung is larger than the left lung. The right lung weighs approximately 620g while the left lung weighs about 570g; together, in a healthy adult, they weigh between 1.18 and 1.19kg.

Functions The main function of the lungs is to purify blood and supply it with oxygen. The entire blood supply (4-4.5 l) washes through the lungs about once a minute.

LIVER

Liver is the *largest gland* in the human body, situated on the right side of the stomach. It is dark brown in colour and divided into two lobes, varying in weight from 1.359 to 1.812 g. The *gall bladder* is attached to the liver and stores the bile produced by it (storage capacity: 30-60 ml). *Functions* The liver secretes bile, forms and stores glycogen, and plays an important role in the metabolism of proteins and fats. The liver is responsible for

(a) metabolism of the products of digestion,

(b) storage and release of substances (principally glucose) to maintain a constant level in blood,

(c) synthesis, conjugation and transformation *of* substances (e.g., formation of proteins, dioxication of poisonous substances, production of carbohydrates from proteins, etc.).

The *bile* produced by the liver is an important agent for digestion, especially fats. It contains water, bile salts and pigments. It does not contain digestive enzymes and as such, does not take part directly in digestion. It contains salts like bicarbonate, glycocholate and taurocholate of sodium. The sodium bicarbonate neutralizes the acid and makes the churned food called chyme alkaline whereas glycocholate and taurocholate of sodium break down the fats of tissues into small globules.

KIDNEY DISEASES

Acute renal failure is one of the primary diseases of the kidney. It is characterized by sudden failure of renal function so that little or no urine is produced, and water and waste products accumulate in the body. It may be caused by haemorrhage or shock leading to greatly decreased blood supply to the kidneys and resulting in renal necrosis (tissue death). A second cause is the accumulation of toxins in the kidney.

Inflammatory diseases of kidney (pyelonephritis, glomerulonephritis), high blood pressure, and obstruction of the lower urinary tract that can lead to chronic renal failure. In this disease there is progressive degeneration of the nephrons resulting in uranic poisoning from the accumulated wastes.

Both acute and chronic renal failure may be treated by dialysis, an artificial filtration of the blood through semi-permeable membranes to remove urea and other wastes, or by transplantation of the another human kidney from a donor.

The excretory tract is subject to benign and malignant tumours, infections and inflammations, and obstruction by calculi.

The kideny stones composed of inorganic substances, largely calcium phosphate, or oxalate or organic matter like uric acid.

REPRODUCTIVE SYSTEM

Reproduction is the production of a new generation of individuals of the same species. It is one of the fundamental characteristics of living organisms. It involves transmission of genetic material from one generation to the next, ensuring that the species survive over long periods of time, even though individual members of the species die. There are two basic types of reproduction, asexual and sexual.

Asexual Reproduction is reproduction by a single organism without production of gametes. It usually results in the production of genetically identical offspring, the only genetic variation arising as a result of random mutation among the individuals.

Sexual Reproduction is the fusion of two gametes to form a zygote, which develops into a new organism. It leads to genetic variation, which is advantageous to the species because it provides the raw material for natural selection and, therefore, evolution. Eventually, new species may form, the process known as speciation. Increased variation can be achieved by the mixing of genes from two different individuals, the process known as genetic recombination.

REPRODUCTION IN HUMAN

The male reproductive system consists of two testes each of which has two functional components : (i) *seminiferous tubules*, and (ii) *interstitial cells* or *leydig cells*.) suspended in the pouch of scrotum. The Scrotum have a paired duct system each consisting of *epididymis, vas deferens, ejaculatory duct* and *male urethra,* and *secondary sex organs* including a prostrate, two seminal vesicles, two Cowper's glands and a penis. **Testes produce sperms and secrete testosterone;** prostrate, seminal vesicles and Cowper's gland secrete fluids which mix with sperm to form semen; the duct system conducts the semen to the exterior.

The female reproductive system consists of *two ovaries*, and a duct system of *two fallopian tubes*, and *uterus and a vagina.* **Ovaries produce ova and secrete oestrogens and progesterone.** The fallopian tubes conduct the ovum towards the uterus; the uterus lodges the growing foetus and opens to the exterior through the vagina.

Gametogenesis is the formation of gametes for sexual reproduction. Gametogenesis is carried out in the *gonads*. The gametogenesis in male gonad is called *spermatogenesis*. It is the production of sperms in the testes. The gametogenesis in female gonad is called *oogenesis*. It is the formation of ova in the ovary.

Spermogenesis or transformation of spermatogonia (male germ cells present in seminiferous tubules) into spermatozoa occurs in seminiferous tubules in four stages: *(i) Proliferation phase :* In this stage the spermatogonial cells have diploid number *of* chromosomes (46 in man) which undergo several mitotic divisions to increase their number, *(ii) Growth phase:* The spermatogonia cells increase in the dimensions and are called primary, spermatocytes in this stage, *(iii) Maturation phase;* Primary spermatocytes undergoes first meiotic division to produce two smaller secondary spermatocytes and these two further divide to give four spermatids and; *(iv) Transformation phase;* The spermatid in this final stage acquires a tail and anterior acrosomal cap (head cap) and is transformed into spermatozoan.

Oogenesis is the transformation of oogonia (female germ cells) into ova. It takes place in the Graafian follicle of ovaries and is completed in the three stages: *(i) Proliferation phase:* The oogonia cells which have a diploid number of chromosomes undergo several mitotic divisions in the foetus upto six months; *(ii) Growth phase:* The oogonium increases in size and is transformed into a primary oocyte; and *(iii) Maturation phase:* The primary oocyte undergoes meiosis in two steps. The first reduction division leads to the formation of two unequal daughter cells-the larger constitute the secondary oocyte, whereas the smaller, consisting mainly of the nucleus, forms the first polar body, that subsequently degenerates. An ovum and a second polar body result from the second meiotic division or second maturation division prior to fertilization. Like the first, the second polar body also disintegrates after some time. Thus, a single mature cell is produced from one primary oocyte.

Menstrual Cycle

The reproductive cycle of human females and other higher primates differs from non-primates in two ways. First, the receptivity of the female is more or less continuous. Secondly, there is bleeding or menstruation phase which is not met within the non-primates.

Menstrual cycle occurs only when the released ovum is not fertilized. The lack of menstruation is indication of pregnancy, but some times it may be caused due to complexities.

In human females, the duration of the menstrual cycle is about 28 days with inner variations. This cycle is divided into four following phases :

Menstrual Phase

It lasts for 3-5 days during which blood is discharged out. The bleeding is caused by the rapid regression of the uterine lining, rupturing of its blood vessels and sloughing away of portions of endometrium. The day of the beginning of menstruation is counted as the first day of the menstrual cycle.

Proliferative Phase

During this phase, the uterine endometrium regenerates and becomes thickened-under the influence of the hormone, ***oestrogen***. This process lasts for about 10 days and extends from 6th to 14th day of the cycle.

The gonadotropins hormone (Luteinising hormone and follicular stimulating hormone) increase during this phase stimulate follicular development and secretion of esterogen by growing follicule. The luteinising hormone (LH) and follicular stimulating hormone (FSH) are at peak during the mid-cycle (14th day). The secretion of LH during the mid-cycle cause rupture of graafian follicle. This releases the ovum.

Ovulatory Phase

This normally occurs on the 14th day of the menstrual cycle and lasts for only 6 hours. During this phase, an ovum is released from the Graafian follicle (ovulation) to make its entry into the Fallopian tube.

Luteal Phase

After ovulation, the Graafian follicle is transformed into corpus luteum which secretes the hormone, ***progesterone***. As a result, the uterine glands get active and endometrium becomes more thick for implantation of the fertilized ovum. In the absence of fertilization, the menstrual cycle begins afresh.

The menstrual cycle ceases at age around 50 years. This is termed as *menopause*.

Fertilization and Embryo Development

During sexual union, the sperms are discharged into the vagina. Each discharge of semen contains millions of sperms. However, only one of them fuses with the ovum to fertilize it. The sperms deposited in the vagina swim up to the uterus and further up through the fallopian tubes where if a sperm meets an ovum, it fuses with it resulting into the formation of a zygote. The zygote moves down the oviduct, reaches the uterus and gets embedded in the endometrium on the 24th day of the menstrual cycle.

The zygote divides repeatedly to form an *embryo.* At first the embryo is nourished by the secretions of the uterus. But it soon implants itself into the uterine wall which has been prepared to receive it. The cells of the embryo now arrange themselves to form the three primary germs—layers, viz., the *outer ectoderm,* the *middle mesoderm* and the *inner endoderm,* which in course of time establish the different organs system of the body.

The implanted embryo soon develops two membranous coverings, an outer *chorion* and an inner *amnion.* The embryo lies within a pool of watery fluid contained in the amnion, and is therefore well-protected. The chorion in combination with another membrane, called the *allantois,* forms finger-like projection called *embryonic vilii,* These fit into corresponding depressions in the soft wall of the uterus. The maternal and embryonic tissues that come into intimate contact thus establish an important organ called *the placenta.* It is through this organ that materials are exchanged between the maternal and embryonic blood. The edges of the amnion come together and form the *umbilical cord,* which is a tube that connects the placenta with the digestive tract of the embryo. The umbilical cord contains blood vessels that transport materials between the placenta and the embryo. In the placenta, the maternal blood, the embryonic blood do not mix. Exchange of materials between the maternal blood and the embryonic blood takes place chiefly by diffusion through the membranes that separate them. With the growth of the embryo, the placenta also grows. Apart from serving as the respiratory, nutritive and excretory organs of the embryo, the placenta also serves as an important but temporary endocrine gland.

The process delivery of foetus (childbirth) is called *parturition.* The mammary gland of female during pregnancy undergo differentiation to produce milk towards the end of pregnancy. This is called *lactation.* The milk produced during the initial few days of lactation is called *colostrum.* It contains several antibodies which develop resistance to new born babies.

DIGESTIVE SYSTEM

DIGESTION IN HUMANS

The human digestive system consists of (1) the digestive tract, or the series of structures and organs through which food passes during its processing and (2) other organs that contribute juices necessary for the digestive process.

The digestive tract begins at the mouth and ends at the anus.

The Mouth

Ingestion and mastication, or chewing, takes place in the mouth with the help of teeth. The tongue helps to work the food into a ball or bolus so that it can be swallowed. When food is swallowed the soft palate closes the opening to the nasal cavity and the epiglottis closes the opening to the trachea. The bolus is pushed along the oesophagus to the stomach by *peristalsis.*

Teeth

Teeth is cone-shaped structure present in the mouth cavity. A teeth has following structure enamel. Dentine, neck, root and cementum.

Each teeth in human is embedded in a socket of jaw bone. This type of attachments is called **thecodont.** In frog teeth are not embedded in jaw but are the part of same bone. It is called **acrodont.** In human two set of teeth are produced during life time, this is called **diphyodont.** In adult human 32 teeth are of four different types (**Heterodont**) as incisors (I), canine (C), premolar (PM) and molar (M).

The Stomach

The stomach is a muscular bag in which a meal is temporarily stored. Its contents are passed on gradually to the small intestine. *Peristalsis* (type of movement) helps to mix the food with gastric juice, and so turn it into a watery paste called *chyme.* The mucous helps to protect the stomach wall from its own secretions of hydrochloric acid and pepsin. Some absorption of small molecules such as glucose, salt, alcohol takes place in the stomach.

The Small Intestine

The first, slightly wider part of the small intestine is called the *duodenum.* The duodenum is about 25 cm long. The middle part of intestine is called *jejunum* which is about 8 feet long. The *ileum*, is the longest part of the gut. The ileum is about 12 feet long. The later stages of digestion takes place in the small intestine. The walls of the ileum produce intestinal juice, and the digestive processes of the duodenum continue for a time in the ileum. Bile and pancreatic juice is also emptied into the duodenum. Nearly all the absorption of digested materials takes place through the wall of the ileum through the villi.

Large Intestine or Colon

Large intestine is about 5 feet long. The contents of the intestine contain a high proportion of water. The walls of the large intestine absorb much of this water, so it is not lost from the body. The semi-solids which remain are called faeces. They are stored in large intestine and passed out at intervals through the anus. Faeces is a mixture of substances which include undigested food, mainly the cellulose cell wall of plants and dead bacteria and mucous and dead cells from the gut walls. The cells lining the gut have a limited life. They are constantly dying or wearing away and being renewed. Surplus bile and other secretions colour the faeces. The walls of the colon absorb vitamin K which is synthesised by some intestinal bacteria.

Function of Liver

The liver is found only in vertebrates. Liver is about 1.5 kg. It is the largest gland of body. The liver stores carbohydrate as glycogen, lipids, mineral salts, vitamins A, D, and B_{12}. The liver helps to keep the blood sugar (glucose) level constant, which in turn helps to keep the osmotic pressure of the blood constant. The liver synthesize a variety of products. These include most of the *plasma proteins* and *bile.* Bile is stored in the gall bladder and passed into the duodenum to help in digestion. Bile contains salts which help in emulsification of fats and absorption of food. The liver converts toxins into harmless substances. Many of the toxic by-products of the body's own metabolism are made harmless in the liver. Example : the conversion of nitrogenous waste products to urea.

Absorption

About 90 per cent of digested food and 10 per cent of water and minerals are absorbed by the small intestine. In order to enhance the absorption capacity of the small intestine its epithilial lining is thrown into a number of folds called *villi.* The membrane of each villus is further folded into a number of smaller *microvilli.* The villi have a rich supply of blood capillaries. Simple sugars and amino acids are absorbed, through the intestinal wall into the blood capillaries. These are then carried by the portal vein to the liver before release into general circulation. The glycerides and fatty acids are transported usually, via the lymph vessels (lacteals) and thoracic duct to the blood. Absorption in stomach occurs only to a limited extent. The large intestine absorbs much of the residual water from undigested food.

HORMONAL CONTROL OF DIGESTION IN HUMAN

The activities of gastrointestinal (GI) tract are coordinated by nervous and endocrine systems of the body. Gastrointestinal peptide hormones are the hormones secreted by the endocrine cells found scattered in the mucosa of stomach and intestine. These hormones regulate the digestive activities. Most of the gastrointestinal hormones are "local hormones" as act upon the same part of gut which secrete them.

Enzymes

An enzyme is a protein which acts as a catalyst in the metabolism of an organism.

Characteristics

All enzymes are proteins and share common properties. They form colloidal solution and are of high molecular weight; (ii) enzymes catalyse every chemical reaction that occurs in the living system; (iii) enzymes generally accelerate biochemical reaction by reducing the energy requirement (activation energy); (iv) enzymes are sensitive to change in pH in the reactions medium; (v) enzymes are specific in their action; (vi) many enzymes cannot act on their own and require the help of some substances called activators for their activation; (vii) certain substances called inhibitors slow down the rate of enzymatic reaction; (viii) most enzymes can work in either direction.

SENSE ORGANS

THE EYE

Structure of the eye

The eye is the organ of the sense of sight situated in the orbital cavity. It is almost spherical in shape and is about 2.5 cm in diameter. It is possible to see with only one eye but three – dimensional vision is impaired when only one eye is used. There are 3 layers of tissue in the wall of the eye.

They are:

1. The outer fibrous layer : sclera & cornea
2. The middle vascular layer : choroid, ciliary body and iris.
3. The inner nervous tissue layer : retina.

Structures inside the eye ball are the lens, aqueous fluid (humour) and vitreous body.

Sclera and Cornea

The sclera is the white of the eye and forms the outermost layer of the eyeball and anteriorly is continuous with the cornea. The sclera maintains the shape of the eyeball.

The cornea is a clear transparent membrane. Light rays pass through the cornea to reach the retina. The cornea is convex anteriorly and refracts or bends light rays to focus them on to the retina.

Choroid

The choroid is the middle layer and rich in blood vessels and is a deep chocolate brown in colour.

Ciliary body

This consists of muscle fibres and epithelial cells. It is located anterior to the choroid. It is attached to the suspensory ligament which in turn is attached to the capsule enclosing the lens.

Contraction and relaxation of the ciliary muscle changes the thickness of the lens which refracts light rays entering the eye to focus them on the retina. The epithelial cells secrete aqueous fluid into the anterior segment of the eye. i.e. the space between the lens and the cornea.

Iris

The iris extends anteriorly from the ciliary body and lies behind the cornea and in front of the lens. It is a circular body composed of pigment cells that gives the eye its black, brown, grey or green colour. In the centre there is an opening called the pupil.

Pupil varies in size depending upon the intensity of light. In bright light the pupil constricts. In dim light the pupil dilates.

Lens

The lens is a highly elastic, circular, biconvex, transparent body, lying immediately behind the pupil. The thickness of the lens is controlled by the ciliary muscle through the suspensory ligament. It is enclosed within a transparent capsule. The lens bends light rays reflected by objects.

Retina

The retina is the innermost layer of the wall of the eye. It is extremely delicate. It is composed of several layers of nerve cells and nerve fibres. The retina has a layer highly sensitive to light, containing cells called rods and cones.

The rods and cones contain photosensitive pigments that convert light rays into nerve impulses. The rods are for light vision. The cones are for colour vision.

The rods contain rhodopsin (visual purple) a pigment which is bleached in dim light. Vitamin A is needed for its synthesis.

Near the centre of the posterior part there is an area which appears yellow in colour called macula lutea. In the centre of this area there is a little depression called fovea centralis which consists of only cone-shaped cells.

About 0.5 cm away from the macula lutea, all the nerve fibres of the retina converge to form the optic nerve. The small area of the retina where the optic nerve leaves the eye is the optic disc or blind spot.

Chambers of the eye

In the anterior segment of the eye, the space between the cornea and the lens is incompletely divided into anterior and posterior chambers by the iris. Both chambers contain a clear aqueous fluid (humour) secreted into the chambers by the ciliary glands.

Behind the lens and filling the cavity of the eyeball is the vitreous body (humour). This is a soft, colourless, transparent, jelly-like substance composed of 99% water and some salts.

The fluid in both the chambers help to maintain the shape of the eyeball.

PHYSIOLOGY OF VISION

In order to achieve clear vision, light reflected from objects is focused onto the retina of both eyes. The processes involved in producing a clear image are:

1. Refraction of the light rays

2. Changing size of the pupils and

3. Accommodation of the eyes.

A co-ordination of these three processes is necessary for effective vision.

1. Refraction of the light rays

When light rays pass from a medium of one density to a medium of a different density they are refracted or bent. This principle is used to focus light on the retina. Before reaching the retina light rays pass successively through the conjunctiva, cornea, aqueous fluid, lens and vitreous body.

The lens is the only structure in the eye that can change its refractive power. Light rays entering the eye need to be bent to focus them on the retina. To focus light rays coming from near objects onto the retina the lens changes itself to a more convex shape with the aid of suspensory ligament and ciliary muscle. The relaxing of the ciliary muscle makes the lens thinner and thereby focuses light rays from distant objects on the retina.

2. Size of the pupils

The size of the pupil controls the amount of light entering the eye. In bright light pupils are constricted. In dim light they are dilated.

The iris consists of one layer of circular and one layer of radiating muscle fibres. Contraction of the circular fibre constricts the pupil. Contraction of the radiating fibres dilates it.

3. Accommodation of the eyes to light

Accommodation is the process whereby light emerging from distant as well as near sources is brought to focus on the retina. In order to focus on near objects within 6 metres, the eye should make the following adjustments.

They are:

1. Constriction of the pupils

2. Convergence of the eyeballs

3. Changing the power of the lens

Objects more than 6 metres away from the eyes are focused on the retina without adjustment of the lens or convergence of the eyes.

Functions of the Retina

Light rays falling on the retina causes chemical changes in the photosensitive pigments in the rods and cones. This generates nerve impulses which are conducted to the cerebrum via the optic nerves. The rods are stimulated by dim light and are necessary for night vision.

The cones are sensitive to bright light and colour. Visual purple (rhodopsin) is a photosensitive pigment present only in the rods. It is bleached (degraded) by bright light and is quickly regenerated when an adequate supply of vitamin A is available. This is the visual cycle.

Dark adaptation : When an individual moves into a darkened area where the light intensity is insufficient to stimulate the cones, temporary visual impairment results while the rhodopsin is being regenerated within the rods. When regeneration of rhodopsin occurs, normal sight returns.

Refractive errors of the eye

In the normal eye (emetropic) light from near and distant objects is focused on the retina.

Hypermetropia (Farsightedness) : A near image is focused behind the retina because the eyeball is too short. A biconvex lens is used to correct this.

Myopia (nearsightedness) : The eyeball is too long and distant objects are focused in front of the retina. A biconcave lens is used to correct this.

Astigmatism : This results in blurred vision when there is abnormal curvature of part of the cornea or lens that prevents focusing on the retina. Cylindrical lenses are used to correct this.

THE EAR

The ear is the organ of hearing. It is supplied by the eighth cranial nerve, i.e., the cochlear part of the vestibulocochlear nerve which is stimulated by vibrations caused by sound waves.

With the exception of the auricle (pinna), the structures that form the ear are encased within the temporal bone.

Structure

The ear is divided into three distinct parts.

1. External ear
2. Middle ear (tympanic cavity)
3. Internal ear

External Ear

The external ear consists of the auricle (pinna) and the external acoustic meatus.

The auricle

The auricle is the expanded portion projecting from the side of the head. It is composed of fibroelastic cartilage covered with skin. It is deeply grooved and ridged and the most prominent outer ridge is the helix.

The lobule is the soft pliable part at the lower extreme composed of fibrous and adipose tissue richly supported with blood capillaries.

External acoustic meatus

This is a slightly 'S'-shaped tube about 2.5 cm long extending from the auricle to the tympanic membranes (ear drum). The lateral third is cartilaginous and the remainder is a canal in the temporal bone. The meatus is lined with a thin layer of skin, continuous with that of the auricle. There are numerous ceruminous glands in the skin of the lateral third. These are modified sweat glands that secretes cerumin (wax), a sticky material. Foreign materials, e.g., dust, insects and microbes, are prevented from reaching the tympanic membrane by wax, hairs and the curvature of the meatus. Movements of the temporomandibular joint during chewing and speaking 'massage' the cartilaginous meatus, moving the wax towards the exterior.

The tympanic membrane completely separates the external acoustic meatus from the middle ear. It is oval-shaped with the slightly broader edge upwards and is formed by three types of tissue:

1. The outer covering of hairless skin
2. The middle layer of fibrous tissue
3. The inner lining of mucous membrane which is continuous with that of middle ear.

Tympanic Cavity or Middle Ear

This is an irregular – shaped cavity within the temporal bone. The cavity, its contents and the air sacs which open out of it are lined with mucous membrane. Air fills the cavity, reaching it through the eustachian (auditory) tube which extends from the nasopharynx. It is about 4 cm long and is lined with ciliated epithelium. The presence of air at atmospheric pressure on both sides of the tympanic membrane enables it to vibrate when sound waves strike it.

The lateral wall of the middle ear is formed by the tympanic membrane.

The roof and floor are formed by the temporal bone.

The medial wall is a thin layer of temporal bone in which there are two openings:

1. Oval window (fenestra vestibule)

2. Round window (fenestra cochleae)

The oval window is occluded by part of a small bone called the stapes and the round window, by a fine sheet of fibrous tissue.

Auditory ossicles

These are three very small bones that extend across the cavity from the tympanic membrane to the oval window. They form a series of movable joints with each other and with the medial wall of the cavity at the oval window.

They are the malleus, incus and stapes.

The malleus is the lateral hammer – shaped bone. The handle is in contact with the tympanic membrane and the head forms a movable joint with the incus.

The incus is the middle anvil-shaped bone. Its body articulates with the malleus, the long process with the stapes, and it is stabilized by the short process, fixed by fibrous tissue to the posterior wall of the cavity.

The stapes is the medial stirrup-shaped bone. Its head articulates with the incus and its base fits into the oval window. The three ossicles are held in position by fine ligaments.

Internal Ear

The internal ear contains the organs of hearing and balance and is generally described in two parts, the bony labyrinth and the membranous labyrinth.

a. Bony labyrinth

This is a cavity within the temporal bone lined with periosteum. It is larger than the membranous labyrinth of the same shape which fits into it, like a tube within a tube. The space between the bony walls and the membranous tube is occupied by perilymph. The membranous labyrinth also contains fluid, the endolymph.

The bony labyrinth consists of:

1 vestibule

1 cochlea

3 semicircular canals

The vestibule is the expanded part nearest to the middle ear. It contains the oval and round windows.

The cochlea resembles a snail's shell. It has a broad base where it is continuous with the vestibule and a narrow apex, and it spirals round a central bony column. The cochlea is divided by a septum called basilar membrane.

The semicircular canals are three tubes arranged so that one is situated in each of the three planes of space. They are continuous with the vestibule. One end of each canal is dilated to form ampulla. The semicircular canals are the organs of equilibrium.

(b) Membranous labyrinth

The membranous labyrinth is the same shape as its bony counterpart and is separated from it by perilymph. It contains endolymph. It is divided into the same parts: the vestibule which contains the utricle and saccule, the cochlea and three semicircular canals. The utricle and saccule are oval membranous sacs. A cross-section shows the triangular shape of the membranous cochlea. Neuroepithelial cells and nerve fibres lie on the basilar membrane or base of the triangle. Many of the neuroepithelial cells are long and narrow and are arranged side by side. These cells are called hair cells and their nerve fibres from the true organ of hearing, the organ of Corti. The hair cells are attached to a thin membrane called tectorial membrane. The nerve fibres combine to form the auditory part of the vestibulocochlear nerve (eighth cranial nerve), which passes through a foramen in the temporal bone to reach the hearing area in the temporal lobe of the cerebrum.

Physiology of Hearing

Every sound produces sound waves or disturbances in the air, which travel at about 332 metres (1088) feet per second. The auricle, because of its shape, concentrates the waves and directs them along the auditory meatus causing the tympanic membrane to vibrate.

Tympanic membrane vibrations are transmitted through the middle ear by movement of the ossicles. At their medial end the footplate of the stapes rock to and fro in the oval window, setting up fluid waves in the perilymph. These indent the membranous labyrinth and the wave motion in the endolymph stimulates the neuroepithelial cells of the organ of Corti. The nerve impulses produced pass to the brain in the cochlear portion of the eighth cranial nerve (VIII). The fluid wave is finally expended into the middle ear by vibration of the membrane of the round window. This nerve, the vestibulocochlear nerve, transmits the impulse to various nuclei in the pons varolii and midbrain. Some of the nerve fibres pass to the hearing area in the cerebral cortex where sound is perceived.

Semicircular Canals

The semicircular canals have no auditory function although they are closely associated with the cochlea. They provide information about the position of the head in space, contributing to maintenance of equilibrium and balance.

There are three semicircular canals, one lying in each of the three planes of space. They are situated above and behind the vestibule of the inner ear and open into it.

Structure of the semircular canals

The semicircular canals, like the cochlea are composed of an outer bony wall and inner membranous tubes or ducts. The membranous ducts contain endolymph and are separated from the bony wall by perilymph.

The utricle is a membranous sac which is part of the vestibule and the three membranous ducts open into it at their dilated ends, the ampullae. The saccule is a part of the vestibule and communicates with the utricle and the cochlea.

In the walls of the utricle, saccule and ampullae there are fine specialized epithelial cells with minute projections, called hair cells. Amongst the hair cells there are the minute nerve endings of the vestibular part of the vestibulocochlear nerve.

Functions of the semicircular canal

The semicircular canals, utricle and saccule are concerned with balance. Any change of position of the head causes movement in the perilymph and endolymph which stimulates the nerve endings and the hair cells in the utricle, saccule and ampullae. The resultant nerve impulses are transmitted by the vestibular nerve to the cerebellum.

The cerebellum also receives nerve impulses from the eyes and the muscles and joints. Impulses from these three sources are coordinated and efferent nerve impulses pass to the cerebrum where position in space is perceived, and to muscles to maintain posture and balance.

ENDOCRINE GLAND

The glands of the body may be divided into those with an external secretion (exocrine glands) and those with an internal secretion (endocrine glands). Example of exocrine glands are the sweat, Lachrymal and mammary glands which pass their secretion along the ducts to the external surface of the body and the glands of the mouth, stomach, and intestine which pass their secretions along ducts into the alimentary tract. The endocrine or ductless gland on the other hand have no ducts or openings to the exterior. The secretions are passed directly into the blood stream and transmitted to the tissues.

A hormone is a chemical substance produced by the endocrine glands and their overall function is to regulate the activities of various body organs and their functions. The first hormone was discovered by Bayliss in 1903.

The main endocrine glands in the body are :

1. Thyroid
2. Parathyroid
3. Islets of Langerhans
4. Adrenal gland
5. Pituitary and
6. Sex glands

THYROID GLAND

The largest of the endocrine glands is the thyroid, which is located in the neck region. The thyroid gland weighs 25 gms in a healthy adult. It has two oval parts called the lateral lobes on either side of the trachea. These two lobes are connected by a narrow band called isthumus. The entire gland is enclosed by a connective tissue capsule. This gland produces hormone, thyroxine rich in iodine.

Thyroid gets iodine from the blood stream. Iodine is formed by the reduction of iodide. It is then fixed with the amino acid tyrosine to form mono and di-iodo-tyrosine compounds. Two molecules of diiodo-tyrosine combine to form thyroxine. By eating vegetables grown in iodine-containing soils or by eating sea-foods and iodised salt our diet will have enough iodine necessary for the production of thyroxine. Thyroid stimulating hormone (TSH) produced by the anterior pituitary lobe increases the activity of thyroid gland. Whenever the thyroxine level falls below a particular level TSH is stimulated,

Functions of Thyroxine

1. Helps to regulate tissue growth and development.
2. Increases the B M R and thus raises the body temperature.
3. It controls the metabolism by regulating the anabolic and catabolic process.
4. Stimulates the cells to break down proteins for energy.
5. Decreases the breakdown of fats.
6. Increases the breakdown of body glucose and enhances the glucose absorption.
7. Calcium and phosphorus are removed from the bones and excreted in increased amounts.
8. Helps in the conversion of Beta-carotene into vitamin A.

Thyroid Disorders

It is of 3 types. They are:

1. Hypothyroidism
2. Hyperthyroidism
3. Simple goitre.

Hypothyroidism

It results due to lack of thyroid hormone secretion. It results in cretinism in children and myxoedema in adults.

Cause of Hypothyroidism

1. Failure or arrest of normal development of thyroid gland.
2. Failure to form genetic enzymes normally.
3. Deficiency of iodine in the body.
4. Administration of antithyroid drugs in excess.
5. After surgical removal of thyroid gland.

The Chief Features of Cretinism are as follows

1. Stunted growth
2. Broad nose
3. Thick lips
4. Lobling tongue
5. Muddy dry skin
6. Milestones of development in children get delayed e.g., Holding up the head, sitting, standing, walking gets delayed.
7. BMR is depressed.

This disease can be cured if thyroxine or iodine is administered sufficiently.

In adults hypothyrodism causes myxodema which is more common among females than in males.

The Chief features of hypothyrodism in adults (Myxoedema)

1. Decreased BMR
2. Sexual dysfunction
3. Lack of energy
4. Lack of memory
5. Loss of hair
6. Dullness
7. Loss of appetite
8. Slow heart rate
9. Gain in weight
10. Puffy face due to tissue fluid retention.

Hyperthyroidism

Occurs due to the excessive secretion or over action of thyroxine.

Symptoms of Hyperthyroidism

1. Enlargement of thyroid gland results in the protrusion of eye ball from the orbit.
2. Flushed skin and high temperature
3. Increased O_2 consumption and CO_2 output
4. Tendency to lose weight
5. The pulse and heart rate are high
6. Nervousness and irritability
7. Low resistance to withstand stress and strain
8. High blood pressure
9. Mild diabetes
10. Emotional restlessness

The clinical condition of hyperthyroidism is exophthalmic goitre in which the thyroid gland is usually enlarged and there is characteristic protrusion of eye balls from the orbit.

Simple Goiter

A lack of dietary iodine may cause endemic goiter. Thyroid gland is enlarged and has increased number of follicles. This leads to low level of thyroid hormone in the blood, and derangement of body functions.

PARATHYROID GLAND

These are two tiny oval pairs (6mm x 2m) of glands situated at upper and lower poles of lateral lobes of thyroid gland. It secretes the hormone, parathyroxine.

Functions of Parathyroxine

1. Increases the concentration of organic acid in the bone.
2. Increases the calcium and phosphorus solubility
3. Increases the reabsorption of calcium from the bones resulting in increased serum calcium level.
4. Increases phosphate excretion in the urine.
5. Increases the reabsorption of calcium from the renal tubules.
6. Promotes the absorption of calcium and phosphorus from the intestine.
7. Stimulates the process of lactation in mammary gland.

Deficiency of Parathyroxine

1. Serum calcium level falls.
2. Blood reaction is more alkaline owing to excessive loss of CO_2.
3. Decalcification of bones.
4. Increase in the heart and respiration rate.
5. Rise in body temperature.
6. General mental depression.
7. Tendency to cataract formation.
8. Under development of teeth.
9. Brittleness of nails.
10. Dryness of skin.
11. Lowered general resistance.
12. Nervous irritability.
13. Twitching of muscles causing Tetany.

Tetany is a condition, in which there is hyperexcitability of nervous system with intermittent tonic spasms of muscles chiefly of the limbs, face, and back of the neck. When the small muscles of hands are affected, the hand is held in the same position. It is known as Carpo - Pedal spasms. When the laryngeal muscle are affected laryngeal spasm is seen. If tetany is not treated it may lead to paralysis of respiratory muscle and cardiac arrest. Finally death may occur.

ISLETS OF LANGERHANS IN THE PANCREAS

The Pancreas is both an exocrine gland secreting digestive juice through a duct into the duodenum and an endocrine gland secreting hormone into the blood stream. It consists of head, body and tail. The head fits into the curve of duodenum The body and tail are directed towards the left. The pancreatic islets represents the endocrine part of the pancreas. Most of the islets are located in the tail and only a small number in the head of the pancreas. There are two different types of cells in the islets of langerhans. The alpha cells and beta cells are very important. The alpha cells secrete a hormone Glucagon whereas the beta cells secrete insulin.

Functions of Glucagon

1. Increases the blood glucose level
2. Breaks down the liver glycogen into glucose.
3. Stimulates the break down of lipid in adipose tissue.

Functions of Insulin

1. Converts glucose into glycogen and accelerates the transport of glucose from the blood into the cells.
2. Decreases the blood sugar level.
3. Builds up the glycogen store in the liver.

Deficiency of Insulin

Hyposecretion of insulin results in Diabetes mellitus. It is caused due to elevated blood sugar level. This condition is known as hyperglycemia. This condition leads to the condition 'glycosuria' in which sugar is excreted in the urine. Carbohydrates as well as protein and fat metabolism are affected in the diabetics.

Symptoms of diabetes are:

1. Excessive thirst, hunger and urination
2. Loss of weight.
3. Weakness, restlessness and fatigue.
4. Decreased resistance to infection.
5. Itching of the genitals.

Diabetes can be kept under check by taking a high protein and low carbohydrate diet. If Diabetes cannot be controlled by diet alone, insulin must be administered by injection.

ADRENAL GLAND

The adrenal or supra renals are two small glands each one situated above a kidney. Adrenal gland consists of two different parts each of which acts as a separate gland. The inner area is called the medulla which is brown in colour while the outer area is called the cortex which is lighter in colour.

Adrenal Cortex

It is composed of three layers. They are (a) Zona glomerulosa (outer layer) (b) Zona fasciculata (middle layer) and (c) Zona reticularis (inner layer).

The adrenal cortex secretes three hormones. They are:

1. **Glucocorticoids :** Acts as antagonists to insulin and cause increase in blood sugar.
2. **Mineralocorticoids:** Acts on sodium and potassium and help in the conservation of sodium in the body.
3. **Sexsteroids :** Stimulates the development of the reproductive organs in childhood. It is responsible for development of secondary sex characteristics and reproductive function.

Functional insufficiency of the adrenal cortex and tuberculosis of the adrenal gland gives rise to Addison's disease. Its early signs are dark pigmentation of the skin, especially of the hands, neck and face, anemia, loss of energy, weakness, decreased appetite, nausea, and vomiting. Patients are very sensitive to cold and pain and susceptible to infections. This can be treated by administering the hormone in combination with a diet high in sodium and low in potassium.

Over activity of adrenal cortex increases the secretion of this hormone, and sexsteroids, this results in an acute change of secondary sex characteristics. For example, female may develop male secondary characteristics like growth of beard, low pitch of the voice, lack of menstruation and male may develop female secondary sex characteristics.

Adrenal Medulla

Adrenal medulla secretes two hormones. They are Adrenalin and Nor-adrenaline.

Functions of Medullary Hormones

1. Dilation of the pupils and improves visual acuity.

2. Increases both rate and amplitude of contraction of heart and raises the cardiac output.

3. Increases both rate and amplitude of respiratory movements and causes dilation of the bronchioles.

4. Raises the blood sugar level by means of glycogenolysis.

5. Increases the Basal Metabolic Rate and thus raises the body temperature.

6. Dilation of the walls of intestine and the urinary bladder.

The functions of adrenalin are similar to that of Nor-adrenalin except in a few instances. For example, adrenalin increases the heart rate whereas Nor-adrenalin decreases heart rate.

PITUITARY GLAND

The pituitary is a small gland about the size of a cherry. It is situated at the base of the brain. It plays a peculiar role in the system of endocrine glands. It is referred to as the 'master' gland of internal secretion because it controls the activities of other endocrine glands.

The pituitary gland is divided into two main parts (1) Anterior pituitary and (2) Posterior pituitary.

The Anterior Pituitary

This part secretes a large number of hormones. Many of them stimulate other glands. Its main hormones are:

1. **Growth Hormone:** It facilitates the growth of the bone and cartilage tissue. Over activity of the anterior pituitary lobe in childhood results in excessive growth and height. This condition is known an gigantism. A decreased activity of the anterior pituitary causes a severe growth retardation leading to dwarfism.

Excessive production of growth hormone in an adult leads to excessive development of certain regions such as fingers and toes, feet, hands, nose, lower jaw, tongue, thoracic and abdominal organs. This condition is known as acromegaly.

2. **Thyrotropic Hormone (TSH):** This hormone stimulates the activity of the thyroid gland. Administration of this hormone causes overgrowth of thyroid tissue.

3. **Adreno Cortico Tropic Hormone: (ACTH):** This hormone stimulates the cortex of the adrenal gland and increases the production of the hormones of adrenal cortex.

4. **Follicle Stimulating Hormone (FSH):** This hormone influences the growth, development and maturation of the vesicular follicles in the ovary. In males, the hormone stimulates the formation of sperm in the testes.

5. **Lactogenic Hormone:** It acts on the mammary gland and helps in the formation and flow of milk during lactation.

6. **Luteinising Hormone:** It is required for the growth of follicle in the ovary and stimulates ovulation. In the absence of the hormone, no ovulation and production of the corpus luteum can occur. In males it stimulates the interstitial cells of testes to secrete testosterone.

Posterior Lobe of the Pituitary

This lobe is just behind the anterior lobe, it produces two hormones-Oxytocin and Vasopressin.

Oxytocin acts on the smooth muscles especially that of the uterus and produces powerful contractions of the uterus and helps in parturition. Vasopressin acts on the smooth muscle of the arterial system and increases the blood pressure. This hormone helps in the reabsorption of water from the distal convoluted tubule. Vasopressin deficiency is the cause of diabetes insipidus in which water is not reabsorbed. So great amounts of urine are excreted with no sugar in it. Such patients feel constantly thirsty.

The Sex Glands

The sex glands including the ovaries of the female and the testis of the male are important endocrine structures. The secretion of these glands play an important part in the development of the sexual characteristics. The male sex gland secretes hormone called testosterone and is responsible for secondary sex characteristics. The female sex gland secretes a hormone called estrogen and it stimulates the development and functioning of the female reproductive organs.

There is one other hormone produced by the female sex glands and it is called progesterone. This hormone assists in normal development of pregnancy.

—————————

FAMILY 8

DEFINITION

Family is universal and typically consists of a married man and woman and their children. Family means a group of related people who share a common home. Members belong to a family through birth, marriage or adoption.

Three characteristics of family emerge from here. These are, a couple is married and hence has legitimate status to sexual relationship between husband and wife. Second, it implies a common place of residence for all its members. Of course, it is seen that sometimes one or more members of a family may temporarily live away from the house for reasons of work or otherwise. Similarly, some members like old and aged parents/uncles/aunts or even cousin may stay with the family and are considered a part of the family.

Thirdly, a family consists of not just the married couple but also children, both natural and adopted. Natural children are those born to the couple and others may be legally adopted by the couple.

Clearly, therefore, the family is the first organized unit of a society. Now let us find out the functions of a family.

Functions of a Family

There are several important functions which a family performs.

(i) It gives protection: Indeed, it provides the best setting for the rearing and care of newborns and infants, adolescents, the sick and the infirm or aged.

(ii) It provides emotional support of a degree and kind that is not available otherwise. Such bonding is indispensable for the healthy development of children. In fact, the family is the primary group which allows intimacy and affection to be freely expressed.

(iii) It educates its members, who learn to live life in the setting of a family. Children are taught the do's and don'ts of the society, how to interact with others, respect and obey elders, etc.

(iv) It provides financial security. Basic needs such as of food, shelter, clothing are provided for members and they share responsibilities and work.

(v) It acts as a source of recreation. A family can be a source of happiness, where members can talk to one another, play and do various activities together. These may range from house-hold work to celebration of festivals and other events like birth, engagement or marriage.

(vi) Family also performs the function of socializing children. Parents give their children the first lessons in how to live with other people, to love, share, help in time of need and take on responsibilities. The family nurtures attitudes and values in children and influences their habits. Traditional skills are also picked up within the family. The family also prepares its young members to get formal education in school and beyond.

(vii) Family also fulfills the sexual function which is a biological need of every human being.

(viii) Reproductive function is fulfilled as a result of sexual relationship between married man and woman. Children so born are the future members of the society.

TYPES OF FAMILY

1. Joint Family

2. Nuclear Family

A great deal of importance is attached to the family as a unit. In our country, Indian families, generally, are very stable and child-centered. Let us learn about the characteristics of both joint and nuclear families.

Joint Family is made of a combination of nuclear families, and consequently it is much larger. It is made up of a man and his wife, their unmarried daughters, married sons, their wives and children. The men are of the same family and women enter the family by marriage. However, where the woman is the head of the family, it is the mean who enter the family through marriage. It is a group of more than one or even two generations living together.

Typical characteristics of a joint family therefore, are as follows

(i) All member live under the same roof.

(ii) Members eat food cooked in a common kitchen.

(iii) Members are co-owners of property of the family. The eldest male member of the joint family looks after the finances and the property i.e., there is a common purse.

(iv) Members participate in common family events, festivals and religious ceremonies.

(v) Daughters of the family get married and move out to their husband's house while sons remain in the house with their wives and children.

(vi) The decision making power in a joint family is with eldest adult male member. The eldest woman also plays a role in decision making but in a subtle way.

Traditionally, joint families used to be the rule in our society. Things are changing now especially in urban areas. However, the joint family system still continues in agricultural and business families.

There are several advantages of a joint family:

● It encourages family members to be co-operative and accommodating. Work, especially agricultural work, can be shared.

● It allows for the old, the helpless and the unemployed in the family to be looked after and cared for.

● Rearing of small children becomes easier, especially when both parents work.

● A child gets emotional and economic support in the event of the death of a parent.

● There is greater financial security.

Joint families also have their problems.

● Women are sometimes badly and unequally treated.

● Often disputes arise among the members over property or the running of a business.

● Some of the women have to do all the housework, and they get very little time or opportunity to develop their personality.

The Nuclear family is usually a small unit made up of the husband, the wife and their unmarried children. Sometimes a brother or unmarried sister of the husband may be living with them. This would be an extended family.

There are some advantages of living in a nuclear family:

● Members of a nuclear family are generally more independent and show greater initiative and selfreliance.

● The children are frequently encouraged to make decisions. This increases their self-confidence.

● Deeper emotional ties develop among the members. This is on account of the greater privacy and also opportunities for mutual interaction which are available in a nuclear family.

● It is seen that as a society becomes more industrialised and urbanized, the incidence of nuclear families increases.

● One of the foremost reasons for families to be nuclear, especially in big cities is housing problem. Larger families need larger space to live in. If families have to live conveniently there is little option but to stick to a "nuclear" family.

Disadvantages of a Nuclear Family

- There is no adult support to the young couple. No experienced person of the family is readily available for advice.

- When both the parents are working no one from the family is there to take care of children.

- In case of adversity there is no one to support the family financially or emotionally.

- Social values like 'adjustment', sharing or cooperation are difficult to learn.

CHANGING FAMILY SCENARIO

As we have said earlier, industrialization has brought about many changes in the type of family and as a result, in the roles and responsibilities of members of a family. So far, in a traditional family, the sons 'took on' the family business or profession. The father or male members used to earn the money and were responsible for the 'outside' work. The women looked after the home and the children.

Now children, boy or girl, are more educated and have greater and better opportunity for jobs. They leave their home to work elsewhere, most often to urban areas from rural areas and suburbs. This has resulted in more nuclear families. Because of smaller families, requirements of the family have changed, for example ration requirements are less and also different because the number of people at home are less.

Being on their own, women have a greater responsibility of looking after the home and outside work. Similarly, the men also have to help out at homes looking after the children, etc. In some cases women have taken up jobs outside the house and have the added responsibility of earning and looking after the home and children.

The children too have to be more self-reliant and have to do their share of work at home.

Family life was earlier rigidly patriarchal, where children and wives had few rights and privileges and were not free to voice an opinion. It is now undergoing a change.

In the modern home women have greater freedom and social importance. The children too have rights of their own. Their interests and desires have to be considered. They also are able to voice their opinion on family matters which concern them. Duties, which are divided in a joint family because of presence of grand parents, uncles, aunts and siblings become concentrated with the parents.

As the nuclear family is far away from the rest of the family and relatives, the larger community of neighbours, colleagues, friends etc. become important. The family members need to adjust and adapt to them harmoniously.

EMBROIDERY   9

MEANING OF EMBROIDERY

Embroidery is the art of creating decorative effects on the surface of a fabric using designs and stitches made with the help of needle and thread. It can be beautifully described as a painting with needle and thread. Our museums contain beautiful pieces of work from all over the world, each of them different but still sharing a similarity with regard to the use of basic stitches and techniques. Some of the famous traditional Indian embroideries are:

- Phulkari of Punjab
- Kantha of Bengal
- Kasuti of Karnataka
- Chikankari of Uttar Pradesh
- Zardozi of Kashmir
- Sindhi and Kutchi of Gujarat

Remember, these are only a few examples, there are many more embroideries which are created in our country. Do visit the Crafts Museum of Pragati Maidan, whenever you come to Delhi.

EQUIPMENT AND MATERIALS USED FOR EMBROIDERY

(a) **Hand sewing needles:** A good embroidery needle is the most important thing required for embroidery. Use a finer needle for a delicate fabric and vice versa. The needle should be slightly thicker than the sewing thread so that it makes a sufficiently big hole in the fabric for the thread to pass easily. Needles should always have a fine tip so that they can easily move in and out of the fabric. Do not use a needle which is bent, without a point or rusty. This will affect the regularity and neatness of work.

(b) **Thimble:** This is small light weight metallic piece which fits snugly on the middle finger of the needle holding hand. It protects the finger from getting injured with the needle while pushing it into the cloth. Thimbles come in different sizes.

(c) **Scissors:** Embroidery scissors are small, with sharp, narrow, pointed blades. Protect the blade by keeping them in a sheath or cover and get them sharpened occasionally. These are used to cut and neaten the loose ends of thread. Now-a-days thread clippers are also available. These appear like small scissors or like tweezers with sharp edges, which help in cutting the thread neatly.

(d) **Threads for embroidery:** Thread is a very important feature of embroidery. There are a variety of threads available in the market. Different types are used for different kinds of embroidery. The kind of thread used also depends on the end product to be made. Thread may be of cotton, silk, wool or synthetic material. It could have more or less twist. Hence, different threads will differ in fineness and lustre. Some embroidery threads are also available in ply. This means a number of yarns are twisted together.

In the market embroidery threads are commonly available as cotton embroidery threads, silk floss (also known as pat) – it is a low twisted silk yarn which has a lot of shine but low strength, silk thread (resham ka dhaga) – it is a twisted silk yarn, has good shine but lower strength than cotton. Woollen yarn can also be very beautifully used to produce good embroidery pieces.

(e) **Embroidery frames:** To get good results embroidery is usually worked using frames. Frames hold the fabric tightly and evenly, hence the stitches are more likely to be neat and accurate than if the fabric were held in the hand while working. There are two main types of frames:

1. **Round frame:** This is also known as hoops. It consists of two pieces, a smaller hoop which fits into a larger one. There is usually a spring or screw adjustment to keep them fitting snugly. The fabric for embroidery is placed over the smaller hoop and the larger hoop is pressed over the fabric, fitting it snugly on to the smaller hoop. These frames are either of wood or metal. While framing a very delicate fabric, it is advisable to place tissue paper over the inner hoop or twist or wrap the inner hoop with a thin material to prevent markings on the fabric.

2. **Rectangular frame:** The rectangular frame consists of four pieces attached to each other in a rectangular form. The fabric to be embroidered is stretched on the frame on all the four sides, where the fabric is tacked onto the end of the frame with the help of needle and the thread.

(f) **Fabric:** Correct use of design, needle and thread on various fabrics can produce lovely embroidered fabrics.

DESIGN

Design has been defined as "a plan or a drawing produced to show the appearance of something before it is made".

In other words it is the process and art of creating, planning and making a detailed drawing of something to be made. It can be an embroidery design or a furniture design, garment/fashion design, a design for a house to be built etc.

A far as embroidery is concerned we can easily say that design is a decorative pattern which aims at increasing the beauty of the article on which it will be embroidered.

Types of Design

Designs fall into five basic categories–

(i) Geometrical designs

(ii) Simplified designs

(iii) Naturalized designs

(iv) Stylized designs

(v) Abstract designs

(i) **Geometrical designs:** Designs created by using various geometrical shapes, such as lines, circles, squares, rectangles, triangles etc. are called geometrical designs. It is possible to draw many man-made objects using geometrical shapes.

(ii) **Simplified designs:** These designs comprise of slight curves and few details. See the following designs, observe and compare the geometrical and simplified designs. Simple lines and curves with few details create simplified designs.

(iii) **Naturalized designs:** As the name suggests, these are the designs inspired from Nature. Patterns in Nature change all the time, different seasons unfold different colours and scenes. Man is inspired by all that is happening around him.

(iv) **Stylized designs:** These are made to make the design look more beautiful. The design loses its natural form as it becomes more decorative and stylized. Thus the designs which have more curves and details and are away from their natural form and look more complicated are called stylized designs.

(v) **Abstract:** An abstract design does not have any specific inspiration. Both natural and abstract designs use the same source of inspiration but results would be quite different. The natural design of a leaf will look like a leaf but an abstract design of the same can be created by only using its texture, veins, patterns or colour to produce an attractive design. Every day objects, when viewed from different angles, can be an exciting source for abstract designs.

MOTIF, PATTERN AND DESIGN

Often the terms design, motif and pattern are used interchangeably. A design starts with a motif. When a motif is repeated at certain intervals over a surface it is called a pattern. Repetition of this pattern creates a design. Certain principles are used when repeating the motif or the pattern to create different design.

EMBROIDERY DESIGNS

Whenever we select a design we keep the following points in mind.

– The embroidery design must fulfill its purpose, for example, we use a cartoon on children's garments.

– Choose the embroidery design according to shape and size of the garment.

– Select the design according to the texture of the fabric, e.g., light embroidery will be suitable for delicate fabrics like chiffon and heavy embroideries will be more appropriate for thicker fabrics like cotton.

– The design varies with occasion. Heavily embroidered garments are appropriate for a wedding but will definitely look out of place in office.

– The sex of the wearer also influences the selection of the design. A design for women's garment will not look appropriate on a man's garment.

– Select the design keeping the age of the wearer in mind. Certainly what looks appealing on a teenager's dress may not look nice on grandmother's clothes.

– Embroidery design must use the background of the fabric effectively in terms of colour combination and texture.

– Decorate the area near the points of emphasis, e.g., collars, pockets, neckline etc.

– Take care to see that it is comfortable. Embroidered article must not be so heavy that is becomes difficult to carry. Nor should design be abrasive to the skin of the wearer.

In short, the factors you must consider while selecting a design for embroidery are:-

● purpose

● shape and size of the article

● colour and texture of the fabric

● occasion

● sex of the wearer

● age of the wearer

● comfort

● point of emphasis

COLOUR

CLASSIFICATION OF COLOURS

There are numerous colours all around us. The classification of these colours have been devised to organise and identify colours. A most familiar one is the 12 hue "Colour Wheel". These colours can be classified either according to their origin or properties. The most common classifications are as follows:

1. Primary, Secondary and Tertiary colours

2. Warm and cool colours

3. Neutral colours

4. Metallic colours

1. Primary, Secondary and tertiary colours

Primary colours: The primary colours are red, yellow, and blue. These three colours form the basis from which other colours can be made.

Secondary colours: The colours formed by mixing two primary colours in equal quantities are called secondary colours. These are orange, green, and purple.

Tertiary colours: These are formed by mixing a primary and a secondary colour in equal quantities. For example, blue (primary) and green (secondary) mix to form blue-green (tertiary).

Yellow + orange = yellow orange

Red + orange = red orange

Red + purple = red purple

Blue + purple = blue purple

Blue + green = blue green

Yellow + green = yellow green

The three primary, the three secondary and the six tertiary colours give us our set of twelve colours.

Traditional Indian embroidery uses all these colours in various shades.

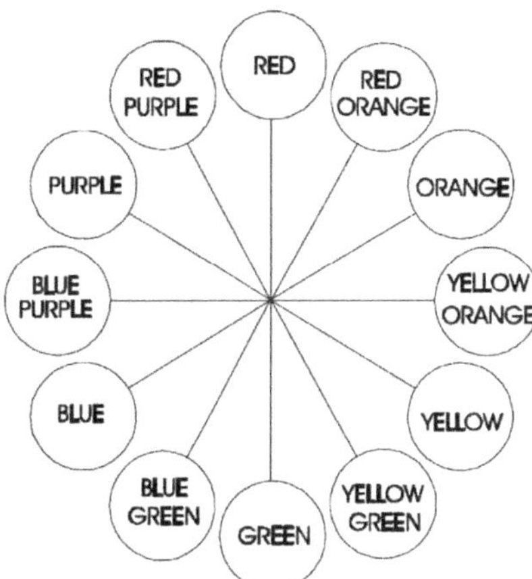

Fig. The colour wheel

2. Warm and Cool colours

Make a colour wheel. Now draw a line vertically down the center of the wheel as shown in the figure. If you split the colour wheel vertically down the center, one side will have all the warm colours and one side will have all the cool colours.

Warm colours: These are red, orange, yellow, etc. These colours have the element of fire or sun within them. They project a feeling of warmth. They create a visual impact of reduced size and length. These are encouraging colours that produce a feeling of excitement and happiness. Since most heavy embroideries are executed for happy occasion like marriage or child birth, selection of such colours is natural.

Cool colours: These are blue, green, purple, etc. They have the element of vegetation or water in them. They project a cool feeling. These are peaceful colours that give a feeling of rest and repose. They also create a visual impact of enhanced size and length. These colours can be used to create embroidered pieces for summers. They also provide a balance to vibrant warm colours. Warm and cool colours are complementary to each other and always create very interesting effects.

The warmth and coolness of colours like green and purple, which are formed by mixing one warm and one cool colour are dependent upon the amount of primary colour used to prepare the secondary colour.

3. Neutral colours

White, black, grey, brown, tan, beige etc. are neutral colours. They are a very important part of any embroidery. They form a very effective background for bright colours. Whenever we are not sure of a right colour scheme, neutral colours come in very handy.

4. Metallic colours

The sparkle and shimmer of metal is always attractive to man. Metal wires were hammered to fineness of a yarn and used in the embroidery. Plain golden or silver wires are called 'Badla' and when these wires are wound around a thread they are called 'Kasab', spangles of metal are 'Sitara' and tiny dots made out of badla are called 'Mukaish'.

CHARACTERISTICS OF COLOUR

Just like every object has three dimensions i.e., length, breadth and height, colour also has three dimensions. They are described by using the terms hue, value and intensity.

Hue: Refers to the name of the colour e.g. red, orange, blue etc.

Value: Refers to the lightness or darkness of a hue. By adding white to a hue a lighter colour can be obtained. It is called tint. By adding black to a hue a darker colour can be obtained. It is called shade or tone. Henceforward, we shall refer to all the light shades as tints and dark shades as tones. Tints and tones are specially useful when you are embroidering a natural design eg. - if you have to embroider a flower, you can use the hue along with two tints and one tone. Motifs like fruits, birds, nature scene etc. can all be embroidered in a similar fashion.

Intensity refers to the brightness or dullness of a colour. If all the colours used in embroidery are bright or dull a balanced look will not be created. So, it is a good idea to use both dull and bright colours in the correct proportions, for example red and golden yellow flowers can be balanced by tints of green leaves and brown stems. To increase the intensity of a colour place the complementary colours next to each other. This kind of placement produces very bright colour schemes, for example, red and parrot green.

COLOUR SCHEMES

A colour combination that matches and looks pleasing to the eye is called a colour scheme. Whenever more than one colour is placed next to another, a scheme is automatically created.

There is a definite scheme through which we can always produce pleasing effects when more than one colour is used. These colour schemes could be:

1. Monochromatic colour scheme
2. Analogous colour scheme
3. Complementary
4. Split complementary
5. Triad
6. Tetrad

1. **A Monochromatic colour scheme** uses a single colour. It consists of tints and shades of the same colour e.g. on a pale blue kurta you may embroider sky-blue, dark blue and navy blue motifs or Lucknow chikankari where white motifs are embroidered on white fabric. This kind of scheme is quite restful, easiest to produce and is always successful.

2. **An analogous colour scheme** is also called adjacent colour scheme. It uses adjacent or neighboring colours on a colour wheel. Such colours have at least one hue in common. E.g. yellow flowers, yellow green leaves and green stems can be embroidered. It is a very pleasing combination.

3. **Complementary colour scheme:** It is a two colour scheme. In this scheme colours that are placed opposite to each other in a colour wheel e.g. red and green, are used.

4. **Split complementary colour scheme:** It is a three colour scheme. It is made by using any one colour and splitting its complementary colours into two parts e.g. yellow, red purple and blue purple, (Purple is the complementary colour for yellow).

5. **Triad colour scheme:** It is a three colour scheme. It combines any three colours that form an equilateral triangle on the colour wheel. eg: yellow, red and blue or orange, green and purple.

6. **Tetrad:** This is a four colour scheme. It combines any four colours that form a square on a colour wheel. These schemes are being used in Kashida of Jammu and Kashmir, Kantha of Bengal and Chamba Rumal of Himachal.

Example: Green, yellow orange, red and blue purple.

The choice of colour is the most important decision a designer will make. Before making that decision the effect of combining colours and the impact that each colour will have both individually and when combined with others, needs to be considered.

If two colours appear striking when used together they are said to contrast well. Complementary colours contrast well. A good contrast also occurs when light and dark shades of two colours are used e.g. pale yellow and dark red. The excellent contrast of black with white is an extreme example of this principle. Contrasts can be emphasized by using black or white outline on a motif. It is seen that a white border seems to deepen a colour. Black or white line separating colours makes each colour show up more.

Colours from the same area of the colour wheel go well together, i.e., they produce a pleasing overall effect called harmony.

Pastel yellow and deep green, or pale pink and purple, are examples of harmonious colours going well to produce a gentle and pleasing effect.

SIGNIFICANCE OF COLOURS IN DAILY LIFE

The history of colour is as old as the history of mankind. Colour, for primitive man, possessed magical properties. Long before man wore clothes, the body was adorned with colours from natural sources like berries.

Different colours have different meanings. Each colour has a different psychological effect on us. Red – out of fire-means heat to us, green-out of freshly sprouted plants – means freshness and gold – out of sunlight – means gaiety. Colours have different meaning in different parts of the world. For example, in the western world, people grieve in black but in India and China people mourn their dead in white. Even in India some brides wear red whereas in certain areas girls get married in white and gold/red. Let us study these effects so that we can use these colours effectively.

Colour	Effect
Dark red	Love, health, vitality
Bright red	Passion, danger
Dark gray red	Evil
Pink	Femininity, festivity, delicacy, innocence
Orange	Ambition, enthusiasm
Brown	Utility, maturity
Yellow	Inspiration, wisdom, gaiety
Dark gold	Luxury, riches
Light yellow, green	Freshness, youth
Blue	Calmness, sincerity, idealism
Purple	Magnificence, royalty

FACTORS INFLUENCING THE USE OF COLOURS IN DAILY LIFE

- Age of person
- Sex of the person using the colour
- Profession
- Occasion
- Season
- Type of garment
- Body structure of person

Children and young adults look better in brighter colours. Older people must appear responsible, so you could choose those kinds of colours for them. Men must look mature and keeping their job profile in mind may have to project an image of dependability and sternness. So, choose colours accordingly.

Occasion also plays a very important role in selection of colour. Before deciding on a colour, make sure that you know what the occasion is-if it is a marriage or a party, whether it is a morning function or an evening one.

Choice of colours is very largely dependent upon the season too. Time and again we have talked about using cool, fresh and soft colours during summers. One can use bright, dark and cheerful colours in winters. The type of the garment also has an influence on the selection of colour. Choice of colour for embroidery on a western outfit will definitely be different from those used on a sari or lehnga. Before deciding on the colour, check a person's height and weight. Check out special body features like long legs, short waist or large hips.

STITCHES

BASIC STITCHES

(i) **Stem Stitch :** Stem stitch is basically an outline stitch. This stitch makes a fine line and is used around edges and for making veins in leaves, stems etc.

In this, the needle is inserted to the right of the line and brought up to the left of the line, making a thick outline. The stitch may be used as a filling by working rows alongside each other.

(ii) **Satin Stitch :** It is basically a filling stitch. The thread is taken out in front and back equally. It gives a very smooth finish to the embroidery. These are straight stitches worked slantwise. For straight areas, work slantwise from top to bottom; for a small circle, work long stitches vertically, centre first, then fill each side; for leaf shapes, work diagonally, starting from the left edge.

(iii) **Long and Short Stitch :** This is used to fill areas in solid and shaded colours. The first row is alternating long and short stitches. The following rows are stitches of equal length worked at ends of short and long stitches. Regularity of the following rows depends on the shape to be filled. Plan the stitches in an area so they fill it naturally and gracefully. It is helpful to mark with pencil the direction of some of the stitches. Here also, the needle works equally in the front and back of the fabric.

(iv) **Chain Stitch :** This stitch appears like a chain on the face of the fabric. It is worked from top down. Bring the needle up through the fabric; hold the loop with your thumb and insert the needle again at the same point. Bring the needle up a short distance away, with the thread looped under needle; repeat. It is used for heavy outlines or as a filling, making rows of chain following the outline of the shape being filled.

(v) **Darning Stitch :** It is also a filling stitch where the stitch is visible only on the face of the fabric.

The needle is taken out in front, one float is taken then the needle goes down and is taken out from the back through the very next yarn in the same row unlike in the satin stitch where floats of thread are the same in front and back. Here only the front has floats.

(vi) **Herring Bone Stitch :** Also known as Machali Tanka in Hindi. It is worked between the lines. Bring the thread up through the lower line, insert the needle in the upper line, a little to the right and take a short stitch to the left. Insert the needle on lower line a little to the right and take a short stitch to the left. May be used for thick seams or to connect two solid areas for softening the effect. It finally seems that the lower and upper threads are interlacing with each other.

(vii) **Button Hole Stitch :** The most common identification of this stitch is the opening into which the button of a shirt is closed. The edge of that opening is finished using a stitch known as the button hole stitch. It is worked from left to right. Bring the needle up through the fabric. Holding the thread under the left thumb, form a loop; then pass the needle through the fabric and over the looped thread; repeat. These stitches are made very close to each other.

This stitch may be used for filling an area or finishing edges and specially the edges in a patch work.

(viii) **Blanket Stitch :** This stitch is very similar to the button hole. The only difference is that the stitches are a little distance apart. The edges of blankets carpets, etc., are finished by this stitch.

(ix) **Cross Stitch :** These are stitches which from x's on the face of the fabric. They are worked from top to bottom - with the needle pointing left, make a row of small horizontal stitches spaced as far apart as they are long. Pull the thread firmly, this produces diagonal floats between stitches; when the row is finished, reverse, working stitches from bottom to top - still with your needle pointing left. Thread floats should cross in the middle forming an "x".

(x) **French Knot :** For making a French knot bring the thread up through the fabric, wrap the thread over and under the needle, crossing the beginning thread, insert the needle into the fabric close to where it came up. A double thread may be used to make larger knots if desired.

FINISHING OF THE EMBROIDERED ARTICLE

During the embroidery and once it has been done, a final finish has to be given to the embroidered article, to make it look neater and presentable. For this, remember the following points:

(i) Do not end the embroidery in a big knot. Keep the back of the embroidered article as neat as the front.

(ii) Clip the extra threads at the back.

(iii) Wash/dryclean the article after embroidery as handling during embroidering makes it dirty.

(iv) Starch and then iron the article well.

(v) Finish the edges of the article appropriately by hemming, picotting, etc.

(vi) If your article is heavily embroidered, store after folding it in mulmul cloth.

Communication

10

MEANING OF COMMUNICATION

Communication means a common ground of understanding. It is a process of exchange of facts, ideas, opinions and as a means that individuals or organizations share meaning and understanding with one another.

FUNCTIONS OF COMMUNICATION

1. **Information**—the collection, storage, processing and dissemination of news, data, pictures, facts and messages, opinions and comments required in order to understand and react knowledgeably to personal, environmental, national and international conditions, as well as to be in a position to take appropriate decisions.

2. **Socialization**—the provision of a common fund of knowledge which enables people to operate as effective members of the society in which they live and which fosters social awareness thereby permitting active involvement in public life.

3. **Motivation**—the promotion of the immediate and ultimate aims of each society and the stimulation of personal choices and aspirations, the fostering of individual or community activities, geared to the pursuit of agreed aims.

4. **Debate and discussion**—the provision and exchange of facts to facilitate agreement or to clarify differing view points on public issues. The supply of information needed to foster greater popular interest and involvement in all local, national and international matters of common interest.

5. **Education**—the transmission of knowledge so as to foster intellectual development, the formation of character and the acquisition of skills and capacities at all stages of life.

6. **Cultural Promotion**—the dissemination of cultural and artistic products for the purpose of preserving the heritage of the past, the development of culture by widening the individuals horizons, awakening his imagination and stimulating his aesthetic needs and creativity.

7. **Entertainment**—the diffusion through signs, symbols, sounds and images of drama, dance, art, literature, music, sports, games etc. for personal and collective recreation and enjoyment.

8. **Integration**—the provision to all persons, groups and actions of access to the variety of messages which they need in order to know and understand each other and to appreciate others living conditions, viewpoints and aspirations.

SCOPE OF COMMUNICATION

The scope of communication is very wide and comprehensive. It is a subject of almost unlimited dimensions and is a interdisciplinary one.

It is a continuous process of exchange of information and uses a set of symbols like words, action, pictures, figures etc.

Communication can be downwards, for example the Head Master giving instruction to the students through the teachers.

Communication can be upward, for example students opinion conveyed to the Principal through the teachers Communication can be horizontal, for example discussions among teachers themselves or the students deciding on some issues related to their club activities.

LEVELS OF COMMUNICATION

(a) **Self Communication or Intrapersonal Communication:** Communication scholars and researchers recently have come to realize the logical way to start improving our communication skills by understanding our own self-communication or otherwise called intrapersonal communication. This involves the internal communication patterns we use to 'talk to ourselves' either consciously or unconsciously.

(b) **Dyadic Communication or Interpersonal Communication:** This represents the type of communication that involves two or more persons communicating directly within a relatively informal two- person or smallgroup setting. Dyadic communication is a transaction between two people. This level of communication can take many forms - conversation, debate, interview, etc. We spend most of our communication time at this level.

(c) **Small group Communication:** This is a form of interpersonal communication that usually involves three or more persons but generally not more than twelve. The group is brought together for some common purpose or goal.

(d) **Large group communication:** This is also a common level in communication where more than thirty people come together to share their ideas, experience, knowledge, etc. They have common interests and aspirations.

(e) **Mass Communication:** In today's interdependent world, one needs to look beyond face to face communication to cater to our need to speak to many people at a time spread all over the world. In mass communication we reach large groups of people. Modern civilization has devised almost magical methods to carry our messages even to the remotest corner of the world with astonishing speed, much beyond the wildest imagination of the earliest generation. The method is known as mass communication.

SUCCESSFUL COMMUNICATION

Involves six elements - communicator (who) sending a useful message (what) through proper channels (how), effectively treated to an appropriate audience (whom) to evoke the desired response (effect).

That is who says what to whom, how and with what effect:

I. A good communicator should
1. know his audience well.
2. know his message well.
3. know the different channels that can be used.

II. A good message must be.
1. clear simple and understandable
2. significant and need based
3. appropriate and applicable.

III. Treatment of message helps in
1. organizing the subject matter
2. relating the message to suit the audience
3. avoiding any misinterpretation.

IV. Channels of communication are the physical bridges between the sender and the receiver of messages
1. Channel will depend on the size of the audience- individual/group/mass.
2. Channel used will depend upon the skills of the communicator and the audience knowledge.
3. Channel chosen will depend on the message to be conveyed.

V. The audience
1. may consist of one person or many or mass.
2. homogenous or heterogenous
3. highly motivated and actively participate
4. communication process

VI. Audience Response

1. reaction of the audience to the message they received.

2. can be verbal or non-verbal.

3. is important to make the communication process complete.

The choice of a channel or method of communication, also called Teaching Methods, generally depends on the number of people (audience) location or the place where communication is taking place, time available for communication and the skills of the communicator.

In any communication process, how you communicate is very important since this determines the effect or impact of the process. The important channels of communication are the teaching methods and the use of audio/visual aids.

TEACHING METHODS

Teaching methods are classified into:

- **Individual Methods:** This method is followed or chosen when the number of people to be contacted are few, are conveniently located, close to the communicator and sufficient time is available for communication. In this, individual attention can be given.

- **Group Methods :** A group may be defined as an aggregate of small number of people. This method is adopted when it is necessary to communicate with a group of people simultaneously and who are located not far off from the communicator, and reasonably good time is available for communication. Individual attention is difficult and may not be possible.

- **Mass Methods :** This method is followed where a large and widely dispersed hetero-geneous audience is to be communi-cated within a short time. There is no personal contact in this method.

METHODS OF TEACHING IN HOME SCIENCE

Communication is the process by which messages are transferred from a source to a receiver. It is also a process of sending and receiving messages through appropriate channels between two people or group of people.

Channel of communication constitutes the medium through which information or message is conveyed. These channels or methods of teaching/ learning or techniques of communication may be classified or discussed in many ways. They include both formal and non-formal teaching methods and use of audio/visual aids. Details of these were discussed in the earlier text. In this chapter we will learn a few selected methods and aids which can be used in the class room by the teachers and students to present ideas and information in simple ways.

Home Science has two distinct situations of teaching, i.e. formal and non-formal. Learners under the non-formal education system differ from learners under the formal system of education, in their background, resources and motivation. The traditional classroom teaching methods used for formal groups may not be equally effective with the non-formal. In a formal situation, teacheroriented methods can be used whereas in non-formal teaching situations learner-oriented methods have to be implemented.

However, whatever may be the teaching situation, the basic values, principles and limitations of the teaching methods remain the same. A communicator should be able to adopt each method according to the situation by modifying or improvising it. For example, in a formal situation, necessary classroom arrangements have to be made if demonstration or workshop methods are to be used, but in a non-formal situation students may be seated under a tree or in the verandah of a school, temple or panchayat office.

ENVIRONMENT   11

POLLUTION AND POLLUTANT

Pollution is the addition of any substance to the environment in excess to what is normally present, thereby making the environment impure.

The substance which causes pollution is known as a pollutant. A pollutant is harmful to our health. When we wash clothes or bathe in the river, the dirt, soap, etc., are the pollutants. They make the water dirty or unsafe for drinking.

AIR POLLUTION

Oxygen is the most important component of air. All living beings are dependent on it for life. Man and animals breathe in oxygen and breathe out carbon di-oxide. During the day, plants take in this carbon-di-oxide and give out oxygen. This helps in maintaining a balance in the composition of oxygen and carbon-di-oxide in the air. If things remain this way there is no problem. But something different is happening today. Most of the time, specially in city areas, the air that we breathe contains various pollutants.

Sources

The sources of pollutants in the air are as follows:

(i) Human Sources

Human beings are the main culprits in causing pollution. Their various activities are worth examining because these are major causes of air pollution.

(a) **Combustion process:** Combustion means burning. Smoke from burning may come from:

- Burning of a household fuel;
- Burning of coal in thermal power stations;
- Exhaust from automobiles;
- Bursting of crackers etc.

All these sources produce so much smoke that it is difficult to breathe. The smoke also affects the eyes and causes blindness.

(b) **Industrial manufacturing process**

- Smoke from factories.

(c) **Agricultural operations**

- Spraying of insecticides through airplanes spreads the poisonous substance in a large area of the atmosphere.

(d) Use of solvents and spray paints.

(ii) Natural sources

Besides human beings there are some natural sources of pollution too. These include the gases emitted from volcanoes, gases produced during jungle fires, and dust which spreads with the wind.

To sum up we can say:

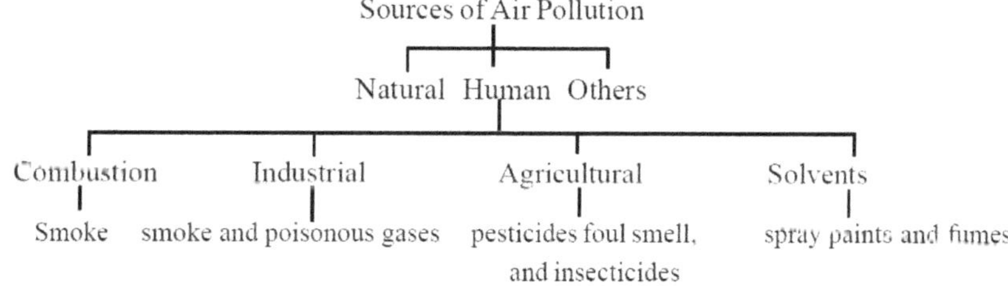

155

Effects

Let us now see some of the effects of air pollution.

(i) **On human beings:** The respiratory system of human beings is affected leading to several diseases like bronchitis, asthama, etc. Certain type of skin allergies like rashes and redness are also common.

(ii) **On plants:** Due to pollution, the plants get less sun light thereby affecting their food manufacturing process. Pollutants are also deposited on their leaves. This causes blocking of pores and restricts respiration.

(iii) **On environment:** Aeroplanes sometimes could neither take off nor land because of poor visibility. This is not only because of fog but also because of the presence of pollutants like smoke and dust in the air.

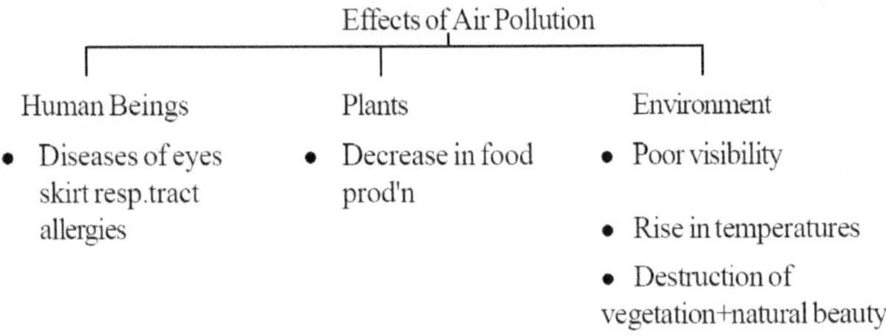

Control of Air Pollution

(i) Use a smokeless chullah at home. Provide a tall chimney to the chullah to carry the smoke away.

(ii) Use biogas which is a smokeless fuel.

(iii) Use a solar cooker at home which uses heat from the sunlight.

(iv) Factories should have chimneys filters. This will help in trapping the poisonous substances in the gases that are let out by them.

(v) Factories must be located far away from residential areas.

(vi) Vehicles must be fitted with special devices to reduce pollution.

(vii) Use of unleaded petrol and CNG should be encouraged.

(viii) Garbage should not be burnt. It should be disposed off hygienically, preferably through sanitary landfills.

(ix) Roads must be metalled so that dust does not rise and mix with air.

(x) Trees should be planted and cared for so that these keep the air fresh and pure.

(xi) Crops should be grown in the fields all the year round so that the soil is not exposed to erosion.

WATER POLLUTION

Polluted water may be coloured, may have suspended particles, a foul smell and a bad taste.

Sources of Water Pollution

Water gets polluted when the following are thrown in it:

1. **Domestic wastes:** Waste water from toilet, bath and kitchen is disposed off in a nearby water source (river, lake or pond) and thus the water gets polluted. Very often garbage is also disposed off in this source of water and dead animals and half burnt dead bodies are also thrown in it. All these cause water pollution.

   Sources of water are used for bathing animals, washing clothes and washing self after defeacation. This also causes water pollution.

2. **Industrial wastes:** Waste and waste water from factories and power plants flows into the rivers, ponds, etc., and causes water pollution.

3. **Agricultural wastes:** Fertilizers, insecticides, etc., go through the soil to the underground water and cause water pollution.

4. **Oil spills:** Some times oil from oil tankers spills over large areas of sea. This also causes water pollution.

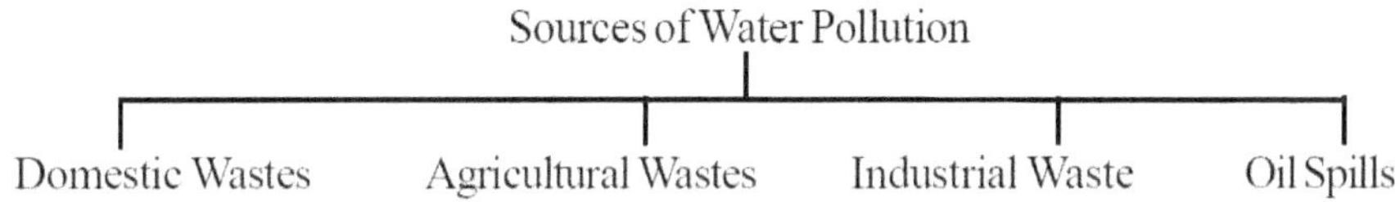

Effects

Drinking unsafe water causes diseases like cholera, typhoid, diarrhoea, dysentery, etc. Bathing in polluted water causes skin diseases and allergies.

Control

(i) Make sure that untreated sewage water is not thrown into the sources of water.

(ii) Industries should not be allowed to throw untreated wastes into the river or pond.

(iii) Defecation in open and near the water source should be discouraged. Use proper latrines for defecation.

(iv) Latrines, soakage pits, dumping grounds and land fills should be far away from the source of water.

(v) Bathing of self, washing clothes or bathing animals in or near the harvested water sources should be banned. Rain water in special ponds/wells should be used for washing clothes and bathing animals.

(vi) Rivers and seas should not be used for disposal of garbage.

Making Water Safe For Human Consumption

This water can be made safe by using the following procedures at home.

(i) **Straining:** Before filling, put a clean muslin cloth on the mouth of the pot and let the water filter or strain through it. Remember, straining helps only in removing solid particles. It cannot do anything to the micro organisms which may be present in the water. Thus, the water may be clean but not safe.

(ii) **Boiling:** Boiled water is safe to drink. Boiling water vigourously for twenty minutes kills many disease causing germs that it might contain. The boiled water should be cooled, filtered and then stored in clean covered pots.

(iii) **Bleaching:** A big family consumes a lot of water which is generally difficult to boil. You can then use bleaching powder to make your water safe. Bleaching powder is available at a chemist shop.

Take fresh bleaching powder and mix one tea spoon in a glass of water. Bleaching powder generates chlorine which helps in killing the germs. Take three tea spoons of this solution and add to a bucket full of water (15-20 litres). Leave it for about half an hour because chlorine requires time to act.

Filters which fit or connect on to the tap only remove the solid particles if there are any.

The other types strain water and also use charcoal, ultraviolet rays or membrane filters to absorb smells and kill germs.

The Storage type filter has two compartments, one fitted on top of the other. The upper receives unfiltered water and the filtered water flows to the lower compartment where it is stored. There are ceramic candles fitted at the base of the upper compartment which retains any unnecessary ingredients present in the water. Clear water gradually trickles down into the lower compartment, where it is stored. These days special one litre bottles with filters attached at the mouth are sold in the market. These bottles can be carried everywhere to get clean drinking water.

Methods of Water Purification

(i) Straining

(ii) Boiling

(iii) Bleaching

(iv) Chlorinating

(v) Filtering

Conserving Rain Water - Water Harvesting

Rain water can be collected and stored in underground or roof top storage tanks to be used in times of scarcity. A part of it can be allowed to percolate into the ground to raise the level of underground water. This process of collecting rain water and conserving it is called rain water harvesting.

SOIL POLLUTION

Soil pollution can be defined as changes in physical, chemical and biological nature of soil to the extent that is has a harmful effect on humans and other living beings. Soil becomes polluted when wastes from factories in the form of chemicals and metals are thrown on it. These poisonous substances in the soil enter the plants that are growing there. It enters the human and/or animal system when we eat it.

Sources

Following are some of the sources of soil pollution

(i) **Domestic wastes:** When household garbage is left on soil it rots and becomes a breeding ground for insects, worms and germs. There may be disease germs already present in the garbage. Defeacation in the open is a common practice in India. When people defeacate and urinate on the soil dirt, germs and worms are generated. When we walk barefoot on this soil these germs and worms enter our system causing stomach disorders. They enter into animal and plant system also, thus infesting all living beings. This way they enter into the food chain and further, into the human body.

(ii) **Defeacation in the open:** Defeacating and urinating in the open is a common practice in India. Early morning people are seen defeacating in the fields or in open spaces. These spots are stinking and filthy. The urine and excreta may contain germs and worms which enter the soil and pollute it. If it rains, the dirt flows into the nearby source of water.

(iii) **Spitting:** We have yet another bad habit of spitting anywhere and everywhere. The sputum not only spoils the surroundings but may carry disease germs. It may dry up and disappear but the germs remain and pollute the soil.

(iv) **Industrial wastes:** Soil becomes polluted when waste from factories is thrown on it. These poisonous chemicals in the soil enter the plants and poison them or kill them. Infact, some chemicals can make the soil totally infertile.

(v) **Agricultural wastes:** If insecticides, pesticides and fertilizers are added in excess then they enter the plants or stick to the surface of the growing fruits and vegetables.

Sources of Soil Pollution

Domestic Waste	Defeacation, Urination and spitting in the open	Industrial wastes Agricultural wastes

Effects

Improproper disposal of domestic waste, defeacating, urinating and spitting in the open are all sources of spread of disease germs and worms into the soil. As mentioned earlier, when we walk barefoot on the soil, these germs enter our body and eventually making us sick. Very often industrial and agricultural wastes leave harmful chemicals in the soil. Plants and vegetables that are grown on such soils absorb these chemicals. Animals and human beings who consume these plants may fall ill.

Control

Some measures to control soil pollution are:

Proper disposal of garbage: Garbage from homes should be properly disposed off so that it does not allow flies, mosquitoes and cockroaches to breed. At home, it must be collected in a bin which should be kept covered.

(a) **Dump outside the city limits:** If dumping of household waste is done in pits which are covered with twigs and plants, the flies and mosquitoes cannot breed on it. After the pit is full, cover it with soil and let the garbage be buried.

(b) **Land fills:** Quite often, specially in big cities, the garbage collected is so much that small pits are no answer. Low lying areas outside the city limits and away from the source of water are selected and garbage is dumped there every day. It produces foul smells and attracts birds, animals and insects. But since it is outside the city it does not affect the people so much except when they pass the ugly site and get the foul smell.

(c) **Composting:** The garbage from gardens is put into a pit in one corner of the garden. At the end of each day, it is covered with ash and leaves. Gradually the lower layers are converted into compost or manure. This manure can be used for gardening.

(d) **Burning of refuse:** Burning is a good way of getting rid of refuse because the quantity is reduced and germs, etc., do not get an opportunity to breed. But burning can produce a lot of smoke which causes air pollution.

(e) **Incineration:** The latest technology in garbage disposal is the use of an incinerator. An incinirator is a furnace in which the rubbish is burnt. This is an expensive method because a lot of fuel is required to burn the rubbish. However, it is sterile and safe. The garbage is reduced to a relatively small heap of ash.

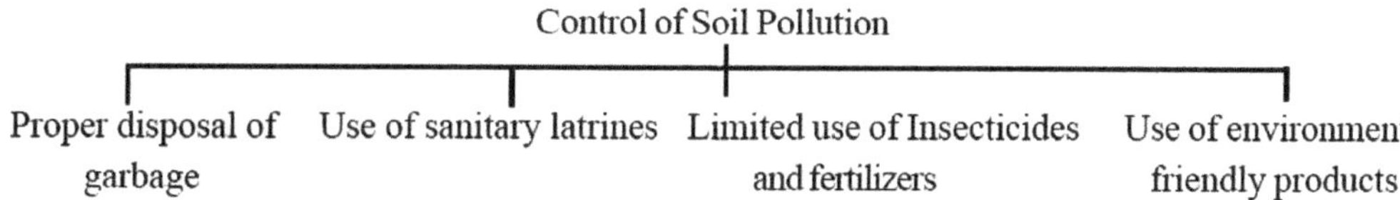

NOISE POLLUTION

Noise pollution is the result of unpleasant sound.

Sources of Noise Pollution

Some of the importnat sources are:

(i) automobiles, trains and aeroplanes

(ii) loudspeakers, radio and television when played at full volume.

(iii) Industries and machines.

Control

It is impossible to get rid of all noises completely, but we can definitely reduce them. Following are some of the suggestions for reducing noise pollution

- Playing the radio and TV at low volume.
- Avoiding the use of loudspeakers.
- Talking in low tones.
- Using the horn only when absolutely necessary.
- Fitting silencers to the engine of vehicles.
- Building factories away from residential areas.
- Building airports far away from city limits.

HOUSEKEEPING   12

WHAT IS HOUSEKEEPING?

Housekeeping in simple words means maintaining a house on a daily or long term basis or looking after its cleanliness, tidiness, upkeep and smooth running. How do you make sure that everything in the house is in usable condition? None of the objects are broken or chipped and fabrics are not torn. All the fixtures like taps, geysers, electric wiring, bulbs, tubes, fans, plugpoints, are in good working condition, geysers are not leaking, electric wiring is proper and there is no danger of fire due to short circuiting, and so on.

The different procedures followed to keep and maintain everything in the house in a good and presentable order, are collectively known as good housekeeping. In other words, we may also say that housekeeping is a process of keeping a place clean, beautiful and well maintained so that it looks and feels pleasant and inviting to all, either living, visiting or working there.

AREAS OF HOUSEKEEPING

Housekeeping is an essential and regular feature in all types of establishments.

In commercial establishments, the housekeeping services are done by a team of specialized people according to different areas. Here is a detailed list of areas which need housekeeping.

(i) **Rooms and corridors:** ceiling and wall paint, wall paper, fans, air-conditioners, electrical switches and sockets, wiring, windows, doors, glass panes, bed, bed-making, carpets, locks, keys, etc.

(ii) **Toilets:** taps, sinks, water closet, geysers, water supply, electrical sockets and switches, supply of towels, toilet paper, toiletries (soap, shampoo, etc.)

(iii) **Linen:** linen (table napkin, tablecloth) towels, bed sheets, bed covers, blankets, garments of guests, staff uniforms, etc.

(iv) **Furniture and furnishings:** furniture, curtains, table lamps, tube lights, chandeliers, bulbs, sofas, dining tables and chairs, etc.

(v) **Gardens:** Plants, pots, lawn (grass), flowers, trees, bushes, hedges, etc.

vi) **Public areas:** stair case, corridors, lobby, conference/ seminar room, waiting halls, recreation room, parking area, clubs, swimming pool, offices, common toilets etc.

GROOMING OF PERSONNEL INVOLVED IN HOUSEKEEPING

A well-groomed personality projects a good image and speaks well of hygiene and efficiency. As far as possible, personnel involved in housekeeping should—

- be fresh, well groomed and clean, not half asleep or unkempt in appearance while reporting on duty
- have their hair neatly cut and tied properly
- have nails neatly trimmed
- dress in simple, clean and well ironed clothes
- avoid rings or other jewellery
- use light makeup, in case of women
- use footwear that is light, without heels and noiseless
- be healthy and not suffer from any skin disease, colds, etc

- avoid bad habits such as nail biting, nose picking, leg shaking, sitting on work table, spitting, chewing pan, smoking, etc.
- bathe daily.

MEANING AND IMPORTANCE OF CLEANING

Cleaning involves sweeping floors, dusting furniture and other surfaces, mopping or washing floors, polishing surfaces, articles and accessories, scrubbing tiles, sinks, toilets, disinfecting drains, rearranging cleaned areas and putting things in their specific place. We can say that cleaning is a process of removing dust, dirt or any other undesirable materials like stains, spots, contents of an ashtray, etc.

'Dust' collectively refers to the loose particles, which are very easily moved by air and settle on any surface. It is easily removed with the help of a dry cloth.

'Dirt' refers to dust which sticks to any surface with the help of moisture or grease. It is more difficult to remove dirt as compared to dust. Dirt has to be removed either with a detergent or any other cleaning agent.

Methods of Cleaning

(a) **Dusting:** When any surface is wiped with a piece of dry cloth, (duster), it carries the loose dust with it and the process is known as dusting. This should be done with a clean soft cloth.

(b) **Shaking and Beating:** When you shake or beat any soft material, like a carpet/rug or a curtain, the dust falls out, making the article dust free to a large extent. This is mostly done in open air so that other things do not get dusty.

(c) **Sweeping:** When a broom or a brush is used to carry the dust laterally along the room, the process is known as sweeping. While sweeping any vertical surface as walls, you should remember to start from the top and sweep downwards. Similarly for lateral sweeping as for floors, start from one end of the room and move to another, preferably a door, and carry the dust all along or collect in a dust pan. All the movable articles kept on the floor should be lifted , swept under, and kept back in place.

(d) **Mopping:** Wiping a surface with a damp cloth is called 'mopping'. The piece of cloth used is known as a 'mop' and is generally coarser than a duster. In this process, both the dust, as well as easily removable dirt, is also removed. Mopping is mostly done on floors. Extra attention should be paid to nooks and corners otherwise it gets tougher to remove fixed grime later on.

(e) **Washing:** Sometimes mopping alone is not sufficient to remove dirt. Such surfaces are then scrubbed with the help of a yard (bamboo) broom along with plenty of water. Eventually the dirt loosens and is carried off by water. This process is known as 'washing'. In case of tougher stains or dirt, detergent may be added to the water.

(f) **Polishing:** When some reagent is rubbed on a surface to bring out the shine, the process is known as polishing and the reagent applied is known as the 'polish'.

CLEANING EQUIPMENT AND MATERIALS

A. Cleaning Equipments

Following are some of the equipments which use during the process of cleaning.

(a) **Dusters:** These are mostly made of soft cotton, flannel or artificial feathers mounted on a stick. These are used to clean loose dust and are also used for wiping various surfaces.

(b) **Dust pans:** These are made of either plastic or metal and have flat surfaces, rounded at the sides. After sweeping, dirt and dust is collected directly into these with the help of a broom and carried to a dustbin. Dustpans save sweeping the entire amount of dust from one room to another. Instead, dust can be collected from each room and disposed of simultaneously. Dust pans should be cleaned after use.

(c) **Mops:** are mostly made of thick, loosely woven cotton cloth. These are used to wipe dust from the floors. These are dipped in clean water and squeezed before wiping the floors.

(d) **Polishing cloth:** these are made of soft absorbent cloth such as flannel. Dry polishing cloth helps to clean and shine the polished surfaces by rubbing them vigorously.

(e) **Brooms:** brooms are either soft or hard. The soft ones are used to sweep the floors, whereas the hard ones (yard broom) are used to wash the floors.

(f) **Brushes:** are available in various sizes and shapes and are made of different materials. Different brushes are used for specific jobs. Brushes with nylon or plastic bristles are used for cleaning carpets or furniture, round feather brushes are used to remove cobwebs, metal brushes are used to clean wire mesh in the windows.

(g) **Buckets or basins:** metal or plastic buckets/ basins of suitable sizes are used to carry water, detergents and chemicals so that there are no spills.

(h) **Dust bins:** these are available in plastic with a lid. These should be lined with paper so that the garbage does not stick to the surface. They should be emptied and washed daily.

(i) **Vacuum cleaner:** it works on electricity and has a fan. This sucks in the dirt and dust from the surfaces and stores it in a disposable bag inside. This bag should be emptied regularly.

B. Cleaning Materials

There are many materials and reagents, which help in cleaning, scrubbing and polishing surfaces. Some of these are commercial preparations for cleaning and you may be already familiar with some of them.

(a) **Water:** Water is the simplest cleaning reagent available to us. Some dirt may be loosened and dissolved in it. Although most of the time, some other cleaning agent is also used along with it.

(b) **Detergents:** Detergents are available in powder, solid (soap, soap flakes etc.) and liquid form. These are used with water to clean various surfaces. The basic ingredients in a detergent are surface active agents, known as surfactants. A detergent may have more ingredients to make it more effective, like alkaline salts, bleaches, foam boosters, germicides and perfumes. The exact nature and use of a detergent will actually vary according to its ingredients. However, there are a few points which should be kept in mind while choosing a detergent. It should –

- be readily soluble in water
- be effective in all types of water and produce no scum
- have good wetting powers so that the solution penetrates between the article and the dirt particles
- have good suspending powers to suspend dislocated dirt and not allow it to settle back
- be effective over a wide range of temperatures
- be harmless to the article and the skin.
- clean quickly
- be easily rinsed away

(c) **Abrasives:** Some of the common abrasives are sand, finely powdered brick, saw dust, wheat bran, emery paper, fine ash, filtered chalk etc. Besides these, steel wool, nylon mesh, coconut fibers are also used to scrub dirt. Their use depends on the surface to be cleaned and the type of dirt to be removed. The extent of cleaning will depend upon the nature of the abrasive used and on the scrubbing action.

(d) **Acids:** Strong acids are used to clean toilets (water closet and sinks) and are available in crystals or liquid form. Milder forms of acids are also used to clean very dirty tiles. Acids should be rinsed off as soon as possible after use and should be stored away from children. Vinegar and lemon are used to clean stains on metals like brass and copper.

(e) **Alkalis:** Baking soda and ammonia are used as grease emulsifiers and stain removing agents.

(f) **Bleaches:** Stains on fabrics are removed by bleaches such as sodium hypochlorite, sodium perborate, hydrogen peroxide, sodium hydrosulphite etc.

(g) **Solvents:** Solvents such as methylated spirit, carbon tetrachloride, kerosene, petrol etc; are used to remove grease, wax and other stains from the surfaces.

(h) **Polishes:** polishes are used on surfaces such as floors, furniture, leather and even metals. When rubbed on a surface, they provide a protective covering to the surface and produce shine. The article also gets cleaned in the process.

Recipes of Some Commonly used Polishes

Furniture cream

INGREDIENTS	METHOD	USE
i. Bees wax 50gm	i. Shred wax and put in a pan. Cover with turpentine.	Use to polish light coloured furniture.
ii. Turpentine 30ml	ii. Heat in a double boiler till wax melts.	
	iii. Cool and allow it to set.	

Furniture polish

INGREDIENTS	METHOD	USE
i. Linseed oil 50 gm	i. Mix all ingredients together in a clean bottle and store	i. This can be applied on furniture with a pad of old cloth
ii. Turpentine 30 ml		
iii. Vinegar 30 ml		
iv. Methylated spirit 30 ml		

Metal polish

INGREDIENTS	METHOD	USE
i. Soap-2 tbs	i. Dissolve soap in boiling water	i. Shake well before use.
ii. Ammonia-1 tbs	ii. Mix with bath brick and ammonia.	ii. Soak soft toweling in the mixture, let it drip dry.
iii. Boiling water- 2½ cup	iii. Cool and store in air tight bottle.	iii. Wipe and rub with this toweling.
iv. Bath brick -50		

Copper cleaner

INGREDIENTS	METHOD	USE
i. Fine sand- 4 tsp	Mix all ingredients and keep in jar.	Rub well into brass or copper surfaces to remove stains.
ii. Flour - 2 tsp	Moisten a small amount of above mixture to a paste by using equal amounts of vinegar and water.	
iii. Salt- 1 tsp		

Note : tbs - table spoon; tsp - tea spoon

CLEANING AND CARE OF WALLS AND FLOORS

Walls and floors are mostly made of cement and concrete or even plastered with mud. Walls may either be painted / white washed or some may be covered with wallpaper, ceramic tiles, fabric or wooden panels. Floors may also be made of marble, granite, mosaic chips, or wood. Maintenance and precautions to be adopted for some of the commonly used surfaces on walls or floors have been discussed in the table below.

Table : Cleaning walls and floors

Surfaces	Maintenance	Precautions
Painted surfaces	i. Dust and remove the cobwebs regularly ii. Sponge with warm water and detergent from top to bottom iii. Rinse with clean, fresh water.	i. Never rub the walls vigorously or scrub with coarse abrasives and brushes. ii. Never use strong chemical solvents
Wallpaper	i. If torn, you should immediately gum it back in place. ii. Rub stains with a piece of soft damp cloth or a sponge. iii. Wipe, if the paper is washable. Use grease absorbers like talcum powder, Fuller's earth, bran, etc., to remove any grease stains.	i. Never scratch the wallpaper.
Ceramic tiles	i. Clean regularly with hot water and detergent. ii. Remove stubborn stains with water sand-paper along with hot water and detergent. iii. Special chemicals are available for cleaning them.	i. Do not use too much of acids as they may become loose and come off. ii. Acids should be rinsed immediately after use.

Surfaces	Maintenance	Precautions
Marble/granite/ mosaic/cement	i. Clean with hot water ii. Occasionally clean them with kerosene oil and sawdust. iii. Rub with lemon juice to keep the marble white and stain free.	i. Wipe corners and sides sides daily as they can get black.

CARE AND MAINTENANCE OF FLOOR COVERINGS

Just as walls and floors have different surfaces and various ways of cleaning them, there are different ways of cleaning floor coverings. It is not necessary that all floors be covered. In fact, in a country like ours, it is felt by most people that the easiest way to keep floors clean is to sweep and mop them. However, in most commercial establishments, the floors are wholly or partially covered, mainly for convenience and an aesthetic look.

Table: Cleaning floor covering

Surfaces	Maintenance	Precautions
Carpet	i. Clean carpets regularly. ii. Once a month take it out, turn it upside down and shake it to remove loose dust. iii. Alternatively, vacuum cleaners can be used effectively. iv. Wash colour fast, dirty carpets with soap solution. Work a lot of lather into the carpet with a brush, using circular motions over small areas at a time. Rinse thoroughly with sponge and dry it in the sun.	i. Put naphthalene balls in rolled up carpets. ii. Air them at intervals. iii. Dry thoroughly before rolling. iv. Remove any stains immediately.
Vinyl/linoleum	i. Clean with wet cloth. ii. Rub stains with a mild detergent.	i. Do not soak with water. Take care to squeeze out excess water from the mop before wiping. ii. Scrub the corners regularly. iii. Do not use hard abrasives and srubbers. iv. Avoid washing soda or alkali as it tends to stick.

Surfaces	Maintenance	Precautions
Coir is made up of coconut fibre.	i. Clean it daily with a coarse broom or brush. Occasionally take it out, turn upside down and shake to remove the dust. ii. If it gets very dirty, wash with soapy water, rinse in cold salty water and dry completely in open air.	i. Do not let it get very dirty. ii. Dry completely.
Doormats	i. Turn it upside and beat with a wooden stick. ii. They can be washed with soapy water, rinsed and dried in the sun.	

CLEANING OF WOODEN SURFACES

Wood is used for furniture, counter surfaces in the kitchen and floors. It is finished in a number of ways so that its pores get sealed. It also needs to be treated for protection against white ants. If left untreated, it is likely to develop permanent marks on account of dirt, oil and other spills.

Table: Cleaning wooden surfaces

Surfaces	Maintenance	Precautions
Plain wood (chopping boards, pastry boards, rolling boards and pins) Maintenance	i. Wash with mild soap and warm water. Rinse and dry in open air. ii. Extra bits of food sticking to the board can be removed by using the back of a knife.	i. Always scrub along the grain. ii Never use hard scrubbing brush. iii. Avoid soaking in water. Never use very hot water as the wood will swell. iv. Avoid strong cleaning agents.
Polished wood	i. Dust and rub with a flannel cloth. ii. Remove water marks by rubbing methylated spirit/ turpentine or a mild solution of ammonia.	i. Avoid spilling on wood. ii. Wipe spills immediately.
Painted wood (doors and windows)	i. Clean with mild soap and water. Rub dry with a flannel cloth to give it a gloss. ii. Repaint periodically to preserve it better.	i. Ensure that all traces of soap are carefully removed, otherwise, stains may still seen on the surface.
Laminated/veneer surface (sunmica)	i. Wipe clean with wet cloth. ii. To remove heat marks, rub metal polish and wash up with mild detergent. Use wax polish or creams to protect veneer surfaces.	i. Avoid scratching and using coarse abrasives. ii. Wipe all spills immediately avoid permanent staining.

CARE OF METAL SURFACES

Utensils/ appliances – may be made of copper, brass, glass, steel, silver, iron, etc. Brass and copper form a poisonous tarnish- a blue-green colour, in humid climates. We would need to maintain each of these surfaces in a different way, some of which have been discussed below.

Table: Cleaning metal surface

Surfaces	Maintenance	Precautions
Brass and copper	i. Use soaps and cleaning powders with mild abrasive action. Rub lemon juice and salt, vinegar or tamarind pulp along with fine steelwool. Use sifted ash to clean utensils at home. ii. Clean engraved brass with an old tooth brush. iii. Use 'Brasso' or mild solution of the hydrochloric acid to clean very dirty ornamental articles.	i. Never use brasso or other chemicals to clean cooking utensils as they are poisonous.
Silver and silver-plated used for tea pots, trays etc.	i. Wash with warm, soapy water immediately after use. ii. Protect from getting tarnished by covering them individually with tissue paper. iii. Scrub lengthwise with a soft cloth. iv. Remove any tea stains by using 2 table spoons of soda and boiling hot water. Rub decorative articles with 'Silvo' (a polish available in the market).	i. Do not use any coarse abrasives as it gets sctatched easily. ii. Use mild abrasives.
Steel	i. Clean with cold or hot water along with detergent. ii. Scrub badly stained pans with mild abrasives. iii. Soak burnt steel utensils in saline water (add salt in water) and scrub with mild abrasive.	i. Do not use hard abrasives as the steel gets scratched.
Iron	i. Clean soon after use. ii. Smear oil on the surface to seal it. iii. Remove stains by using brick powder, bran, saw dust etc.	Dry completely as moisture can result in rusting.
Non stick/Teflon coated (tava, pans, snack toasters, saucepan)	i. Smear oil before use. ii. Rinse immediately after use. iii. Clean with sponge and soapy water, rinse and dry.	Do not use steel wool or hard abrasives.

CLEANING OF GLASS, CANE AND PLASTICS

Glass is used for windows, table tops, partitions and sliding doors. Cane is lightweight and mostly used in chairs and tables. Plastic is used in bottles, mugs, buckets etc.

Table: Cleaning of glass, cane and plastic

Surfaces	Maintenance	Precautions
Glass	i. Clean with a wad of newspapers and water. ii. To give it shine, rinse it with water in which vinegar is added. iii. Remove grease stains with ammonia in warm water. iv. Remove fly specks by rubbing with methylated spirit.	i. Do not use hard scrubbers and abrasives, as it will result in scratches.
Cane	i. Regularly dust and clean to eliminate bugs, spiders, and cockroaches in corners. Use a brush to reach the corners. ii. Wash it with warm salty water (1 Tb spoon salt in 1 litre water) Then dry it completely in open air. iii. Coat with clear varnish to prevent staining. It can also be polished with liquid wax polish.	i. Avoid soaking in water.
Plastics	i. Remove stubborn stains by applying kerosene oil and if possible, put it out in the sun.	i. Do not use strong abrasives as the tend to scratch the surface. ii. Do not use chlorine.

ELECTRICAL REPAIRS

Important Warning

- Always wear rubber slippers.
- Always dry hands completely.
- Always keep a wooden plank/woollen blanket handy.
- Always disconnect the main supply/unplug the appliance.

Electrical Fuse

A fuse is made of a thin metallic wire, normally of a tin, lead and zinc alloy. Some times, due to a short circuit , or a faulty appliance, this wire melts and the fuse blows. Once it blows, you can carry out the following steps –

(a) Put the main switch off.

(b) Identify the faulty appliance, switch off and remove it.

(c) Take out the fuse cut out and examine it. Remove the melted wire and clean the cut out/carrier.

(d) Replace with a new wire. The new wire should pass through the hole if one is provided.

(e) Replace the fuse cut out, close the box and put the main switch on.

3 pin plug

These plugs are mostly of two sizes : either 5 or 15 amperes. Due to high current they sometimes melt, thus exposing raw wires which can lead to electric shock. This plug consists of 3 wires : one for positive, another one for negative and the third one for earthing (neutral). Usually different colours are used to differentiate between them. Green colour is mostly chosen for earthing, red for positive and yellow or some other colour is chosen for negative (these colors can vary).

To change the 3-pin plug, follow the given steps:

(a) Unscrew the main screw placed in the middle of the plug.

(b) Unscrew the small screws on each of the three wires and pull them out.

(c) If needed, expose the inside wires by scraping the outer plastic coating with a blade or a sharp knife.

(d) Replace with a new plug, put positive in one screw band and negative in the other screw band, parallel to it. Tighten the screws. Make sure the two do not touch each other.

(e) Put the neutral wire in the lower screw band and tighten the screw.

(f) Put the cover and tighten the main screw.

Room Coolers

Room coolers consist of a cabinet, a water pump and an exhaust fan. The air first passes through the wet cooling pads and then this cool air is thrown in the room. Some points of attention are:

(a) The cabinet must be well cleaned before installation and also periodically, when in use. If it is made of iron, it should be painted to avoid rusting.

(b) The cooling pads, which are made of grass wool or 'khus-khus' should be changed every summer.

(c) Pump and the fan must be lubricated before summer.

(d) The water inlet in the pump should be covered with a filter, usually wire mesh, to prevent the entry of grass wool or 'khus-khus' particles, which may clog the water pipe.

(e) Care should be taken that the water is always above the minimum level, otherwise the pump will be damaged.

(f) Whenever water is being filled in cooler, make sure that the electricity supply is switched off.

Room Heater

The main part of a room heater is the heating element, which gets heated when electric current passes through it. The heating element can be easily replaced by removing the screws which hold it. The body of room heater should be periodically cleaned to maintain a smooth shiny surface so that maximum heat gets reflected.

OBJECTIVE QUESTIONS

1. What is the definition of health?
   (a) The absence of disease or infirmity
   (b) A state of being easily quantifiable
   (c) A state of complete physical, mental and social well being
   (d) A state of being subjectively assessed by individuals

2. How can health improvements be quantified and measured?
   (a) We cannot
   (b) Using quality and length of life
   (c) Comparing health status to the state of complete physical, mental and social well being
   (d) Using only monetary terms

3. Duty of care means
   (a) accepting responsibility for other people's mistakes
   (b) giving out advice and relevant accident forms to injured members
   (c) having a working knowledge of rules
   (d) accepting responsibility for health and safety in workplace

4. What is the percentage of fats and oils that should be included in the normal diet?
   (a) 10-15%
   (b) 12-15%
   (c) 25-30%
   (d) 30-35%

5. Which of the following is not the way to make sure you meet the highest standards of personal hygiene?
   (a) Limit the jewellery that you wear
   (b) Long hair must be tied back
   (c) Clean your teeth regularly
   (d) Wash your hands regularly

6. Which of the following is not a part of environmental hygiene and keeping your place free from clutter or conditions that allow bacteria and vermin to thrive?
   (a) Follow correct storage and garbage removal procedures
   (b) Maintain and clean equipments at the highest standard of hygiene
   (c) Carry personal hygiene kits (bum bags) with gloves and mask
   (d) Wash your hands regularly

7. Which of the following is not a hazard that can cause injury or harm in your place
   (a) Crowd control
   (b) Spills and slippery surfaces like water, food and oil
   (c) Incorrect storage including flammable materials having special storage requirements
   (d) Environmental conditions such as sun exposure

8. Which of the following causes of injury does not lead to a sprain or strain
   (a) Heavy loads
   (b) Incorrect lifting
   (c) Traumatic stress
   (d) Using equipment incorrectly

9. Which of the following is not a stage of risk management principles
   (a) Hazard control

    (b) Hazard maintenance

    (c) Hazard assessment

    (d) Evaluation/monitoring

10. Artery walls are

    (a) thin walled and near surface of the skin

    (b) strong, muscular and elastic

    (c) strong tiny vessels

    (d) strong and close to skin

11. Damage from lack of oxygen to the brain begins in

    (a) less than 4 minutes

    (b) 3 minutes

    (c) 1-2 minutes

    (d) more than 5 minutes

12. The mobile parts of the spinal column are

    (a) coccyx and sacrum

    (b) vertebrae

    (c) thoracic and lumbar

    (d) ligaments

13. The breathing control centre is located

    (a) front of brain

    (b) base of brain

    (c) in the lungs

    (d) in the medulla

14. Blood escaping from an artery is

    (a) bright red and oozing

    (b) dark red and oozing

    (c) bright red and spurting

    (d) dark red and spurting

15. The trachea and alveoli are part of the

    (a) cardiovascular or circulatory system

    (b) musculoskeletal system

    (c) respiratory system

    (d) nervous system

16. Oxygen is transferred from inhaled air to the blood in the air sacs of the

    (a) heart

    (b) capillaries

    (c) arteries

    (d) lungs

17. The heart's primary function is to pump blood to which two main areas?

    (a) Lungs and heart

    (b) Lungs and rest of body

    (c) Main arteries and the aorta

    (d) Capillaries and lungs

18. One of the most important but often neglected aspects of first aid treatment is

    (a) calling for help

    (b) reassuring the patient

    (c) checking for danger

    (d) assessing the patient

19. Checking for circulation involves

    (a) feeling for pulse

    (b) feeling for pulse and observing patient's colour

    (c) feeling for pulse, observing patient's colour and looking for signs of movement

    (d) feeling for breathing

20. Symptoms of shock include

    (a) rapid, weak pulse

    (b) confusion

    (c) pale, cold clammy skin

    (d) breathless and nausea

21. What is the correct treatment for a nose bleed?

    (a) Stand patient up, tilt patients head backwards, apply cold compress to forehead

    (b) Lay patient down in recovery position, apply soft bandage to nose

    (c) Lay patient on back, elevate knees, reassure patient

    (d) Sit patient down, tilt head forward, squeeze soft part of nostrils

22. What is the definition of shock?

    (a) Loss of effective circulation

    (b) Severe injury

    (c) A reaction of a traumatic event

    (d) Severe infection

23. In a secondary assessment you need to look, listen and feel. What are you feeling for

    (a) Any movement of air from patient's mouth or nose
    (b) Deformity, texture, temperature or swelling
    (c) Patient's breathe on your cheek
    (d) Patient's responses and sounds

24. Symptoms of a fracture
    (a) pain and tenderness
    (b) possible bleeding at wound site
    (c) deformity and swelling at wound site
    (d) possible discolouration

25. How many vertebrae are in the spinal column?
    (a) 13
    (b) 33
    (c) 26
    (d) 40

26. Most deaths from heart attacks occur
    (a) in 1-2 hours after attack
    (b) in 15 - 30 minutes after attack
    (c) within 24 hours of attack
    (d) within an hour of attack

27. What is the most correct procedure for first aid documentation?
    (a) Gather information from bystanders and record in patrol log book
    (b) Record events as witnessed, signed by first aider and kept on file
    (c) Check with patient as to cause of injury, ensure next of kin notified and verbally pass information onto ambulance/paramedics
    (d) Record all events as stated by bystanders and ensure patient signs as correct record

28. Treatment from stings is
    (a) put patient in a warm shower
    (b) rub with sand to stop the burn
    (c) wash with fresh water and apply ice
    (d) wash with sea water and apply ice

29. The most appropriate fluid to give to a conscious patient suffering from hypothermia is

    (a) cool fresh water
    (b) sweet carbonated drinks
    (c) a small amount of alcohol
    (d) warm, sweet drinks

30. The treatment of a sprain
    (a) immobilise
    (b) stretch the muscle
    (c) apply ice, elevation and compression
    (d) apply heat, elevation and compression

31. What are vitamins?
    (a) Building materials for the body
    (b) Energy providers
    (c) Essential organic substances
    (d) Essential fatty acids

32. Complex carbohydrates include
    (a) brown rice, fruit
    (b) honey, biscuits
    (c) cake, sweets
    (d) meat, fish

33. What can an excess of protein intake lead to?
    (a) A feeling of wanting to eat more
    (b) Vitamin A deficiency
    (c) More calcium being excreted
    (d) Constipation

34. Foods high in cholesterol include
    (a) french dressing, burger relish
    (b) soya milk, porridge oats
    (c) lamb's liver, prawns
    (d) olive oil, corn oil

35. Fat soluble vitamins include
    (a) B_6, B_{12}
    (b) B_2, B_3
    (c) D, A
    (d) B_1, folic acid

36. Washing with anti-bacterial soaps before preparing food is better than washing with regular soap and water.
    (a) True
    (b) False

37. Which of the following could be symptoms of diabetes?

    (a) Increased thirst, frequent urination

    (b) Dizziness, hunger

    (c) Disturbed behaviour, over activity

    (d) Impulsiveness, aggressiveness

38. Which enzyme does hydrochloric acid activate?

    (a) Rennin

    (b) Lactase

    (c) Trypsin

    (d) Pepsin

39. Which of the following can be found in the epidermis?

    (a) Elastin

    (b) Melanocytes

    (c) Lymph vessels

    (d) Sweat glands

40. What is the action of the biceps femoris?

    (a) To flex the hip, to extend the knee

    (b) To abduct the leg

    (c) To extend the hip, to flex the knee

    (d) To flex the arm

41. What is mitosis?

    (a) The covering around the cell

    (b) The protection against UV light

    (c) The elimination of toxins from the skin

    (d) The multiplication of cells

42. What is the common name for the zygomatic bone?

    (a) The jaw bone

    (b) The cheek bone

    (c) The forehead

    (d) The skull

43. What can hypersecretion of thyroxin in adults cause?

    (a) Graves disease

    (b) Myxoedema

    (c) Cretinism

    (d) Dwarfism

44. What is the function of venules?

    (a) To carry deoxygenated blood from the capillaries to the larger veins

    (b) To carry oxygenated blood from the capillaries to the larger veins

    (c) To carry deoxygenated blood from the larger veins to the capillaries

    (d) To carry oxygenated blood from the larger veins to the capillaries

45. How is lymph drained back into the bloodstream?

    (a) Through the lymphatic capillaries

    (b) Through the spleen

    (c) Through the lymphatic nodes

    (d) Through the lymphatic ducts

46. What is neuralgia?

    (a) Shooting pains along the course of a nerve

    (b) Pain down the back and outside of the thigh

    (c) Disease of the basal ganglia

    (d) Paralysis or weakness of one side of the face

47. What does lipase digest?

    (a) Starch

    (b) Proteins

    (c) Fats

    (d) Carbohydrates

48. What are the functions of the trachea?

    (a) To moisten and warm the air

    (b) To collect foreign matter or bacteria by the goblet secretory cells

    (c) To allow exchange of gases to take place

    (d) To act as a passageway between the larynx and pharynx

49. Myosin is a contractile protein in

    (a) a myofibril

    (b) a muscle fibre

    (c) a nerve

    (d) the perimysium

50. Eversion is

    (a) moving the side of the sole of the foot outwards

    (b) pointing the toes upwards

(c) pointing the toes downwards

(d) moving the side of the sole of the foot inwards

51. The aerobic system is used by the body for exercise

(a) which lasts for longer than 3 minutes

(b) of short duration

(c) of high intensity

(d) which starts after 10 minutes of exercise

52. What is the aim of the warm up?

(a) To reduce muscle tension and make the body feel more relaxed

(b) To assist the circulatory system to help control adequate venous return and adequate cardiac response

(c) To prepare the neuromuscular response patterns

(d) To provide a controlled duration of exercise at the correct level and for the correct time

53. What is lactic acid defined as?

(a) The highest volume of oxygen a person can consume during exercise

(b) A waste product of aerobic energy production

(c) The physiological stress on the body during exercise

(d) A waste product of anaerobic energy production

54. How long should a cool down in an absolute beginners class be?

(a) 5 minutes

(b) 10 minutes

(c) 15 minutes

(d) 20 minutes

55. Which exercise for the gastrocnemius muscle should you include in your routine?

(a) Heel raises

(b) Toe tapping

(c) Hamstring curls

(d) Lateral raises

56. What safety precautions need to be considered when performing exercises using stretch bands?

(a) Knees tight

(b) Arms straight

(c) Pelvis tilted

(d) Shoulders lifted

57. Contra indications to aerobic exercise requiring medical approval include

(a) smokers

(b) after eating a heavy meal

(c) undiagnosed illness

(d) exhaustion

58. To increase the intensity of an exercise you should include the

(a) feet

(b) arms

(c) hands

(d) shoulders

59. What type of charge does a neutron have?

(a) A negative electrical charge

(b) A positive electrical charge

(c) An interchangeable electrical charge

(d) No electrical charge

60. Localised contra indications to mechanical massage include

(a) bruising

(b) cancer

(c) contagious disease

(d) thin client

61. What is the best thing to use to clean, mold and mildew from your bathroom?

(a) Bleach

(b) Baking soda

(c) Dish soap

(d) Salad dressing

62. When you do laundry, by what criteria should you separate the clothes to be washed?

(a) By designer and fabric

(b) By colour and fabric

(c) By type pants, tops, etc

(d) By fabric only

63. What should you do with the pile of dirt that accumulates on the floor when you sweep?
(a) Sweep it under the rug
(b) Recycle it
(c) Feed it to your pets
(d) Sweep it into a dustpan

64. Which of these is Not a type of vacuum cleaner?
(a) Hand-held
(b) Supersonic
(c) Stick
(d) Upright

65. Which of the following food items may be stored indefinitely?
(a) Peanut butter
(b) Canned fruits
(c) Dry pasta
(d) Canned soup

66. If you eat raw or undercooked eggs, you may get...
(a) botulism
(b) salmonella
(c) leprosy
(d) rabies

67. Which of these ingredients would you Not find in a dish detergent?
(a) Surfactant
(b) Paprika
(c) Chlorine compound
(d) Corrosion inhibitor

68. Why should you buy pans and pots with copper bottoms?
(a) So your kitchen will look good for the photographer from "House Beautiful"
(b) Because copper is a better conductor of heat and cooks faster
(c) They sound better when you bang them together
(d) It just looks cool

69. Which of these would you Not find on a spice rack?
(a) Caraway seeds
(b) Dill
(c) Chorizo
(d) Nutmeg

70. Which of these should you Not do while ironing?
(a) Use a presscloth when ironing lace
(b) Use spray starch before ironing
(c) Iron clothes while they're on your body
(d) Make sure the iron temperature isn't too hot

71. Which of the following statements is False with regard to domestic life?
(a) Domestic groups do not always have the same personnel
(b) Family co-varies with climate
(c) Domestic groups always include co-resident mothers and children
(d) Husbands and wives do not always share the same domicile

72. Nuclear families
(a) are equally important in all cultures
(b) are organised in the same way in all cultures
(c) are universally responsible for the socialisation of children
(d) are found in a majority of cultures, although alternative forms are often more prevalent.

73. Marriage to more than one wife is called
(a) polyandry
(b) polygyny
(c) matrilineality
(d) matrifocality

74. Polyandry is
(a) very common throughout the world
(b) found mainly in China
(c) helps prevent the partition of corporate land by keeping the household undivided

(d) the result of a shortage of men

75. The most common form of marriage in America is
(a) monogamy
(b) serial monogamy
(c) plural monogamy
(d) polygyny

76. One-parent domestic groups are
(a) aberrant forms of family organization
(b) as economically viable as nuclear family groups
(c) are associated with the social and economic conditions that make long term marriage less tenable
(d) all of the above

77. Which of the following is Not true of gender roles?
(a) Males are physically stronger on average than females.
(b) In most societies males pre-empt major centres of public power.
(c) Matriarchies existed in the past but were overthrown by men.
(d) There are many societies without marked gender inequalities.

78. Which of the following is a marriage universal?
(a) Establishes a distinction between legitimate and illegitimate childrearing.
(b) Gives the husband exclusive access to the wife's sexual services.
(c) Establishes a joint fund of property for the benefit of children.
(d) Establishes reciprocal relationships and economic ties between in-laws

79. Bride price is
(a) money or goods presented to the bride by her family
(b) compensation paid directly to the groom
(c) compensation to the family of the groom for their loss of the groom's labour
(d) compensation to the family of the bride for their loss of the bride's reproductive power

80. A dowry
(a) is compensation to the bride's family for losing a daughter
(b) is the transfer of money or wealth by the groom's family for the loss of his labour
(c) is wealth received by the bride from her husband's family
(d) is compensation for taking responsibility for the bride where women are regarded as economic burden

81. Exogamy is
(a) a rule stipulating that one must marry outside one's own group.
(b) a rule stipulating one must marry inside one's own group
(c) a rule observed only by the Nayar
(d) considered incestuous in some societies

82. An important advantage of exogamy is
(a) it ensures that individuals will marry outside a group
(b) it helps establish economic relations with neighbouring groups
(c) it reduces the likelihood of warfare
(d) all of the above

83. The belief that males are spiritually superior to females is
(a) expressed in Christianity, Juadaism and Islam
(b) characterised by male dominated rituals and myths
(c) often not accepted by women who have their own gender ideologies
(d) all of the above

84. Excessive crying can be...
(a) a risk factor for shaken baby syndrome
(b) caused by colic
(c) caused by reflux
(d) all of the above

85. How much sleep does the typical 9 month old need?
   (a) 16 hours, including 12 hours overnight and 3 naps
   (b) 14 hours, including 11 hours overnight and 2 naps
   (c) 12 hours, including 11 hours overnight and 1 nap
   (d) 12 hours

86. When can you start solid baby foods, like cheerios?
   (a) 2-3 months
   (b) 4-6 months
   (c) 8-9 months
   (d) Once he gets his first tooth

87. When do infants get their first tooth?
   (a) 2-3 months
   (b) 4-5 months
   (c) 5-7 months
   (d) 7-9 months

88. At what age do most infants roll over?
   (a) 2 weeks
   (b) 2 months
   (c) 5 months
   (d) 9 months

89. When can you switch formula fed infants to cow's milk?
   (a) 9 months
   (b) 10 months
   (c) 11 months
   (d) 12 months

90. An infant can grasp two blocks and bang them together. How old is he?
   (a) 4 months
   (b) 5 months
   (c) 6 months
   (d) 7 months

91. Textiles can be damaged by
   (a) being creased—this can lead to splitting of the textiles
   (b) light and UV radiation, causing fading and setting off chemical reactions which weaken the textiles
   (c) mould, insects and pollutants
   (d) all of the above.

92. When handling textiles
   (a) try to touch as little of them as you can—always pick them up by one part only
   (b) fold them as neatly and as small as possible to make handling easier
   (c) never pick them up by one corner and always support the weight of the textile evenly
   (d) have clean hands.

93. To label a textile
   (a) write in permanent ink on the corner of the textile, or on the collar of the costume
   (b) write in permanent ink on a sticky label and stick this to the textile
   (c) machine-sew a label to the textile
   (d) write the label onto cotton tape and attach this to the textile with one or two hand-stitches.

94. Which of the following statements is true?
   (a) Historic costume should not be worn if you wish to preserve it.
   (b) Body oils and perspiration will not damage textiles.
   (c) The stress and strain of wearing a garment can cause a great deal of damage.
   (d) Historic costume should be worn on festive occasions especially those involving food and drink.

95. Small flat textiles:
   (a) should be stored in Dacron sausages
   (b) should be stacked one on top of the other
   (c) should always be rolled
   (d) can simply be stored flat, with interleaving if items are to be stacked.

96. When rolling a large textile for storage:
   (a) choose a roller that is longer than the item is wide

    (b) cover the roller with acid-free material to protect the textile

    (c) select a roller with a small diameter so that it does not take up too much space

    (d) fringes and tassels should be kept straight.

97. When displaying textiles:

    (a) be aware that light and UV radiation are the greatest enemies of textiles

    (b) use acid-free materials in the display systems

    (c) ensure that your textiles are well supported

    (d) protect your textiles from fluctuations in relative humidity and temperature, dust, insects and pollutants

98. Historic costume can be:

    (a) stored on wire coat-hangers

    (b) displayed safely on mannequins if measures are taken to modify the mannequin to the appropriate shape

    (c) worn regularly with the right undergarments

    (d) protected in storage by hanging them on padded hangers and covering them to keep off dust.

99. To clean textiles:

    (a) proceed with caution and use a vacuum brushing technique

    (b) wash them in washing machines

    (c) use the full suction of your vacuum cleaner to ensure you remove all the dirt

    (d) use a carpet beater.

100. A fabric in which a nonwoven web is combined with a woven, knitted, or stitch-bonded layer is called:

    (a) supplemented fabric

    (b) built up fabric

    (c) supported fabric

    (d) supukwenkin fabric

101. Cotton wax, a natural substance that is present in small quantities on the raw cotton fibre and make it water resistant, is removed by

    (a) stripping

    (b) chemicals

    (c) steaming

    (d) scouring

102. _______is a term used by wool sorters for short staple taken from the under neck and belly parts of the fleece.

    (a) Smalls

    (b) Throw-aways

    (c) Brokes

    (d) Bits

103. A variety of long staple, upland cotton grown along the Mississippi River in U.S.A and some of its tributaries is called _____.

    (a) Valley cotton

    (b) Huck cotton

    (c) River cotton

    (d) Sippi cotton

104. Fibre that is 0.01 denier per filament of less is called _____.

    (a) ultrafibre

    (b) ultimate fibre

    (c) ultrasonic fibre

    (d) untrafine fibre

105. Which of the following is a term for the straight, lustrous fibres generally found in the wool from sheep that have been badly bred or poorly fed? (They resemble kemp and will not dye of blend well.)

    (a) Ganse

    (b) Garber

    (c) Gare

    (d) Garlix

106. Which of the following is a general term for waterproof fabric?

    (a) Imberline

    (b) Tarnate

    (c) Canvas

    (d) Tarpaulin

107. Manufactured filaments or staple fibres that have been coloured by incorporating pigments in the melt or polymer solution from which they are extruded are called:
   (a) preproduction pigmented
   (b) dye extruded
   (c) polymer pigmented
   (d) producer coloured

108. _______ is a brownish-black, tough fibre obtained from the leaves of the jaggery palm. Uses: scrubbing, horse and brewery brushes, large cables for tying up ships, etc.
   (a) Piri
   (b) Pila
   (c) Kittul
   (d) Betal

109. _______ is a gold and silver wire thread made in India, used in weaving
   (a) Goshoo
   (b) Silgol
   (c) Golbute
   (d) Goghari

110. The paddle-shaped tail of a fat-tailed sheep can weigh up to:
   (a) 5 lbs
   (b) 10 lbs
   (c) 20 lbs
   (d) 40 lbs

111. Which of the following is a process for transforming designs from specially prepared paper to textiles?
   (a) Decating
   (b) Decalcomania
   (c) Transference
   (d) Decorticating

112. Below grade is a term used in the floor covering industry to refer to _______.
   (a) cheap, lesser quality floor covering
   (b) carpet pieces that do not pass quality control
   (c) remnants
   (d) areas that are below ground level

113. In textiles, SASE stands for: _______.
   (a) Stress at Specific Elongation
   (b) Strong and Safe Engineering
   (c) Stress at Seam Ends
   (d) Self Addressed Stamped Envelope

114. _______ is a method for bonding a nonwoven web. Achieved by spraying it with droplets of adhesive.
   (a) Wet bonding
   (b) Gluette bonding
   (c) Web bonding
   (d) Spray bonding

115. Houndstooth check is --------.
   (a) a way to evaluate the alignment of a zipper.
   (b) a fabric pattern originating with an outer garment worn by shepherds in Scotland that was black-and-white checked.
   (c) a pointed check effect produced by 2 up, 2 down twill and yarns of contrasting colours in groups of four in both warp and filling.
   (d) a test to evaluate the effectiveness of fabric to resist runs and tears.

116. _______ is a method of quilting thermoplastic fabrics without thread using ultrasonic energy.
   (a) Sonic sewing
   (b) Pinsonic quilting
   (c) Sonic welding
   (d) Threadless quilting

117. Wool removed from carcasses of sheep slaughtered by packing houses is called _______.
   (a) skin wool
   (b) blood wool
   (c) slaughter house wool
   (d) pulled wool

118. Mediumweight fabrics suitable for wear during the fall season are called _______.
   (a) midweight

(b) autumn weight

(c) fallen wool

(d) fall weight

119. Very fine woven fabric, often nylon, with coarse, strong warp and filling yarns spaced at intervals so that tears will not spread is called __________________.

(a) ripspot

(b) rippling

(c) ripstop

(d) riseau

120. A K-Value is a numeric value that expresses the rate of ______________ by a textile or other material.

(a) saturation of dye

(b) stretch recovery

(c) absorption of liquid

(d) conduction of heat

121. Digestion of food starts in:

(a) mouth

(b) liver

(c) stomach

(d) intestines

122. The smallest living thing that can cause disease in the human body is:

(a) flea

(b) bacteria

(c) a protozoa

(d) viruses

123. What is essentially required to digest the food in stomach?

(a) Air

(b) Water

(c) Enzymes

(d) Minerals

124. A person suffering from which of the following cannot see with clarity the horizontal and vertical lines simultaneously?

(a) Myopia

(b) Hypermitropia

(c) Astigmatism

(d) Squint

125. Bile is secreted by:

(a) pancreas

(b) small intestine

(c) stomach

(d) liver

126. Which of the following is a genetically transmitted disease?

(a) Myopia

(b) Long sightedness

(c) Colour blindness

(d) Night blindness

127. Respiration is:

(a) to change the food into energy

(b) the process during which food is oxidized and its chemical energy is transformed into useful form

(c) a sort of exercise

(d) interconversion of food and energy

128. Dialysisis:

(a) the same process as osmosis

(b) the diffusion of sugar molecules through water

(c) the process involved in the diffusion of toxic substance through a membrane

(d) the evaporation of surplus sugar

129. What does the urine of a man contain mainly?

(a) Urea

(b) Sugar

(c) Salt

(d) None of the above

(e) All the above

130. Deficiency of insulin causes:

(a) Beri-Beri

(b) Fever

(c) Cancer

(d) Anaemia

(e) Diabetes

131. The main endocrine gland present in the human body is:

(a) Adrenal gland

   (b) Pituitary gland
   (c) Thyroid gland
   (d) Pancreas gland
   (e) None of the above

132. Which one of the following is called a growth gland?
   (a) Adrenal
   (b) Thyroid
   (c) Pituitary
   (d) None of the above

133. Which type of nerves carry impulses from the sense organs in response to stimulus?
   (a) Motor
   (b) Sensory
   (c) Secretory
   (d) All the above

134. The amoeba type organisms in the human body, causing malaria and amoebic dysentery are known as:
   (a) bacteria
   (b) virus
   (c) fungi
   (d) protozoa

135. The normal temperature of the human body is:
   (a) 32°C
   (b) 27°C
   (c) 37°C
   (d) 40°C

136. The function of calcium in our body is:
   (a) to increase the supply of blood to the heart
   (b) to provide strength to the bones and teeth
   (c) to provide oxygen to the blood
   (d) to provide more sugar in our blood
   (e) to help digestion

137. The drug most widely used to relieve pain is:
   (a) opium
   (b) aspirin
   (c) morphine
   (d) baralgan

138. Which one of the following blood groups is universal recipient?
   (a) AB
   (b) A
   (c) O
   (d) B

139. Arrange in right order from childhood onwards the growth of the following teeth:
   1. incisors   2. canines
   3. pre-molars   4. molars
   (a) 1, 2, 3, 4
   (b) 1, 2, 4, 3
   (c) 2, 3, 1, 4
   (d) 4, 1, 3, 2

140. A person in normal health requires per day:
   (a) 1,000 - 1,800 calories
   (b) 4,000 - 5,000 calories
   (c) 2,500 - 3,000 calories
   (d) 3,000 - 4,000 calories
   (e) 3,500 - 5,000 calories

141. Red blood corpuscles are produced in:
   (a) spleen
   (b) liver
   (c) bone marrow
   (d) kidneys

142. For the treatment of which organ dialysis is resorted to?
   (a) Lung
   (b) Liver
   (c) Kidney
   (d) Brain

143. Liver helps to:
   (a) promote digestion of food
   (b) store glucose as glycogen
   (c) promote respiration
   (d) All the above

144. Excessive perspiration makes a man feel weak especially during summer. This is because of:
   (a) loss of salts through evaporation
   (b) loss of more water through evaporation
   (c) the weakening of nerves due to heat
   (d) All the above

145. Reserpine is used to:
  (a) alleviate high blood pressure
  (b) alleviate low blood pressure
  (c) cure heart ailments
  (d) None of the above

146. Radium is used to cure which disease?
  (a) Cancer
  (b) Bright's disease
  (c) Haemophilia
  (d) Typhoid fever

147. By taking the pulse rate of the human body, a doctor determines:
  (a) heartbeat
  (b) functioning of heart valves
  (c) the amount fo blood in body
  (d) the condition of liver

148. The rate and force of the heartbeat, the secretion of glands of the alimentary tract and the contraction of involuntary muscles are controlled by the:
  (a) cranial nerves
  (b) spinal nerves
  (c) central nerves system
  (d) autonomic nervous system

149. Filtration of wastes from the blood in human body is done by:
  (a) Heart
  (b) Lungs
  (c) Kidney
  (d) Intestines

150. Excessive intake of alcohol damages a person's:
  (a) Kidney
  (b) Liver
  (c) Stomach
  (d) All the above to a certain degree

151. Which children you would like to teach?
  (a) Those who are having high levels of intelligence
  (b) Those who are hardworking
  (c) Those who love discipline
  (d) All types of children

152. Home work should be given to students:
  (a) according to their interest
  (b) keeping their ages in view
  (c) keeping their intelligence levels in view
  (d) keeping in view their needs of the final examination

153. If, on a certain day, children are not in a mood to study,"then:
  (a) they should be freed
  (b) they should be ordered to remain seated in the class (without talking)
  (c) they should be told to conduct an interesting activity on that day
  (d) the teacher should sit along with them, laugh along with them and have fun

154. If students are not taking an interest in the lesson, then the teacher should
  (a) tell the students that taking interest in their studies would amount to their welfare
  (b) ask them why they are not taking an interest in the lesson
  (c) himself find out the causes for lack of interest and remove such causes
  (d) file a complaint with the Principal in this context

155. Which one of the following is the best method of teaching?
  (a) Dialogue method
  (b) Text book method
  (c) Project method
  (d) Audio-visual method.

156. By which trait of the teacher, the students are generally impressed?
  (a) His knowledge/learning
  (b) His high moral character
  (c) His tough discipline
  (d) His relationship with the Principal

157. Whose behaviour affects students the most?
  (a) That of the Principal

(b) That of a politician.

(c) That of a teacher

(d) That of a tutor

158. If a student does not complete his home work on a regular basis, what will you do to rectify him?

(a) You will complain to the principal and get him punished

(b) You will call the student in privacy and explain to him that (completion of) home work has many advantages

(c) You will like to get the cooperation of he student in question

(d) You will clearly tell the student that if he continues to ignore his home work, he would not be allowed to appear in the final examination

159. By which method, students learn to the maximum extent and with the utmost speed?

(a) By seeing

(b) By reading

(c) By listening

(d) By doing themselves

160. You think that taking surprise tests is justified because:

(a) students remain frightened due to these

(b) you do not have to get yourself prepared at home for this purpose

(c) you can escape the teaching session due to the alibi of taking a surprise test

(d) the abilities and knowledge levels of students can be truly judged through such tests

161. In order to participate in a conference or seminar, which is related to teaching, you would:

(a) take leave from the school

(b) get the permission of the Principal

(c) not get the permission of the Principal

(d) quietly leave the school and attend the conference or seminar

162. In your opinion, what should be the age for sending little children to school?

(a) When the child starts speaking

(b) When the child develops an interest in studies

(c) When the child attains the age of plus five years

(d) When the child attains the age of plus three years

163. Some students quietly run away from school. In order to check this habit of such students, you would:

(a) try to know why they run away from school

(b) Worm the Principal about their habit of running away from school

(c) inform the parents of such children about their habit of running away from school

(d) try to make class teaching more interesting

164. For whom, education is deemed more important:

(a) For boys

(b) For girls

(c) For adults

(d) For all of these

165. Why is the use of different methods useful in teaching?

(a) In order to make teaching easily understood

(b) In order to make teaching more interesting

(c) In order to attract the attention of students

(d) All of these

166. Should a teacher play along with students in games?

(a) Sometimes

(b) Never

(c) Yes

(d) As and when the Principal wishes

167. The true objective of education is:

(a) making students able so that they can earn a living

(b) preparing students for jobs

(c) helping students acquire knowledge

(d) facilitating the all-round development of students

168. Suppose that a person does not agree with your viewpoint. In such a situation, you would:

(a) present the rationale of your view point before him

(b) not like to talk to that person

(c) consider him to be your opponent

(d) behave with him in a rude manner

169. Children's literature is useful for little children because:

(a) they are entertained due to this

(b) it contains attractive study material

(c) it increases the interest of children in studies

(d) it contains stories that enhance knowledge levels

170. With the help of a cumulative archive:

(a) the moral levels of children can be evaluated

(b) the pace of educational progress of children can be known

(c) children can be disciplined

(d) the development of children can be gauged

171. What is your opinion about giving home work to students?

(a) Highly intelligent students need not be given home work

(b) Weak students should be given simple home work

(c) All the students should be given the same home work

(d) It would be beneficial to give home work to students according to their abilities and capacities

172. The student, who helps other students:

(a) passes with good marks

(b) is respected in the society

(c) becomes a good teacher

(d) becomes a good citizen

173. How can the habit of stealing be removed from among children?

(a) By giving harsh punishment

(b) By giving them the threats of coercion/ punishment

(c) By reprimanding them

(d) By giving them good advice and keeping a vigilant eye over them

174. From your viewpoint, whose development is the most important among children?

(a) Dedication towards work

(b) Self-confidence

(c) The importance of labour

(d) An affinity for religion

175. Which method would be more effective to generate an interst among children for sports/ games?

(a) Showing them big-league matches

(b) Giving new sports gear to children

(c) Telling students that sports and games are as important as studies

(d) Playing yourself in the playground along with children

176. Nowadays, children do not have a zeal to study. The reason for this is that:

(a) they are unable to get enough of motivation to study

(b) they feel that their future would not be bright even after they complete their studies

(c) they do not get a conducive environment for pursuing their studies

(d) they opine that there is no need to study with special dedication (or zeal) to pass the examination

177. The best method of language teaching is the:

(a) textbook system

(b) practice of writing again and again

(c) conversation technique

(d) practice of pronouncing correctly

178. The practical method of make children understanding the meanings of difficult words is to:

(a) give their synonyms

(b) give their antonyms

(c) teach them the usage of such words in sentences

(d) None of these

179. Whose habits does a little child adopt?

(a) Of his friends

(b) Of the classmates and friends of his school

(c) Of his family members

(d) Of teachers

180. Informal education of the child:

(a) is carried out in a planned manner

(b) starts from his environment

(c) is given to him by an institution

(d) is effected with efforts

181. The most abundant gas in air is

(a) nitrogen

(b) hydrogen

(c) oxygen

(d) ozone

182. The most commonly found acid in nature is

(a) hydrochloric acid

(b) sulphuric acid

(c) lactic acid

(d) acetic acid.

183. This bomb is used to destroy living beings but would not damage the buildings and other property

(a) napalm bomb

(b) neutron bomb

(c) hydrogen bomb

(d) None of the above

184. If the Richter scale shows a value of 7.2, then the seismograph indicates

(a) an earthquake of low intensity

(b) an earthquake of very high intensity

(c) an earthquake of moderate intensity

(d) either (a) or (c)

185. Common coal used in our households is

(a) Anthracite

(b) Bituminous coal

(c) Lignite

(d) all of the above

186. The time taken by the Sun rays to reach the earth is

(a) 9 minutes

(b) 10 minutes

(c) 7 minutes

(d) 8 minutes

187. The outer planets are

(a) Moon, Earth, Mercury, Venus, Pluto

(b) Jupiter, Saturn, Uranus, Earth, Mars

(c) Jupiter, Uranus, Saturn, Neptune, Pluto

(d) None of the above

188. Which one of the following diseases would be caused by bacterial infection?

(a) tetanus

(b) rabies

(c) cancer

(d) malaria

189. Which one of the following types of coal contains a higher percentage of carbon than the test?

(a) Bituminous Coal

(b) Lignite

(c) Anthracite

(d) Peat

190. In India, an active volcano is situated at

(a) Lakshadweep

(b) Chhotanagpur Plateau

(c) Andaman and Nicobar

(d) Malawa Plateau

191. An of the following are plant products except

(a) silk

(b) cork

    (c) hemp

    (d) linen

192. Insecticides or medicines could be harmful

    (a) to the insects and weeds as they kill them instantaneously upon consumption

    (b) to the habitat as the environment could become polluted due to excessive usage of chemicals in our crop management processes.

    (c) to the human beings and animals who consume the food adulterated by the insecticides and weedicides

    (d) to the transporters and movers of the crops who could inhale noxious fumes of insecticides and weedicides

193. This country is the largest producer of cotton in the world.

    (a) India

    (b) China

    (c) Egypt

    (d) the USA

194. Which one of the following is not a sedimentary rock?

    (a) slate

    (b) limestone

    (c) clay

    (d) sandstone

195. Salal Hydro Electric Project is situated on the river.

    (a) Beas

    (b) Jhelum

    (c) Chenab

    (d) Sutlej

196. Polar ice is melting due to greenhouse effect. This would lead to

    (a) more melting of the polar glaciers and hence, subsequent submerging of land areas of earth

    (b) increasing temperatures on polar caps

    (c) reduction in temperature of ocean waters and rise in temperature of the Arctic circle waters as well as those of the Antartic circle waters

    (d) no impact

197. The plants, which can resist high temperatures, are known as

    (a) thermophilic

    (b) thermophobic

    (c) thermoduric

    (d) both (a) and (b)

198. Which one of the following vaccines is used for controlling tuberculosis among the cattle?

    (a) Cell Culture Vaccine

    (b) Goat Tissue Adapted Vaccine

    (c) Adjuvant Vaccine

    (d) BCG Vaccine

199. Which one of the following chemicals is carcinogenic if inhaled?

    (a) carbon dioxide

    (b) suspended particulate matter

    (c) lead oxide

    (d) sulphur dioxide

200. Which types of roses are grown in India for industrial applications?

    (a) *R centripetala* and Bushra Rose

    (b) *R damascena Var bifera*

    (c) *Rosa damascena*

    (d) (a), (b) and (c)

201. The size of clay particles is

    (a) greater than 0.2 mm

    (b) 0.02 mm-0.2 mm

    (c) 0.002 mm - 0.02 mm

    (d) less than 0.002 mm

202. Which one of the following plants is of great medicinal value?

    (a) *Ranwolfia serpentiana*

    (b) *Thea sinesis*

    (c) *Coffea robusta*

    (d) *Ficus religiosa*

203. Biological control agents of soil borne plant pathogens act by

    (a) rapidly repleting nutrients and thereby, causing starvation and death of the pathogen

    (b) secreting toxic metabolitics

    (c) direct parastism or predation on the pathogens

    (d) all of the above

204. Nearly 80 percent of sugarcane in India is planted during

    (a) July -December

    (b) May-August

    (c) June - August

    (d) December-April

205. Soluble salt content of soil is determined by measuring its

    (a) pH Value

    (b) organic matter content

    (c) Sulphur content

    (d) electrical conductivity

206. Operation Flood is related to whereas development of fisheries is related to .....

    (a) white revolution, block revolution

    (b) white revolution, blue revolution

    (c) green revolution, blue revolution

    (d) blue revolution, green revolution

207. "Mixed Farming" refers to

    (a) farming by traditional and modern methods

    (b) agriculture and dairy farming clubbed together

    (c) farming without synthetic fertilisers but with traditional manure

    (d) farming with synthetic fertilisers and with traditional manure

208. The main constituent of Gobar Gas is

    (a) butane

    (b) carbon monoxide

    (c) methane

    (d) octane

209. Which gas does not pollute air (for human and animal consumption)?

    (a) carbon monoxide

    (b) nitrogen dioxide

    (c) sulphur dioxide

    (d) carbon dioxide

210. FAO does not give technical assistance in the following project?

    (a) dairy

    (b) soil and water management

    (c) fisheries

    (d) civil aviation

ANSWERS

1	2	3	4	5	6	7	8	9	10
(c)	(c)	(d)	(a)	(a)	(d)	(a)	(c)	(c)	(b)
11	**12**	**13**	**14**	**15**	**16**	**17**	**18**	**19**	**20**
(d)	(b)	(b)	(c)	(c)	(d)	(b)	(b)	(b)	(c)
21	**22**	**23**	**24**	**25**	**26**	**27**	**28**	**29**	**30**
(d)	(a)	(d)	(c)	(b)	(d)	(b)	(d)	(d)	(c)
31	**32**	**33**	**34**	**35**	**36**	**37**	**38**	**39**	**40**
(c)	(b)	(d)	(a)	(c)	(a)	(b)	(d)	(b)	(c)
41	**42**	**43**	**44**	**45**	**46**	**47**	**48**	**49**	**50**
(d)	(b)	(a)	(a)	(d)	(a)	(c)	(b)	(b)	(a)
51	**52**	**53**	**54**	**55**	**56**	**57**	**58**	**59**	**60**
(c)	(b)	(b)	(b)	(d)	(c)	(a)	(a)	(d)	(a)
61	**62**	**63**	**64**	**65**	**66**	**67**	**68**	**69**	**70**
(a)	(b)	(d)	(b)	(c)	(b)	(b)	(b)	(c)	(c)

71	**72**	**73**	**74**	**75**	**76**	**77**	**78**	**79**	**80**
(a)	(d)	(b)	(c)	(c)	(c)	(c)	(c)	(d)	(d)
81	**82**	**83**	**84**	**85**	**86**	**87**	**88**	**89**	**90**
(a)	(d)	(b)	(c)	(b)	(c)	(c)	(c)	(a)	(d)
91	**92**	**93**	**94**	**95**	**96**	**97**	**98**	**99**	**100**
(d)	(c)	(b)	(a)	(b)	(a)	(d)	(d)	(b)	(b)
101	**102**	**103**	**104**	**105**	**106**	**107**	**108**	**109**	**110**
(d)	(c)	(a)	(d)	(c)	(d)	(d)	(c)	(a)	(d)
111	**112**	**113**	**114**	**115**	**116**	**117**	**118**	**119**	**120**
(d)	(d)	(a)	(d)	(c)	(b)	(a)	(d)	(c)	(d)
121	**122**	**123**	**124**	**125**	**126**	**127**	**128**	**129**	**130**
(a)	(d)	(c)	(c)	(d)	(c)	(b)	(c)	(a)	(e)
131	**132**	**133**	**134**	**135**	**136**	**137**	**138**	**139**	**140**
(b)	(b)	(b)	(d)	(c)	(b)	(b)	(a)	(a)	(c)
141	**142**	**143**	**144**	**145**	**146**	**147**	**148**	**149**	**150**
(c)	(c)	(b)	(b)	(a)	(a)	(a)	(d)	(c)	(d)
151	**152**	**153**	**154**	**155**	**156**	**157**	**158**	**159**	**160**
(d)	(c)	(c)	(c)	(c)	(b)	(c)	(c)	(d)	(d)
161	**162**	**163**	**164**	**165**	**166**	**167**	**168**	**169**	**170**
(d)	(d)	(a)	(d)	(d)	(c)	(d)	(a)	(c)	(b)
171	**172**	**173**	**174**	**175**	**176**	**177**	**178**	**179**	**180**
(d)	(d)	(d)	(b)	(d)	(b)	(c)	(c)	(c)	(b)
181	**182**	**183**	**184**	**185**	**186**	**187**	**188**	**189**	**190**
(a)	(d)	(b)	(b)	(a)	(d)	(c)	(a)	(c)	(c)
191	**192**	**193**	**194**	**195**	**196**	**197**	**198**	**199**	**200**
(a)	(c)	(b)	(a)	(c)	(a)	(c)	(d)	(c)	(d)
201	**202**	**203**	**204**	**205**	**206**	**207**	**208**	**209**	**210**
(d)	(a)	(d)	(d)	(d)	(b)	(b)	(c)	(d)	(d)

———————